William F. Macmichael

The Oxford and Cambridge Boat Races

1829-1869

William F. Macmichael

The Oxford and Cambridge Boat Races

1829-1869

ISBN/EAN: 9783954272648
Erscheinungsjahr: 2013
Erscheinungsort: Bremen, Deutschland

© maritimepress in Europäischer Hochschulverlag GmbH & Co. KG, Fahrenheitstr. 1, 28359 Bremen. Alle Rechte beim Verlag und bei den jeweiligen Lizenzgebern.

www.maritimepress.de | office@maritimepress.de

Bei diesem Titel handelt es sich um den Nachdruck eines historischen, lange vergriffenen Buches. Da elektronische Druckvorlagen für diese Titel nicht existieren, musste auf alte Vorlagen zurückgegriffen werden. Hieraus zwangsläufig resultierende Qualitätsverluste bitten wir zu entschuldigen.

OXFORD AND CAMBRIDGE

BOAT RACES.

THE

OXFORD AND CAMBRIDGE

BOAT RACES.

A CHRONICLE OF THE CONTESTS ON THE
THAMES IN WHICH UNIVERSITY CREWS
HAVE BORNE A PART,

FROM A.D. 1829 *TO* A.D. 1869.

COMPILED FROM THE UNIVERSITY CLUB BOOKS AND
OTHER CONTEMPORARY AND AUTHENTIC RECORDS;
WITH MAPS OF THE RACING COURSES, INDEX OF NAMES,
AND AN INTRODUCTION ON ROWING, AND ITS VALUE
AS AN ART AND RECREATION.

BY

W. F. MACMICHAEL, B.A.
OF DOWNING COLLEGE, CAMBRIDGE; LATE SECRETARY OF THE
CAMBRIDGE UNIVERSITY BOAT CLUB.

CAMBRIDGE
DEIGHTON, BELL, AND CO.
LONDON: BELL AND DALDY.
1870.

TO THE RIGHT REVEREND

GEORGE AUGUSTUS, D.D.,

LORD BISHOP OF LICHFIELD,

THIS CHRONICLE OF BOAT RACES

IS, WITH HIS LORDSHIP'S KIND PERMISSION,

𝔇𝔢𝔡𝔦𝔠𝔞𝔱𝔢𝔡

WITH EVERY FEELING OF RESPECT

BY HIS MUCH OBLIGED AND MOST OBEDIENT

HUMBLE SERVANT,

THE AUTHOR.

PREFACE.

IN offering this chronicle of the successive contests between the Boat Clubs of the two Universities, I beg my readers to make allowance for my difficulties when they see the many imperfections with which it abounds Having been obliged to some extent to review the actions of those who have gone before, and to balance the probabilities in cases where incompatible statements were made by the two sides, I have found how difficult it is to form an impartial judgment in a matter in which one is in any degree interested. There are two opposite dangers, which it is equally difficult to avoid; the one of unfairly favouring one's own side, the other, of running to the opposite extreme from the very desire to be impartial, and thus doing injustice, or scant justice, to those who will naturally feel aggrieved by unfair criticism coming from their own side. I am afraid that on different occasions I may have fallen into both these errors, and I hope that any one, who may think that I have done so, will point it out, so that I may correct it if an opportunity occurs.

My general plan of work has been to compare the entries in the official books of the two University Clubs and the newspaper accounts. In carrying this out, I have received most valuable and kindly assistance from Mr J. C. Tinné and Mr W. D. Benson the late and present Presidents of the O.U.B.C., and from my own predecessor and successors in office as secretary of the C.U.B.C., viz. Mr J. W. Pinckney, Mr F. J. Young, and Mr J. H. Ridley, who lent me the club-books for a considerable time, and I fear to their own inconvenience;—from Mr T. S. Egan, who besides helping me in many other points lent me an album containing the "*Aquatic Register*" of *Bell's Life* from 1831 to 1854;—from the aquatic editor of the *Field*, from Mr Thoms, and all the staff of the *Field*, who have shewn me the greatest possible consideration, allowing me to take clippings from their spare numbers wherever I wanted them;—and from the aquatic editor of *Bell's Life*.

And here I may mention that passages

marked as extracts and quotations are not necessarily—and in fact hardly ever—copied verbatim; I have found it necessary to make alterations and omissions in almost every instance.

The author of the article in *London Society* of 1865 about the first boat-race has kindly permitted me to copy it, but annexed the condition that his name should remain unpublished.

The Biographical Notices are, I am sorry to say, very incomplete. In particular it will be noticed that they are wholly wanting in the case of Henley crews. When I first took the work in hand I only intended to treat of *matches* between Oxford and Cambridge, and so began to collect notices of those only who rowed at Putney; but as I proceeded, I found that there would be no consecutive history at all unless I included the contests at Henley Regatta, and then it was too late to work up the biographical notices of the men who rowed in them only. There is only one exception to this rule, and that is in the case of the seven-oared race in 1843. Besides the fact that this is quite an exceptional case, I received, through the kindness of Mr F. N. Menzies, the biographical notices of all the 'seven' together with those of the crew of 1842. For obvious reasons I have not given any notices of the crews of the last nine races. In collecting the biographical notices I have received great assistance from many friends too numerous to recount; I take this opportunity of thanking them all, but more especially Mr J. M. Ridley of Jesus College, who was captain of the crew of 1842, for the great trouble he took to help me. I have also made great use of "The Eton School Lists," by Mr. H. E. C. Stapylton.

To Mr S. Vincent of Lincoln's Inn my most cordial thanks are due for revising all the proof-sheets from the year 1840, and for supplying a large number of the biographical notices. Without his assistance I should have been obliged to send the book to press in a very imperfect condition indeed. To Mr Vincent's suggestions likewise are due the larger portion of the foot-notes in the latter part of the book.

For the medical definitions in Appendix I. I am indebted to my friend and fellow-collegian, Mr W. A. Brailey.

The maps of the racing courses are copied

with slight alterations of outline from the Ordnance Survey. In entering the names on the Metropolitan course I have had the advantage of Mr Egan's thorough knowledge of the river, and I have also made use of an excellent map of the Thames from Putney to Mortlake, published a short time ago by Mr Eugéne Monteuuis, (London Rowing Club) Surveyor. The places on the Oxford course were all supplied me by Mr J. Cross of Exeter College, and an important correction in the outline of the river by Mr W. D. Benson.

That University rowing has, through the annual boat race, become a matter of public interest is undeniable: to shew that it has also a claim on the public confidence for its own sake as a manly art, a wholesome discipline and a healthy recreation, is the general aim of the Introductory Chapter.

W. F. M.

DOWNING COLLEGE,
March 21, 1870.

ADDENDA ET CORRIGENDA.

Page 71, line 19, *for* Cox *read* Cocks.
,, 97, ,, 17, *for* Breadon *read* Breedon.
,, 121, ,, 21, *for* D'Arth *read* D'Aeth.
,, 138, ,, 4, *for* Cloves *read* Cloves[1].
,, 148, ,, 3, *for* E. J.⎫ Sykes *read* J. J. Sykes.
,, 172, ,, 8, *for* J. E.⎭
,, 172, ,, 7, *for* B. Greenall *read* R. Greenall.
,, 214, *after* T. H. Blundell *insert* E. Hooper[1].
,, 216, ,, 7, *for* H. F. Johnson *read* F. W. Johnson.
,, 225, ,, 12, H. R. Mansel Jones. A barrister on the Home Circuit.
,, 248, ,, 12, *for* Loyd *read* Lloyd.
,, 252, *after* J. Hall *insert* R. Wharton[1].
,, 254, ,, 35, *for* T. Havart *read* W. J. Havart.
,, ,, ,, 40, *for* T. Hall *read* J. Hall.

INTRODUCTION.

ROWING pursued as an art at the Universities dates no further back than the middle of the reign of George the Fourth. It is not difficult to account for the fact that it was so late in being adopted by the Undergraduate body. The first regatta ever held in this country was in the beginning of the reign of George the Third, and this may, I suppose, be taken as a proof of the statement that Rowing was not pursued otherwise than as a means of getting a livelihood much before that period.

Now when we consider the amount of energy that a man must possess and apply in order to do justice to his powers in practising this most beautiful art, I think we shall find a very sufficient reason why at the Universities Rowing was unknown till the third decade of this century.

The history of George the Third's long reign comprises little more than a series of wars: wars too the most popular, the most thoroughly national probably, of any in the whole course of our annals. To bear their share in these, flocked the flower of the nation's youth. From the noble to the artisan the whole of the active, material energy of the people was enlisted to fight the nation's wars.

To the Universities, on the other hand, would go the mental energy of the upper and middle classes, those who were not physically fitted for the toils and hardships of active service, and those whose tastes and inclinations led them to follow intellectual pursuits. These, we may presume, used the time allotted to their Undergraduate career with a view mainly to mental culture and the pursuit of arts,—the primary objects doubtless which Alma Mater sets before us at our matriculation.

While the bulk of Undergraduates was thus constituted, it was natural that Rowing should not find a place at the Universities, even if its supporters elsewhere had been of a class likely to give it an air of respectability. I am afraid, however, that the opposite was the case; and that in early times the class of men who supported aquatics were much on a level with the frequenters of prize-fights. I say those who *supported*, for the aquatic amateur was hardly known. Those who have read *Ten Thousand a year* (and who has not?) will remember that Mr Tittlebat Titmouse used to alternate his morning pastime between the prize-ring and the boating-match, and found in either an equally pleasant and ready way of relieving himself of the burden of his newly acquired wealth.

When, therefore, we consider that the Undergraduates of sixty or seventy years ago were men in whom, as a class, the mental powers were cultivated rather than, and somewhat to the detriment of, the physical; and when too we must confess that the class of persons who affected Rowing were not quite so estimable as they might have been, we shall not wonder that the Art of Rowing was wholly ignored at the Universities.

When, however, the wars had ceased, and a universal peace settled on the troubled waters of History, then it was that the Universities began to draw within their maternal arms much of that physical energy which had hitherto been engaged in the wars. This was in the nature of things sure to find an outlet in some direction, and as the wars had ceased, it had to be satisfied with perfecting itself in athletic exercises.

Of these Cricket, which had already got a firm hold on the nation at large, was the first to be seized on, as well for its intrinsic worth, as also because no bad odour attached to it. Rowing, however, has that about it which could not let it remain long in the shade. For calling into action and cherishing the higher qualities of our nature, few sports can vie with it. While no art requires more pains and patience than Rowing, in order to attain to excellence, both as regards each individual oarsman and the whole crew together, there is not the same opportunity for individual display as there is in cricket, or almost any other athletic game.

To take the instance of Cricket; I have often noticed myself, and heard it remarked by others, that players are tempted to subordinate, to a certain extent, the interests of the side to their own score: it is in the nature of the game to encourage individual display. One of the chief pleasures consists in making a good cut, a long drive, or bowling a well-pitched ball or a maiden[1] over; in fact, doing a neat *bit* of work, which will make up for general mediocrity: but who ever was heard to say to any but the veriest tyro in a tub, "Magnificent stroke, that!"? or what crew would be thought worth its salt, which occasionally kept time for half-a-dozen strokes together? Excellence in Rowing is nothing, unless it be constant and enduring. Individual excellence is useless, unless it work in harmony with the rest of the crew. All must be animated by one spirit, all subjected to one will. In a crew of amateurs selfishness can find no place: the very ambition to excel requires the elimination of self-seeking; for the very highest excellence consists, if not wholly, in a large measure in adapting one's movements to those of one's neighbour, and in acting in unison and simultaneously with the rest of the crew: every individual is indeed a separate power, but exists as a power for good only so far as he is a part of a uniform and consistent whole.

Again, it is but few sports that can vie with Rowing in drawing forth and cherishing pluck and determination; what calls for so much endurance under physical distress, or demands so much perseverance under difficulties, as a matter of duty both to oneself and to others? A man who has

---

[1] For an explanation of the technical terms used in the following pages see Appendix I.

conscientiously stuck to it "between first and second wind" is not likely to be daunted at trifles, or to give in without a struggle when difficulties come upon him.

Football, no doubt, possesses many of these advantages in common with Rowing. Both require and educate that spirit which animates the patriot and leads him to subordinate private advantage to the public good. Both, though doubtless in a different manner and in a somewhat different phase, encourage pluck and determination. Football teaches intrepidity, Rowing endurance. In order to attain excellence in either there must be the same steadiness in individuals, the same unity of purpose.

Besides presenting to the moralist so many points worthy of approval, Rowing possesses many material advantages, which are even more conspicuous than the moral ones in their absence from other sports. The chief of these is that its practice is confined to no particular season of the year, but can be pursued in all. Hardly any sun is too hot, any rain too heavy, any storm too severe to keep the rowing man out of his beloved ship; the only thing that can put an effectual stoppage is ice. It will be seen hereafter that occasionally the crew of one or other University has been prevented from practising by the river being blocked. This, however, is but seldom; and as nearly all the ice which we have in this country usually visits us during the Christmas vacation, it comes to pass that the average number of days, on which a University-man during his Undergraduate career is prevented from rowing by the state of the weather, may be counted on the fingers of one hand.

Then again the exercise itself is one of the healthiest and, to the sound man, the least injurious of all those that offer the same advantages.

I dare say this may sound strange to some ears, but I feel convinced it is none the less true. In making this statement, I omit from consideration all such injuries as may be called accidental, that is, such as do not depend upon the practice of the exercises themselves. For instance, in rowing, an injury that might happen to the coxswain as easily as to the rest of the crew, would be in this sense of the word *accidental*. But if an oarsman were to enlarge his heart, or injure himself by over exertion in rowing, this would not be an accidental injury. In walking, again, if a man put his foot into an unseen hole, and sprained his ancle, this would be an accidental injury; but if he got cramp and, by persisting in walking, injured the tendon or muscle, this would not be an accidental injury, because it would depend solely on the practice of the exercise in question. Accidental injuries then being put out of sight, as likely to interfere with the more important question, I hope to be able to shew that Rowing contrasts favourably with other kindred sports, and that the most serious objections to it are due to the deductions which have been drawn by their authors from a very limited and partial knowledge of facts.

The most formidable objection to Rowing is that training for boat-racing, and especially training for the "Long Race," dissipates or impairs the "vital energy." This objection is none the less formidable in appearance because this phrase, "vital energy," is not fully understood by most persons.

Webster defines "Energy" to be "inherent power, power of operation, whether exerted or not." "Vital" means "pertaining, contributing, necessary to life." Thus Vital Energy should mean "the inherent power of living," which every person possesses in a greater or less degree up to the last moment of his life; it is therefore the same as "Vitality," with this reservation, that it is only applied to animal life, whereas Vitality is applied to vegetable life also. The exact phrase, however, I cannot find in the medical books to which I have access. But "Vital Force" is thus spoken of in Valentine's *Text-Book of Physiology*[1]:—

"The assumption of such a vital force is neither useful as affording a clue to a series of phenomena otherwise unknown, nor even harmless in its influence on our ideas. It impedes a correct recognition of the fundamental principles on which the existence of living creatures is based, and leads to results which are decisively opposed to more exact physiological investigations."

The objection divides itself into two parts.

[1] P. 2.

The first states that the muscular system is developed at the expense of the vital energy; the other, that the violent exertions which a man has to make continually, as well in practising as in the trial of skill itself, tend materially to impair this vital energy.

I propose to consider these two branches separately with a view of shewing that the objectors have exaggerated the case against Rowing, which is in reality much less open to such objections than many other exercises.

Though I think that more than this is true, I maintain that this is sufficient for my purpose, which is to shew the advantages which Rowing possesses over all the other recreations (some or other of which are necessary to a reading man) which are open to him at the University.

According to the objectors' theory, then, that exercise is the least injurious which dissipates the " Vital Energy" in the least degree.

Now I take it for granted that development of muscle, however great, is not necessarily accompanied by loss of vital energy: but that this loss is solely dependent on the way in which the development is attained. If the development be gradual and not restricted to too small a range of muscles, it is natural to suppose that the loss of vital energy will be reduced to a minimum; and on the other hand, where a man suddenly takes it into his head to develope muscle, and especially any particular set of muscles, and devotes the whole of the time which he sets apart for exercise, and directs all his energies to the attainment of this object, it is not wonderful if some portion of the elements of his food which ought to go to the general strengthening of his constitution should be diverted to some particular channel, and so his vitality should be impaired.

Now in order to attain any excellence in the art of Rowing it is almost essential that a man should develope the muscles, which are especially required, very gradually. It is a well-known fact, that men, who have the misfortune to be called upon to row races within a few months of their beginning to learn to row, contract faults which it is almost impossible to eradicate, however great pains be taken with them afterwards. It is for this reason (among others) that small college men as a rule contrast unfavourably with those of larger colleges. The college cannot afford to wait for its men till they are educated, so they are put into a racing crew in their second, often in their first term; whereas in the larger college there is generally a sufficient number of senior men to fill the racing boats of the club, without making use of the freshmen.

Considering then the amount of proficiency in Rowing that so many men do attain to, and also noting that there must be, and as we know are; very many who may be said to have mistaken their vocation when they attempted to acquire the art of Rowing, and never could have made oarsmen however they went about learning the art, it is obvious that the majority of boating men must commence to adapt their muscles gradually to the exercise, and so, that little injury is likely to result to their constitution.

Besides this, the number of muscles brought into play in rowing is very large, and their range is confined to no part of the body in particular, but is widely diffused over the whole. The muscles of the fore-arm, the arm and nearly all the muscles of the back, a few on the chest, most of all the abdominal muscles and those of the hips, are all of them brought constantly into use; and, what is perhaps more satisfactory, none of them are suddenly called upon to sustain an unwonted effort. The use of each set of muscles is not only constant, but it is regular.

In dealing with this part of the question, I must not omit to notice what is said by Mr Maclaren in his book on training. He says[1]:—

"A little examination will prove, I think, what at first may not have been surmised, that the legs have the largest share of the work in rowing. For while all other parts employed, back, loins, and arms, act somewhat in detail and in succession, the legs act continuously throughout the stroke, and the individual efforts of each, and the concentrated efforts of all the other parts of the body employed, are transmitted through them to the point of resistance, the stretcher.

[1] P. 23.

* * * * * * *

"Rowing thus gives employment to a large portion of the back, more to the loins and hips, and *most of all to the legs;* but it gives little to the arms, and that chiefly to the fore-arm, and least of all to the chest. Moreover as there is but *one* movement in rowing, namely the stroke, indefinitely repeated with the most rigid precision, and as it is in the rearward half of this movement only that any real muscular effort is made or resistance encountered, it follows that every muscle of the body not employed in this action is excluded from the exercise; moreover every muscle included in it is employed but in one line of action, while it is qualified and designed to act in many, and will be developed and strengthened in proportion as these manifold modes of its use are observed; and moreover again, as, with few exceptions, all muscles have antagonistic muscles, designed to perform counter movements, it follows that as rowing consists but of one motion the antagonistic muscles of those employed in executing this motion must be virtually unemployed.

"Thus, as I have said, the legs have strong employment in rowing, but it is the *extensor* muscles alone which have actual employment; the *flexors* are comparatively idle; they perform no exercise, they gain no bulk, they obtain no increase in power. They are excluded from the work, they have no share in the reward.

"Now it is the circumscribing of the line of

muscular operation, the concentrating of the physical exertion into the narrowest channel, that has brought rowing to its present point of artistic excellence,—which gives to the rower that statuesque appearance when resting on his oar, and that automatic precision of movement when in action, which constitute the very ideal of an oarsman, and of a crew."

This extract is taken from a part of Mr Maclaren's book in which he proves that neither Rowing nor any other exercise, practised to the exclusion of others, develops "every muscle of the body," a phrase one continually hears on the lips of enthusiastic admirers of some exercises.

It is therefore the more valuable for my purpose, when it shews that the range of muscles employed is so large as it does. "Rowing gives employment to a large part of the back, more to the loins and hips, and most of all to the legs."

I confess that I cannot quite agree with the whole of the quotation, but I thought that as I wanted part of it, I ought to give it *in extenso*, and state in what points I must differ from him.

First, I think he attaches too much importance, not to the part which the legs play in rowing, but to the consequent development of muscle. Experience shews that rowing does not develope even the extensor muscles of the legs to any great extent, and that it must be supplemented by running and walking exercise, to effect this object.

Secondly, he omits all mention of the muscles

which the amateur oarsman at least must have found to develope in the most remarkable manner of all—I mean the abdominal muscles; and neglects in too great a degree the improvement which is observable in the chest and arms. Curiously enough too, he ignores all work in that part of the motion of rowing in which these very muscles are brought into play, namely, the feather. It is not improbable that, having theoretically determined in his own mind that no such work existed, he saw no reason for examining whether any other muscles were employed besides those, which it was evident must be employed on the stroke itself. However, that graceful drop of the shoulders at the end of the stroke, which adds so much to the beauty of amateur rowing, and which is of such assistance in keeping the weight of the body on the stretcher till the end of the stroke, necessitates the employment of many muscles in the abdomen, in order to effect the rapid recovery which is so essential in light boat rowing.

In the act of dropping the handle of the oar and the turning of the wrist, in the swift motion of the hands forward (which is so necessary to prevent the handle of the oar catching the knees, as it is liable to do in roughish water if the motion be deferred till after the knees are bent upwards by the forward motion of the body), several muscles of both parts of the arm and the chest are brought continuously into play and are developed in a corresponding manner.

In the arms too both the flexor and extensor muscles are used. It is however, as he says, only the muscles of the fore-arm which gain much strength from rowing exercise. For the advantage of any who study the science of medicine, I insert a description of the "muscular action in rowing," communicated to the *Lancet*[1], by F. C. Skey, Esq., C.B., F.R.C.S., the eminent surgeon, who has on former occasions expressed most unreservedly his opinion that rowing is very injurious. It will be seen that I am right in the chief points in which I have demurred to Mr Maclaren's statements.

"Presuming the rower to occupy his seat and sitting upright, the handle of the oar being held or grasped by both hands, the first action is a compound one, and consists of two movements—first of the trunk or body, and secondly of the entire upper extremity on the trunk: *i.e.* the body is drawn forwards to an angle of about 45°, allowing for the slight curvature of the spine, at the same instant that the arms are extended forwards to the fullest range in the same direction. The second action may be said to be simple or compound, in accordance with the different systems or styles adopted by different authorities. It consists in the recovery of the trunk to the vertical position synchronously with, or to be immediately followed by, the retraction of the shoulder and the flexion of the arm at the elbow-joint. A supplementary action, consisting of rapid extension of the wrist

[1] See *The Lancet*, Oct. 2, 1869.

by the three extensors, for the purpose of feathering the oar, completes the movements engaged in the act of rowing, so far as regards the trunk and upper extremities.

"At the moment which commences these movements, the muscles of the abdomen are brought into action, but for no other purpose than to steady the contents of the cavity—a function they perform on every occasion of a shock to the trunk, whether present or immediately prospective. They cannot influence the position of the trunk itself in its relation to the lower extremities. The body is drawn forwards by the psoas and Iliacus muscles, at least two-thirds of the exerted power being seated in the psoas magnus. When we consider that the full action of these two muscles is sufficient to raise the trunk from the horizontal, or lying, to the upright or sitting posture, the power required to draw the trunk forward from the vertical or upright position is very slight. Synchronously with this action is the extension of the arms to their fullest length, by the combined action of the serratus magnus, by which the scapula is drawn forwards from its position at rest on the back to the side of the trunk, with the pectoralis minor; the fore-arm is extended by the well-known action of the triceps and its small coadjutor the anconeus. The hands are slightly elevated, and the blade of the oar is lowered into the water.

"All the above movements are made preparatory to those by which the boat is propelled, the major action of the whole circle. This is either simple or compound, or rather it consists of two movements that may be either simultaneous or consecutive. It is effected by the drawing back of the trunk, by the retraction of the scapulæ or shoulders, and by the flexion of the arms.

"The first of these movements is generally referred to the muscles of the back. But this is an error. The muscles of the back, under the general name of erector spinæ, act upon a nearly inflexible pillar and nothing more. The sum of their action cannot exceed in its range a greater length than from one to two inches, while the trunk has to move through a space equal to 45°, or the one-eighth of a circle. We must look, therefore, to other agency, to the influence of some enormous muscular power that can directly influence the relations between the trunk and lower extremities, and operate in drawing backwards the entire trunk from an angle of 45° to an' angle of 90°, and of restoring the body to its upright position, and something beyond it. This can only be effected by the great muscles of the buttock, attached between the trunk and the thigh, which sweep round the back of the os innominatum of the pelvis and the thigh-bone, thus involving the hip-joint or centre of motion, upon which the trunk glides. The great muscle of the rower is the gluteus maximus, by the agency of which the trunk is drawn backwards in the act of rowing, or is thrust vertically upwards, as in the act of rising from a chair. The Oxford principle or practice in rowing—whichever it may be termed—involves the primary actions of these two muscles as the great and prominent feature of the art. When they affirm that they row with the back, they in reality row with the buttock or great glutei muscles, as indeed do all persons engaged in the art of rowing,—if it be an art. The second, and with some authorities the simultaneous movement, consists in the whole arm being drawn backwards with the shoulder. The scapulæ are replaced on the dorsal aspect of the trunk by the following muscles: the trapezius, latissimus dorsi, rhomboidei, aided in some degree by the pectoralis major.

"When the glutei have restored the trunk to the vertical position and a little beyond it, the work is taken up by the flexors of the arm at the elbow-joints. These muscles are the biceps and brachialis anticus, which bend the elbow-joint to somewhat less than a right angle. As regards the relation of the elbow-joint to the side, I consider that greater freedom of action of the arm is obtained by the elbow being drawn slightly outwards from the body, than by being retained in close proximity to it.

"The handle of the oar is held in pronation of the fore-arm, and both pronation and rapid and powerful flexion of the fore-arm are facilitated by a slight elevation of the elbow-joint from the body.

"The prominent and distinctive feature of the

Oxford system consists, I believe, in this, that the action of the glutei in drawing the trunk backwards to something beyond the vertical line, is nearly exhausted before the agents of the flexion of the fore-arm commence their work. The Oxford authorities consider that they row with their trunk, while others more prominently row with their arms. In truth, the muscular systems of both trunk and arms are indispensable in all cases, the only distinction being that in the case of the Oxford oarsmen the greater part of the retraction of the trunk, by the action of the glutei, is accomplished with rigid unbent arms, while in other cases the retractors of the shoulder and the flexors of the fore-arm act somewhat more in unison, or rather, they share the time occupied in the former action." [Mr Skey is inclined to think that the Oxford—or what he might more accurately have called the English—system is the more advantageous, for] "Although it may appear obvious that time would be saved by their concurrent or synchronous contraction, yet I do not think the glutei would contract with that force and freedom of action which they would command if they acted singly and alone....An important adjuvant of good rowing is seated in the lower extremities, the muscles of which are brought into strong action. But to suppose that the muscles of the thigh and leg play a very prominent part in the act of rowing as taught by the Oxford authorities, is a physiological error. A few words of explanation will, I think, render this statement clear. It will be observed from the description given above of the influence exercised by the various muscles whose actions have been described, that the result of their contraction, one and all, is to approximate their extremities in a ratio with their form and magnitude generally to the extent of about 45°. The trunk is drawn backwards, and the arm is bent to nearly or to quite that extent. Now the muscles of the lower extremities are attached between two points, which are all but motionless—the pelvis above and the foot below; the former being fixed on the seat, the latter strapped down to the stretcher or foot-board. The functions of these muscles can only be called forth when the limbs are freely subject to their influence in the acts of flexion and extension.

"In the act of bringing the body forward the extensor muscles, viz. the quadriceps, as well as those which constitute the calves of the legs, are slightly relaxed, and the knees bend a little outwards in the same slight proportion. Concurrently with the action of the glutei, the muscles both of the thigh and leg are brought into powerful contraction, for the double purpose of forming the leg into a firm inflexible pillar and pressing the foot immovably against the footboard, forming, as it were, a fulcrum by which the body is enabled to retain its exact position on its seat during the powerful action of the glutei.

"Without this pillar the glutei would lose half

their force. The sense of fatigue, the aching pain of the lower extremities, that follows active undisciplined rowing, is not evidence that these muscles, though indispensable to the exercise, play in it a more than secondary part."

It will be seen that in the above account Mr Skey dissents somewhat from the universal voice of rowing men in recommending that the elbows be not kept close to the side. I think that he has been led to do so by an error in observation. He says, "When the glutei have restored the trunk to the vertical position, and a little beyond it, the work is taken up by the flexors of the arm at the elbow-joints." His error, as I conceive, lies in supposing that the action of the flexors of the arm continues after that of the glutei has ceased. This, doubtless, is a not uncommon fault, which is known as "lugging with the arms at the end of the stroke," but is no part of the true action of rowing. The action of the glutei *commences* with the arms, back, loins and legs perfectly rigid, the arms extended to their fullest reach; but the arms and shoulders begin their work before the body has quite reached the vertical position, and finish all that part of their work, which assists propulsion, simultaneously with the body reaching its extreme backward position.

The reason which leads one to conclude that this is the most advantageous way of arranging the work, is that it has been mathematically determined that with a given amount of power the greatest velocity is attained if the application of force be constant; and it is assumed that, where this is impossible, the next best thing is to have it as nearly constant as possible.

If, then, the arms continue to work after the body has ceased its backward motion, the body must remain stationary for a perceptible space of time, during which the only force in action is the comparatively weak one of the arms (which is likewise objectionable for other reasons); whereas if the work of both ceases simultaneously, the body begins to move forwards at once, so that the centre of gravity of the crew is moved probably one foot nearer the stern of the boat than it was before. Now the average weight which each man has to carry in an eight-oared boat (including coxswain) is given by Mr Maclaren[1] as 58 lbs. Now supposing the average weight of the crew to be 11 st. 6 lbs. or 160 lbs., it is clear that the very act of moving the centre of gravity of the crew one foot to the rear will produce a considerable force of propulsion to the boat itself. It appears that by regulating the forces in this way a nearer approach to a constant force is attained, and thus a greater velocity will be the result. Since this is the case, it becomes quite a secondary consideration whether or no the arm is in the best position for a "rapid and powerful flexion," and "pronation" with the elbow close to the side soon becomes easy by practice. The more important

[1] P. 162.

consideration is how to get the hands forward again quickly enough, and a rapid extension of the arm is facilitated by keeping the elbows close to the side.

To return, however, to the general argument. We have seen that the muscles which are employed in rowing are very numerous, and comprise in their range nearly every portion of the body; moreover, that these muscles are generally developed in a judicious, that is, in a gradual and natural manner. In many other athletic exercises, however, this is not the case: the range of muscles educated is much more limited, and the development much less gradual. The efforts, as a rule, are sudden and spasmodic. A hundred yards runner takes his full breath at the start, and having thus, as it were, wound himself up, goes off at a burst, holding his breath to the end of the course. This occupies 10 seconds, which is just about time enough for three ordinary respirations. I once heard it stated on what, I believe, was good authority, that a certain celebrated quarter-of-a-mile runner, who four or five years ago used to win victories for Cambridge, used to start as in a hundred yards race and hold his breath for half the course, then take another breath, which he made suffice till he arrived at the winning post. Now the exertions a man makes in running a hundred yards race, though not of long duration, are, I suppose, the most severe and agonizing possible. Owing to the excitement of starting, and the struggle of the race itself, the blood must be sent coursing through the veins at a rate much higher than the ordinary, and, consequently, must require a much larger supply of oxygen than usual. But this extra supply is wholly denied it. One long breath is taken in, which perhaps supplies half as much more oxygen than an ordinary breath. Thus the runner carries with him just half the supply which he should have under ordinary circumstances (and this bottled up in a painful manner), and makes this last him during exertions which demand a far larger supply than ordinary. What wonder, then, that men are often sick and not unfrequently faint after a severe hundred yards race; nay, what a marvel it is that the bad results do not occur much more frequently.

In the other kinds of athletic sports, such as jumping and putting the weight, only a very limited range of muscles is employed, and those in a sudden and spasmodic manner. The whole force of the man is concentrated for a severe struggle in a very small space; these muscles alone are exercised, these alone "obtain any reward."

If athletics had continued to bear the same relation to rowing which they did some seven or eight years ago, little harm and much good would have attended the practice of exercises. Originally nearly all the College Athletic Sports were in connexion with the College Boat Clubs, and were intended to keep up general interest in athletic exercises among boating men. As the expenses of the clubs were small, it was found easy to offer considerable prizes for excellence in running, jumping, &c., whereas the heavy expenses of a boat club happily rendered it impossible to offer such for rowing. Thus self-interest came in the way, and by separating the athlete from the oarsman did injury to both.

The second and most important part of the objection was stated by Mr Skey, whom I have already quoted, in a letter to the *Times* in October, 1867. I cannot venture to attempt to answer his arguments, but I must beg leave to differ from his conclusions, because I think they are not generally borne out by facts. A letter which appeared in the *British Medical Journal*, about the same time, from Dr Humphry, of Downing College, Professor of Anatomy in the University of Cambridge, will be both the most conclusive and the most acceptable thing I can offer.

The letter is taken from the No. of the *British Medical Journal* for Saturday, October, 19, 1867.

Professor Humphry on the Effects of Boat-racing on the Health.

SIR,—You ask my opinion on the effects of boat-racing upon the health as shewn by members of this University. I have no statistics wherewith to fortify it; but my opinion, based upon the experience of more than a quarter of a century, during which I have been acquainted with a large number of members of the University, including, of course, boating men, is that the ill-effects of boat-racing are not so great as Mr Skey and some London physicians seem to think. They perhaps see the few sufferers, and are impressed thereby. We see, in addition, the many who pull year after year in the races and take no harm, but rather thrive upon it. On the whole, boating is unquestionably a great physical and moral good to the students, affording a healthful, agreeable recreation, and imparting vigour both to body and mind. A sight of the eight-oars on the Cam would convince any one of that. There ought to, there must, be something of the kind; and it diverts from more questionable amusements many who have little taste, perhaps because they have little fitness, for cricket and other games. That it should share the character of all sublunary things in having some evil mixed, inseparably mixed, with the good, is not only to be expected, but necessary. To say that it entails no evil, would be to admit that it does no good; still, to place the evil prominently and nakedly forward, and so cause a needless amount of alarm, is likely to destroy or diminish the good. We cannot have boating, such spirited boating as we ought to have, without boat-racing; and the contests between the Colleges naturally lead to the much-abused contest on the Thames, which is no doubt a considerable effort. If it were not an effort, it would not be worthy of the Universities; it would be merely the exhibition of a failure on their part to obey the good injunction, that they should do with all their might whatsoever they take in hand; but, it must be remembered, the pullers in that race are carefully selected—a few from among the great many who have been long and gradually trained in the College-races—with especial reference to their qualification of heart and lung, as well as of muscle, for such a contest; and they are diligently prepared for it. Thus the evil is reduced nearly to the minimum compatible with the good that is done by the race, in maintaining a healthful spirit of emulation among our men; and judging from my own experience (I have on several occasions known all or nearly all the Cambridge men) I should say that it is seldom productive of serious bodily mischief, either immediate or subsequent. I do not dispute the less favourable statements of others. On the contrary, I bear them in mind in the advice I am called upon to give; and I tender here merely the result of my own observations.

The fact is, undergraduates are, as a general rule, when not under the eye of their parents, cautious in what concerns their health, perhaps cautious enough; for too great timidity in that may degenerate into a moral weakness, of which I should say there is as much danger at the present time as of personal damage from boat-racing. They are prone to seek advice when they are in doubt as to their fitness for boating, and are for the most part willing to follow it, provided they feel that it is unprejudiced and grounded upon the real merits of the case. Being regarded as responsible agents, and allowed to judge for themselves, they are amenable to reason, and usually take the right course. At least, I have found so; and as my counsel, I need scarcely say, always inclines to the safe side, I have often had to test their forbearance. If we are to train in our Universities, as we wish to do, and as the country needs, an independent, noble and brave, as well as intelligent and industrious youth, we must leave them, to some extent, free to encounter the risks of sport as well as of work, which their energies involve. Mediocrity in play is inferior only to mediocrity in work; and excellence in neither can be attained without some risk. The nation that is best in one is likely to be best in the other. It is among the glories and hopeful features of England that she excels in sports. Woe betide her, when timid counsels damp the ardour of her youth! Whether is it better that their energies should be stimulated by boating with occasional failure of heart, by alpine-climbing with occasional loss of life, by hunting, shooting, &c., with their several attendant risks; or be restrained by timidity, and doomed to the dully secure saunter, with small stick and cigar, in High Street, King's Parade or Regent Street? The struggles on the Isis and the Cam are the counterparts of those in the schools and in the Senate-House. Both play their rôle in developing the man, and preparing him for the struggles of life; and both do so partly by the courage-exciting risks which they involve.

Even from a medical point, we must not omit to take this view into consideration. I trust the ventilation which the matter has undergone will have the effect of reassuring the public, as well as of increasing the discretion of the young, which even in them is so important an adjunct to valour, and so may tend to maintain the manly pastime of boating in our Universities.   I am, &c.

G. M. HUMPHRY.

CAMBRIDGE, *October*, 1867.

What has been adduced above will, I venture to think, satisfy the unbiassed reader that the case against Rowing is certainly not a formidable one, and that possessing as it does many advantages both morally and physically over most other athletic exercises, Rowing as a national pastime may claim to take rank as among the best, if not the very best, means of exercising, disciplining and perfecting the physical powers of man, necessary in their measure to attain the "summum bonum" of the ancient moralist,

"Mens sana in corpore sano."

Apart from all considerations as to whether Rowing is or is not beneficial generally, we have the undoubted fact that it is the most popular recreation at the Universities. It is "par excellence" the reading man's recreation. By means of it he is enabled in a short time to get sufficient exercise to restore the free circulation of the blood which is enfeebled by close application of the mental powers: it demands his whole attention for the time being, and so prevents his mind recurring to his studies in the time when they ought to be wholly out of his thoughts. It need interfere with no work, for the boats generally go down after lectures are all over: to the vast majority of reading men some *violent* exercise is necessary, to nearly all—to all sound men—it is beneficial; and that recreation naturally becomes most popular amongst reading-men which gives the greatest amount of exercise with the expenditure of the least amount of time: if too, any exercise be found which adds to these recommendations, the further one of being inexpensive, that naturally secures the largest number of devotees. All these advantages rowing does possess. What wonder, then, that it is so popular.

There are some who think and assert, apparently without fear of contradiction, that hard-rowing and hard-reading are incompatible: that the man cannot endure the severe strain on both his mental and his physical powers at the same time. But in an argument facts are more forcible than theories, and most fortunate are we at this time, when men of such eminence and such authority on the one hand, and so many anxious parents on the other, unite to condemn our noble sport, most fortunate in being able to point to the names of great men, the men who, spite of opposition on the part of college authorities, first made rowing popular at the Universities, and who are now in the possession of that health and vigour which *theoretically* ought to have wasted away long since, and who in the midst of, and *in spite of*, their rowing, were celebrated in the schools and carried off University honours, which were only a foreshadowing of the more substantial honours that awaited them in the world, in the church, the senate, the forum. After them we can point to a goodly line of men celebrated for their University achievements, some of whom have already attained to high places in the state, and others who bid fair to leave "foot-prints in the sands of time." Let us their successors then be not slow to remember with gratitude the heritage they have left us, and strive to transmit it undiminished to those who come after us. So shall we be able to show far more satisfactorily than by the most unexceptionable arguments, how groundless are the gloomy forebodings of anxious parents and how unnecessary the not less kindly warnings of medical men. I cannot leave this subject without giving the reader the report of a speech of the Bishop of Lichfield, at a meeting which was held under the presidency of the late Lord Justice Selwyn, in June, 1868, to consider what steps should be taken for the Improvement of the River Cam:—

The Lord Bishop of Lichfield rose to move the first resolution, and was received with loud cheers. He said he did not know whether he should apologise for being present, but he could hardly stay away on an occasion like this without showing an amount of ingratitude for an institution which had materially promoted his success in life. It was the same feeling which had prompted his two brothers (Lord Justice Selwyn and Professor Selwyn) to attend the meeting, viz. that they had begun their career in the racing boats on the Cam. Boating was prominently a University means of education. Some of their amusements wasted time, health, and money; but he did not find that boating wasted much time, and it certainly did not waste health. (Hear, hear.) His brother (Lord Justice Selwyn) and himself bore testimony to the fact of boating not injuring the constitution, for he believed if his constitution had not been much tried before he went out to New Zealand he should have broken down; but, having been a boating man on the Cam, he had been thereby enabled to undergo arduous duties. He certainly might say that boating, properly carried out on strict temperance principles, could not injure a man's constitution. (Hear, hear.) He considered that boating was a high moral lesson; and the training they underwent on the Isis and the Cam proved beneficial in after life. The Bishop of Newcastle was No. 7 in his boat, and Bishops Barker, Sydney, Nixon, and Hopper were all members of racing crews. At the first Henley regatta there were three persons from Cambridge University who took part against Oxford who afterwards became bishops. When speaking at Oxford a short time ago he did not say that they were beaten on that occasion. (Laughter.) He cordially joined in the undertaking to deepen the river, and to prevent the silting up of the little water that remained, as he considered that boating was a training of a highly intellectual kind. But there were two or three things connected with this subject which he wished to mention. There was a great disposition to forget the public good for private advantages; and this had crept into every profession except that of boating. Everybody wanted to be paid, receive praise, signalise or individualise himself; but in the University race everything of that kind was merged in the Dark Blue or the Light Blue. There was a sort of corporate spirit which seemed to exclude all idea of individuality. There was a tendency for active-minded men to become single-harness men, who would not consent to go in a four or an eight, and they were little better than the representative in the standard cabs. In an eight it was quite the contrary—they were all animated with the same spirit, and bound together, as it were, by sinew and bone, No. 7 looking at the shoulders of stroke, and so on throughout the boat. There was no better training-school for a young man than to engage in boating, or perhaps cricket; but what are cricket-matches nowadays? They occupy three days, and, after being out fielding for that length of time, a man will go to the wickets, and perhaps be bowled out the first ball. (Laughter.) With regard to the Cam, it was well known that the amount of pollution going into it was making it more and more unfit every day for the purpose for which it was originally intended. They could not make it equal to the Isis, but they could make it much better than it was. £1500 had been subscribed, and it would not be difficult to double that amount. He believed they would find they were doing a great deal to encourage this beneficial pursuit, and that young men would engage in it in the same spirit that obtained years ago, when the boating man was, as a rule, a scholar, and many became fellows, and several bishops; and it was the best means by which their character was formed. His lordship concluded by proposing the following resolution, hoping that Cambridge would gain as many victories as Oxford had gained over them, "That, in the opinion of this meeting, it is most important to take immediate steps for improving the condition of the Cam."

Beside the above, speeches were made by the chairman, the Rev. Professor Selwyn, Mr Beresford Hope, M.P., the Hon. G. Denman, M.P., Mr J. Clarke Hawkshaw, Mr Leslie Stephen, and the Rev. W. Maule.

These interesting speeches are well worth the trouble of looking out and reading. A good report of them will be found in the *Field* of Saturday, July 4, 1868.

HISTORY OF THE BOAT RACES.

1829.

EIGHT-OARED rowing was in vogue at Oxford some time before it was introduced into Cambridge, where the first eight, built at Eton and belonging to St John's College, was launched in 1826. It was between this year and 1829 that the Cambridge University Boat Club was formed. The earliest records of the Club contain an account of a meeting held in December, 1828; when a *new* set of rules was drawn up. The oldest chart of the races, which I know of, is a parchment one in possession of 1 Trinity Boat Club; it commences with the races for the Lent term, 1827. These may, I think, be looked on as the earliest College Races on the Cam, and we may assume that the Club commences at that date. There were only six boats on the river this term, a ten-oar and an eight-oar belonging to Trinity, an eight-oar belonging to St John's, and three six-oars belonging to Jesus, Caius and Trinity Westminster

At a meeting held on the 20th of February, 1829, Mr Snow, St John's College, was requested to write to Mr Staniforth, Christ Church, Oxford, proposing to make up a University match for the ensuing Easter Vacation, at or near London.

As the rowing at Oxford did not begin till after Easter, it was found impossible to have the race until the summer.

After some correspondence it was finally agreed that the course should be from Hambledon lock to Henley bridge, a distance of two miles and a quarter, and that the race should be rowed on June 10th, in the evening.

The following account of the Race is taken from a number of LONDON SOCIETY, *and is evidently from the pen of an eye-witness.*

THE FIRST UNIVERSITY BOAT-RACE,

JUNE 10, 1829.

COURSE: HAMBLEDON LOCK to HENLEY BRIDGE, 2¼ *miles exactly. Time* 14 *m. Another account* 11 *m.* OXFORD *won by* 60 *yards or* 5 *or* 6 *lengths.*

Everybody who recollects the day will remember that it was as fine a day as our climate allows a June day to be.

I look back upon this event now with some feeling of surprise at the state of the University mind that day. The race between the crews of the Universities was, one need hardly say, not at all what it is now. No one looked upon it then as a water Derby: such a thing had never been heard of till that year. And yet I can appeal to the memory of all my contemporaries, whether they have ever at any time since seen the whole University turn itself out as it did that day. The gravest and the most unexpected men were to be seen riding or even driving on some part or other of that three-and-twenty miles between Oxford and Henley. There were gigs, tandems, pairs; and one party of friends actually approached the scene, and I believe returned in safety, in a four-horse drag driven by one of themselves. At least I saw them safe baiting at Benson on the way back. [The writer then goes on to state that he and three friends drove over with a hamper of provisions. They with a few others managed to get a room in an inn, and added slightly to their stock of food from the host's larder in the shape of a shoulder of mutton and some cheese. For these, on demanding their little bill, they found themselves charged at the rate of 10s. per head, and on remonstrating were silenced by the host telling them, with an air of injured integrity, that they might consider themselves very generously treated in not being charged corkage for their own wine.]

The race was rowed as evening came on; and, as the time for it drew near, the whole crowd of Oxford and Cambridge men swelled down to the river-side and on the bridge; the Oxford men showing their blue favours, the Cambridge pink. I was fortunate enough to get a capital position for seeing the conclusion of the race, on the top of the little bridge-house at the Berkshire end of Henley Bridge. The start was out of sight. The odds, it will be remembered, were offered and taken against Oxford. A defeat was confidently expected even by Oxford men; so that we, who wore blue, on taking our stand as we could to see the end of the race, were not in the highest possible spirits. At last it was known that the boats were off. And I will here set down a story which was told at the time, and generally believed. Our friendly antagonists, at starting, were said to have complained that their oars fouled in the weeds. In consequence of this complaint the start was decided not to have been a fair one, and a second was made. Then the Oxford coxswain steered his men through the same water of which the Cambridge crew had complained, and pleasantly called out to them, "Weeds, weeds!"

I have made it my business to inquire into this story, and am able to say on the best possible evidence, —the evidence of some of the crew of the Oxford boat, —that it is untrue. What really happened was this. The Cambridge men having won the toss for choice of side, chose the Berkshire shore. Then, at the start the Cambridge coxswain steered out into the stream. If the course so steered had been acquiesced in by the Oxford coxswain, the Oxford boat would have sustained a serious loss. He held his course, and a foul ensued. The umpires[1] decided that, there being plenty of water on the Berkshire side, both boats should be allowed to row in it. When the boats shewed themselves rounding the bend of the river, all doubts as to the event were over. The first *corona navalis* was to come to Oxford...The Cambridge boat had no chance at any time after it was seen from Henley Bridge; but I think scarcely sufficient justice is rendered to the skill and resolution of the Cambridge crew by the use of the word "easily" [which is the word used by the *Times* in describing the race]. However, the thing was settled; and in a few minutes the Oxford boat came up to an arch of Henley Bridge, well ahead, and shot under to the landing-place. Never shall I forget the shout that rose among the hills. Anyone who has been at Henley will recollect how well the valley lies for reverberating sound. Men who loved Horace must have thought of his lines to Mæcenas,

"...ut paterni
Fluminis ripæ, simul et jocosa
Redderet laudes tibi, Vaticani
Montis imago."

Certainly the echo, image of the Berkshire hills, made itself heard. It has never fallen to my lot to hear such a shout since. There was fierce applause at the installation of the Duke of Wellington a few years

---

[1] See Appendix II.

after, and there has been applause under a hundred roofs since; but applause that fills a valley is a different thing. I did not see the great pageant of the entry of the Princess Alexandra into London; but I had the good fortune to see her embark with the Prince of Wales at Southampton, on the evening of their marriage. The quays and the Southampton water gave back no such answer to our cheers as the Henley valley gave on the 10th of June, 1829.

The following is a correct list of the crews:

OXFORD.

1	J. CARTER	*St John's.*
2	E. J. ARBUTHNOT	*Balliol.*
3	J. E. BATES	*Ch. Ch.*
4	C. WORDSWORTH	*Ch. Ch.*
5	J. J. TOOGOOD	*Balliol.*
6	T. F. GARNIER	*Worc.*
7	G. B. MOORE	*Ch. Ch.*
str.	T. STANIFORTH	*Ch. Ch.*
cox.	W. R. FREMANTLE	*Ch. Ch.*

CAMBRIDGE.

			st.	lbs.
1	A. B. E. HOLDSWORTH	*Trin.*	10	7
2	A. F. BAYFORD	*Trin. H.*	10	8
3	C. WARREN	*Trin.*	10	10
4	C. MERIVALE	*St John's.*	11	0
5	THOS. ENTWISLE	*Trin. H.*	11	4
6	W. T. THOMPSON	*Jesus*	11	10
7	G. A. SELWYN	*St John's.*	11	13
str.	W. SNOW	*St John's.*	11	4
cox.	B. R. HEATH	*Trin.*		
	Average		11	1⅝

The following account of the race is taken from JACKSON'S OXFORD JOURNAL *of June* 13, 1829.

The Oxford crew appeared in their blue-check dress, the Cambridge in white with pink waistbands. The boats of both parties were very handsome, and wrought in a superior style of workmanship. In their preparation to row down to the start the men were hailed with loud acclamations. The post was marked rather more than two miles below the bridge, near a little island; and after an agreement was made as to which side of the island they should row (the choice of which fell to Cambridge), the race begun. The crews of both pulled gallantly, and with clever and equal stroke. There was no great difference between them till passing on each side of the island, when Oxford made a bold and hearty struggle and, on reaching the main opening of the stream, shot ahead some distance, and then began the race in reality. Each of the boats put out the strength of their arms (!) in excellent style, and with the utmost regularity and precision; but it was seen that the Oxford crew were the more powerful and were gaining the victory, for the opposing crew, though coming a few strokes on them, were unable to make that head which shewed a probability of success.

In this way they rowed up to the bridge, among the cheers of thousands, and the contest ended in the victory of Oxford by several boats' lengths.

There was a magnificent display of fire-works in the evening.

It was reported that the match was for a very large sum; but we have authority for stating that it was by no means a gambling match, but a trial of strength and skill.

JUNE 20.

We forgot in our last to mention the manifest difference in the boats. The Cambridge boat, though London-built and launched new for the occasion and much gayer in appearance than the old Oxford boat, was far inferior in the water, dipping to the oar whilst the other rose to every stroke in fine style; and though the Oxford crew were stronger, the Cambridge might have given them more trouble if they had been equally well boated.

Wordsworth, of Christ Church, who rowed No. 4 in the Oxford boat, played in the 'Varsity eleven in the cricket match, which took place a few days after and in which Oxford again proved victorious.

BIOGRAPHICAL NOTICES.

J. CARTER, took his degree in 1830.

E. J. ARBUTHNOT[1].

J. E. BATES, Perpetual Curate of Litherland, 1841; of Christ Church, Hougham in Dover, 1844; died in 1856.

C. WORDSWORTH, D.C.L., graduated in 1830, was ordained deacon in 1834, and was consecrated to the Bishopric of St Andrew's in 1853.

J. J. TOOGOOD, graduated 1832; ordained 1832; prebendary of Combe the 10th in Wells Cathedral, 1840; rector of St Andrew's, Holborn, 1850-7; rector of Kirby Overblow, 1858.

T. F. GARNIER, D.D., graduated 1830; fellow of All Souls, 1830; ordained 1833; chaplain to House of Commons, 1849-50; rector of Trinity St Marylebone, 1850-59; dean of Ripon, 1859-60; dean of Norwich, 1860; died 1861.

[1] Of this gentleman I can obtain no trace.

G. B. MOORE, M.A., graduated 1831; and was ordained deacon, 1833; rector of Tunstall in the diocese of Canterbury.

T. STANIFORTH, M.A., graduated 1830; ordained 1830; instituted rector of Bolton by Bolland in the diocese of Ripon 1831, inducted 1832, resigned 1859; now living at Storrs Hall, Windermere. Captain of boats at Eton, 1826.

W. R. FREMANTLE, M.A., graduated 1829; ordained 1833; rector of Middle Claydon, and of East Claydon w. Steeple Claydon, 1841. Author of *Eastern Churches, Sermons*, &c.

A. B. E. HOLDSWORTH, died many years ago.

A. F. BAYFORD, LL.D., is now the principal registrar of the Court of Probate, and chancellor of the diocese of Manchester. He graduated LL.B. 1830, bracketted Senior in Civil Law.

C. WARREN, M.A., graduated 1831; ordained 1832; vicar of Over, near St Ives, Huntingdon. Author of *The Lord's Table the Christian Altar; The Ministry of the Word for Absolution;* editor of *Synodalia*, a Journal of Convocation.

C. MERIVALE, D.D., graduated in 1830 as 4th in the first class of the Classical Tripos, and a Senior Optime. He was elected fellow and tutor of St John's College. In 1848 the College presented him to the parish of Lawford, Manningtree, Essex, in the diocese of Rochester. He was select preacher in 1838; Whitehall preacher in 1840; he was appointed chaplain to the

House of Commons, and has just lately succeeded Dr Goodwin in the deanery of Ely. Author of the *History of the Romans under the Empire.*

THOS. ENTWISLE, a gentleman of fortune, living near Christchurch, Hants; called to the Bar at Middle Temple, Nov. 1834.

W. T. THOMPSON, fellow-commoner of Jesus College, took holy orders and for a time served the English Church at Brussels. He was in the University eleven as well as the eight, and neither his rowing nor his cricketing could be easily impugned. He was alive in 1838, but died of heart disease before 1841.

G. A. SELWYN, D.D., was born at Richmond (Surrey) in 1809. He was the second son of William Selwyn, Esq., Q.C., and was educated at Dr Nicholas', Ealing, then at Eton, and afterwards at St John's College, Cambridge, from which College he took his degree in 1831, as second in the first class of the Classical Tripos, and as Junior Optime. He was elected fellow of his College, and after being tutor to Lord Powis' sons at Eton, he became curate of Windsor, where he remained until nominated Bishop of New Zealand in 1841. At Eton he was celebrated for his powers of swimming, and was mainly instrumental in establishing the swimming school there, which Etonians will know under the name of "Passing," and which has been so beneficial, that since its foundation there has been no case of drowning at the school.

He went to New Zealand in 1841. He was wont while there to go the round of his diocese every year, employing for this purpose a small schooner of 21 tons, which he used to navigate almost entirely himself; from 1848 he used also to pay a yearly visit to the Islands of the South Pacific, bringing home from thence boys to be trained at the mission school at Auckland. He returned to England in 1854, but went out again to New Zealand in the next year and stayed there till summoned home for the Lambeth Conference in 1867. His later voyages were made in a vessel called the *Southern Cross*, given him by his friends in England. During the war in New Zealand he served with the troops as chaplain.

When the bishopric of Lichfield became vacant by the death of Dr Lonsdale, the late Lord Derby pressed Dr Selwyn to accept it. In accepting it, Dr Selwyn made it a condition that he might return to settle matters in New Zealand.

In July, 1868, he sailed for New Zealand, and having taken leave of his diocese, returned to England by the end of the year.

W. SNOW, M.A., educated at Eton and St John's College, graduated as Junior Optime in 1828; afterwards he changed his name to Strahan, and was a banker in London.

B. R. HEATH, educated at Eton and Trinity College, Cambridge; took no degree at the University; late Captain of East Sussex Militia; died 1851.

1834.

There does not seem to have been any attempt to get up another race between the two universities until 1834. In that year Cambridge was very desirous to have a race, but owing to certain differences of opinion between the two parties as to the most convenient arrangements, it never came off.

On the 26th of April the C. U. B. C.[1] passed the following resolutions :—

1. That a Challenge be immediately sent to Oxford.

2. That the Thames between Westminster Bridge and Hammersmith should be the water proposed to Oxford to race on.

3. That a Committee be formed of five captains, who should choose a captain for the Cambridge crew either from their own body or the University at large; and who, after having chosen

[1] Cambridge University Boat Club.

a captain, and observed the rowing of men in the respective crews on the river, should make a report of their observations and choice.

4. That the crew thus formed should be open to challenge from any and every crew in the University.

A challenge was sent in accordance with these resolutions: to which the Oxford men replied, through Mr Lane, of Queen's College, that they accepted the challenge to row,—but named Henley as the *venue*, first, because it was chosen in the first match; secondly, because it was equally fair for each party (?); and, thirdly, because it would be more free from interruptions.

Hereupon a very lengthy correspondence ensued; in which the Cambridge men, while adhering to the tidal water, extended the choice to any part between Westminster and Richmond, and the Oxford men admitted Maidenhead as the alternative to Henley: no compromise was arrived at, and the match was dropped.

In consequence of this, the Cambridge men had the following inserted in the *Cambridge Chronicle* and *Bell's Life;* it seems a very fair statement of the facts of the case :—

> We are sorry to state that the proposed boat-race between the two Universities will not take place, owing to the Oxford crew having declined the contest, unless the match took place either at Henley or Maidenhead. The challenge was on the part of Cambridge, and the terms proposed were, that the race should come off on any day between the 4th and 21st of June, on any part of the river Thames, between Westminster and Rich-

mond bridges, at any state of the tide, and either with or against it. Had this challenge been accepted, the scene of action would have been equally distant from both Universities, and the water equally unknown to both parties.

Before this year there was a lock in the river Cam at Chesterton: it was situated opposite to the Pike and Eel Inn, just above "Charon's" ferry. The College races used to take place between these locks and the boat-houses; and, though bumping races, they differed considerably from those we have now. Each boat had as now a separate starting-post. These posts were placed alternately on opposite sides of the river, and were placed at such distances apart that each boat overlapped the one in front. The boats were started all together, and the object of each was to bump the boat in front, and to avoid being bumped by the boat behind. As the boats were placed so near together, this would of course have been too trifling a matter, had there not also been what was called a "bumping" post, allotted to each boat higher up the river. It was unlawful for any boat to make a bump on the boat in front of it until it had passed this post. The tortuous course of the river between the Jesus sluice and Chesterton lock rendered some such arrangement necessary.

This lock the conservators of the Cam decided on removing, much to the alarm of the U.B.C., who made most strenuous efforts to prevent it. Here is an instance of the way in which human nature so constantly magnifies the evils that are but dimly seen, nay sometimes makes evils out of things that are in reality benefits, and afterwards turn out to be the very greatest blessings.

These locks held up the water some 5 or 6 feet, probably, and it was looked upon as a certainty that when they were removed the river would become too shallow for rowing in. Men probably thought and said that boating would be an impossibility, and all the hopes of the U.B.C. would be dashed to the ground. Whereas the removal of the locks only obliged them to stir themselves, and look for another course; they found one further from home, it is true, and therein less convenient, but far better and more suitable in every other respect. They also set about finding out the probable cost of deepening and widening the stream; but found that the widening alone would cost between £1000 and £2000, which sum it was utterly beyond the power of the Club to raise; and so the matter dropped.

When it was first decided to challenge Oxford it was agreed to have no bumping races that term; but as the answer to the challenge was some time in arriving, it was decided that unless it should have come before a certain day, that the races should go on, but that no boats should be obliged to row if any of the crew were rowing in the University boat. Those boats which were exempted on this account were allowed to retain their places on the river in the following year.

1836.

In this year, curiously enough, challenges were sent simultaneously from Cambridge and from Oxford; the former renewing in exactly the same terms the challenge of the year 1834, and the latter making a fresh one.

It was agreed that the coxswains must be members of the Universities, but there was considerable discussion about the state of the tide at which the race was to be rowed.

The Oxford men wanted to row on the 16th or 17th of June, and proposed to row against the tide from Putney to Hammersmith. The Cambridge men objected to rowing against the tide, as they considered that fouling would be almost unavoidable if that were agreed to. As, however, both parties were fully determined to have a race at all hazards, these disagreements were happily settled at a personal conference which was held at the Star and Garter, Putney, on the 16th of June, when, after considerable discussion, it was agreed to row the race the next day at 20 min. past 4 in the afternoon (it being then flood[1] tide) from Westminster Bridge to Putney Bridge.

The following list of the crews is from the

---

[1] This word is crossed out in the C.U.B.C. book, but no other has been substituted for it.

Cambridge books, and the account below is taken from *Bell's Life:*—

THE CAMBRIDGE CREW.

1	WILLIAM HAMMOND SOLLY	*Trinity.*
2	FREDERICK GREEN	*Caius.*
3	EDMUND STANLEY	*Jesus.*
4	PERCEVAL HARTLEY	*Tr. Hall.*
5	WARREN MILLER JONES	*Caius.*
6	JOHN HENRY KEANE	*Trinity.*
7	ARTHUR WILSON UPCHER	*Trinity.*
str.	AUGUSTUS KER BOZZI GRANVILLE	*C. C. C.*
cox.	THOS. SELBY EGAN	*Caius.*

THE OXFORD CREW.

1	GEORGE CARTER	*St John's.*
2	FERDINAND THOMAS STEPHENS	*Exeter.*
3	WILLIAM BAILLIE	*Ch. Ch.*
4	T. HARRIS, M.A.	*Magdalene.*
5	JUSTINIAN VERE ISHAM	*Ch. Ch.*
6	JOHN PENNEFATHER	*Balliol.*
7	WILLIAM S. THOMPSON	*Jesus.*
str.	FREDERICK LUTTERELL MOYSEY	*Ch. Ch.*
cox.	D. T. DAVIS	*Jesus.*

The Cambridge men wore white cotton elastic rowing shirts; and the Oxford similar shirts striped blue and white, and blue handkerchiefs, the latter of which were thrown on one side previous to the start.

"The preliminaries having been satisfactorily

arranged, and the boats having taken their stations (the toss for choice being in favour of Cambridge), the signal was given for starting at 21 minutes and a half past four, it being then just the top of high water. Both crews went away from the bridge in excellent style, the Cambridge however taking the start, the Oxford lying close alongside, and off the wharfs in Milbank Street were, for a few seconds, stem and stem with Cambridge, who then went to work most gallantly, drew in advance at every stroke, and at Vauxhall Bridge were well ahead. It was evident, even at this period of the match, that Cambridge had it all their own way; and at Battersea, notwithstanding the Oxonians made several determined pushes to come up with their opponents, the odds were 10 to 1 in favour of the Cantabs, who pursued the "even tenour of their way," and reached Putney about one minute in advance of Oxford. The distance was rowed in 36 minutes by the winning boat. They had scarcely any tide with them the whole way, and the ebb met them about Wandsworth. We cannot say much in praise of the rowing of either party. Their style is bad for the Thames, whatever it may be for Cambridge and Oxford waters. Nos. * and * in the Oxford boat were particularly bad rowers, the former especially —it is surprising he did not shake his head off his shoulders by his frequent bobbings. We saw the Cambridge when they first went out after their arrival in London, and remarked upon their style of rowing as being nothing like that of the crack men of the Thames. They invariably begin to row where the London men leave off, and appear to have no notion of bending forward : we must confess that there was a decided improvement in this respect on the day of the match, a circumstance no doubt attributable to some eight or ten days' practice in our river, under the advice of one of the best of the London watermen. The Cambridge had the best boat. The one rowed by the Oxonians is too flat bottomed for the Thames; she may do very well in shallow water, but she ought never to be brought to London again for a similar purpose.

The Red House, Lintell's, the Old Swan, Battersea, and the Baron de Berenger, at the Stadium, fired their artillery as the contending boats passed; and Avis's, the Bells, and the other houses at Putney, greeted the parties with a volley on their arrival."

BIOGRAPHICAL NOTICES.

W. H. SOLLY, graduated 1837; of Serge Hill, Herts.; b. 1814; magistrate for Dorsetshire, Hertfordshire, and the Liberty of St Alban's.

F. GREEN, graduated 1837; formerly curate of Everdon, Northampton; Curate of Marston Bigot, 1842.

E. STANLEY, Captain of the boats at Eton, 1835; graduated 1849; resident in Belgium.

PERCEVAL HARTLEY, Scholar of Trinity Hall from 1836—41; graduated in Civil Law, second class 1839—40; secretary of C.U.B.C. 1836,

W. M. JONES, graduated 1835; secretary of C.U.B.C. 1834; died young.

J. H. KEANE, LL.B., educated at Rugby and Trinity College; graduated 1841; late Captain of Waterford Militia; Justice of the Peace and Deputy-Lieutenant for the county of Waterford; of Cappoquin House, Waterford.

A. W. UPCHER, M.A., Senior Optime 1837; ordained 1839; rector of Ashwellthorpe with Wreningham, diocese of Norwich.

A. K. B. GRANVILLE, M.A., graduated 1838; ordained 1839; late Perpetual Curate of St James, Hatcham, and Reader at Christ Church, Newgate Street, London; vacated his living in 1868; now living at Beechwood, Iffley, Oxon.; domestic chaplain to the late and present Earl of Ripon.

T. S. EGAN, M.A., graduated 1839. He has always devoted himself to aquatic sports, and used to steer boats at Henley for many years after he ceased to steer the University boat. He is one of the most faithful friends the C.U.B.C. has ever had; his time and talents have over and over again been put at the disposal of the officers of the club whenever they were in difficulty, and he has never failed them when asked to help. In 1852 he had the compliment paid him of being put in charge of the Oxford crew while in training for the University race of that year, and he brought them to the start in the highest state of perfection. Since then he has been mentor to the Cambridge boats on several occasions, and in 1864 the C.U.B.C., to shew their appreciation of the valuable services he had rendered, presented a life-boat to the National Life-Boat Association as a testimonial to him. This life-boat is called *The Tom Egan*, and is stationed at Tramore. There are frequent allusions in the minute books to the services it has rendered in saving the lives of shipwrecked seamen.

GEORGE CARTER, M.A., 4th Class of Lit. Hum. 1836; ordained 1836; rector of Compton Beauchamp, Farringdon, Berks. 1848; domestic chaplain to Earl Craven.

F. T. STEPHENS, Rector of St Mawgan-in-Pydar, Cornwall, 1846.

Sir W. BAILLIE, Bart. of Polkemmet, Linlithgow, M.P. for county Linlithgow 1845—7, educated at Eton and Christ Church.

T. HARRIS, B.D., graduated 1833; Fellow of Magdalene College; Curate of Marton, Warwick; Perpetual Curate of Horsepath, Oxon. 1844; Rector of Swerford Eustone, Oxon. 1849.

Sir J. V. ISHAM, Bart., educated at Eton and Christ Church; died 1846, aged 30.

J. PENNEFATHER[1].

W. S. THOMPSON[1].

F. L. MOYSEY, M.A., graduated and ordained 1838; curate of Trin. Church, Bath, assistant minister of St Margaret's Chapel, Bath, 1839; vicar of Combe St Nicholas, Somerset, 1840—1861.

D. T. DAVIS, M.A., curate of Pontypridd, Glamorganshire, formerly of Eglwy's Drindod.

[1] Of these gentlemen I can find no trace.

1837.

Again, in 1837 a race was proposed between the two Universities; the Cambridge men as before wished to have the London course, the Oxford men persisted in having the race at Henley. At last the Cambridge men proposed Ely, which presents most of the advantages and disadvantages of Henley (only the course is a fairer one); the only difference being that its advantages are common to both, whereas the disadvantages militate against Oxford, just as the Henley ones are adverse to Cambridge. Hereupon the correspondence dropped.

When it was evident that Oxford did not intend to make up a match, Cambridge challenged the Leander Club. This club had been in existence for eighteen or nineteen years, and by its rules it was limited to fifteen members. From its commencement it had ranked high, not only as a general crew, but also from the majority of its members having frequently distinguished themselves both in scullers' and oars' matches. Of late years it had increased so much in celebrity that it was generally considered that nothing on the river could rival them in speed. Although they had never before entered into an eight-oared contest, they often competed in other matches, and were the first to patronise and lend a helping hand in bringing out young watermen who shewed promise of aquatic fame. It was therefore considered a bold, and by some an imprudent, thing for the Cambridge men thus to beard the lion in his den. The match, however, was made; and notwithstanding the prestige of Leander, the betting commenced at 5 to 4 on Cambridge, people thinking that their youth and vigour would win the day against the more matured strength of their opponents, who averaged 36 summers. (*Bell's Life.*)

It was agreed at the wish of Leander that the coxswains should be watermen. At this period it was the custom on the London water to allow "fouling;" that is, to let one boat impede the other whenever it chose and was able to do so. This of course made the office of coxswain one of far greater importance than it is now; and at this time there were two London watermen, Parish and Noulton, who were celebrated rivals in this part of a coxswain's work. As, however, the object of the Cambridge men in challenge was to discover which crew was best, they made it an express stipulation that no fouling was to be lawful.

The race was fixed for Friday, June 9th, 1837. As the day drew near a sudden change took place in the betting, and six and seven to four were offered on the Leander, which odds on the day of the race "went a begging." Many of the best judges, indeed, looked on the event as a certainty for Leander. The crews were

The Cambridge Crew.

1. W. N. Nicholson .... *1st Trin.*
2. F. Green .... *Caius.*
3. G. Budd .... *LadyMarg.*
4. J. H. Keane .... *Trinity.*
5. W. B. Brett........................ *Caius.*
6. C. T. Penrose..................... *1st Trin.*
7. R. Fletcher .... *LadyMarg.*
str. Augustus Ker Bozzi Granville... *Corpus.*
cox. W. Noulton.

The Leander Crew.

1. Mr Shepheard.
2. Mr Layton.
3. Mr Wood.
4. Mr Lloyd.
5. Mr Sherrard.
6. Mr Dalgleish.
7. Mr Lewis.
str. Mr Hornby[1].
cox. J. Parish.

The course was from Westminster to Putney, and ended after a most manly and splendid struggle in a victory for Cambridge, who came in seven seconds ahead. The winners rowed the course in thirty minutes twelve seconds.

Bell's Life (April 7, 1839) says:

It was perhaps the most severe eight-oared contest ever witnessed, and, to the delight of their friends and

---

[1] In the Cambridge book this is given as Horseman.

the dismay of the betters of odds, Cambridge won the match, but only by seven seconds.

On the 10th June, 1837, a match came off at Henley between Queen's College, Oxford, and St John's College, Cambridge. The course was from Greenfield Cottage to Henley Bridge, about $2\frac{1}{2}$ miles, against stream. The Lady Margaret won the toss, but lost the race. The distance was rowed by the winners in $12\frac{1}{4}$ minutes.

1838.

In 1838 a return match was proposed by the Leander on the same terms as before; but resulted in a series of "fouls" from the beginning of the course to the end. The Leander men came in first by a length; but an objection was raised by the Cambridge men on the score of the fouling. Mr Searle, the umpire, having heard both sides, decided that it was "no match," neither being winners. The crews on this occasion were

THE CAMBRIDGE CREW.

1	A. H. SHADWELL	*St John's.*
2	W. W. SMYTH	*Trinity.*
3	WALTER R. GOUGH	*Trinity.*
4	H. YATMAN	*Caius.*
5	C. T. PENROSE	*1st Trin.*
6	A. PARIS	*Corpus.*
7	W. B. BRETT	*Caius.*
str.	E. STANLEY	*Jesus.*
cox.	W. NOULTON.	

THE LEANDER CREW.
1 SHEPHEARD.
2 SHERRARD.
3 LLOYD.
4 LAYTON.
5 WOOD.
6 DALGLEISH.
7 BISHOP.
str. LEWIS.
cox. J. PARISH.

1839.

There is no account in the Cambridge books of the Club transactions in 1838 or 1839, and the Oxford books do not begin till the end of the latter year. The Cambridge men, however, seem to have made good use of their time since 1836, and to have profited greatly by their contests with the "crack men of the Thames" in 1837-38. In 1836 it was said of them that they had no notion of bending forwards, but of Mr Stanley, who rowed stroke in 1839 (he was likewise No. 3 in 1836), it has been said that he was a "splendid man and the beau ideal of an oarsman." *Bell's Life* says that the "stroke was really terrific, one of the severest we ever saw. It was as long as the men could stretch forward, and at the same time tremendously swift."

The following account of the race is taken from *Bell's Life in London:*—

At the early part of the present year the Oxonians, having determined on another trial with their old opponents, and having formed a crew which they considered worthy of being entrusted with the honour of the University, sent off a challenge, which the Cambridge gentlemen were not slow in accepting. After some difficulties in the preliminaries had been got over, both crews went into close training, the Oxonians under the care of Jones, a London waterman, the Cantabs availing themselves of the experience of T. Selby Egan.

The terms of the match were that the race was to be rowed in eight-oared cutters, in the Easter vacation, from Westminster Bridge to Putney; no fouling to be allowed, and the boats to be steered by gentlemen.

Wednesday, April 3rd, was fixed for the race; and on Wednesday, March 20th, the Oxford crew went to the London water, followed by Cambridge on the next Friday.

The Oxonian boat was built by King of Oxford; she was 52 feet long, beautifully constructed and tastefully—nay, splendidly—"turned out." She was painted white and blue, and pricked with gold, having the arms of the University emblazoned on the rudder, with the words "Dominus Illuminatio Mea." She was named the *Isis*, and numbers of persons went to Roberts' boathouse to look at her. For the Cantabs Messrs Searle, of Stangate, built a new boat, but they had not sufficient time to complete her painting, and she had to be launched with only a priming coat of lilac inside. Both boats seem to have been models of perfect construction, and, as oak cutters, had perhaps never been surpassed in lightness.

Both crews pulled so extremely well in practice as to make it a matter of the greatest uncertainty which way the race would terminate, and speculators were at their wits' end to know which side to lay their money on. In fact, each party was so confident of success, that they backed themselves at odds freely. Cambridge, however, seem to have been slightly the favorites.

The crews, after several changes, were finally settled as follows:—

CAMBRIDGE.

1	ALFRED HUDSON SHADWELL	*St John's Coll.*
2	WARINGTON W. SMYTH	*Trinity.*
3	J. ABERCROMBIE	*Caius.*
4	A. PARIS	*Corpus Christi.*
5	C. T. PENROSE[1]	*Trinity.*
6	W. H. YATMAN	*Caius.*
7	W. B. BRETT[1]	*Caius.*
8	E. STANLEY[1]	*Jesus.*
cox.	T. S. EGAN[1]	*Caius.*

OXFORD.

1	STANLAKE LEE	*Queen's Coll.*
2	BERDMORE COMPTON	*Merton.*
3	SAMUEL EDWARD MABERLY	*Ch. Ch.*
4	WM. JAS. GARNETT	*Ch. Ch.*
5	R. G. WALLS	*Brazenose Coll.*
6	R. HOBHOUSE	*Balliol.*
7	PHILIP LYBBE POWYS	*Balliol.*
8	CALVERLEY BEWICKE	*University Coll.*
cox.	WOODFORDE FOOKS	*Exeter.*

None of the members of the Oxford crew, it will be seen, had pulled in the last race in 1836, whereas in the Cambridge boat Stanley, the stroke-oar, had rowed No. 3 in 1836; also the steerer was the same as in that year. Penrose and Brett had rowed in the first race with Leander, and all but Abercrombie had rowed in the second race.

[1] Were members of a former crew.

Mr Vialls of Trinity (who rowed stroke in the following year) had been several weeks in practice with the crew, but was obliged from illness to give place to Mr Yatman, on the Monday before the race.

Wednesday, the day of the race, was exceedingly cold, cloudy and windy, and just the very worst sort of day for an aquatic expedition: nevertheless many thousand persons collected to witness the start. As the time of this drew nearer Cambridge became more and more the favourites.

The river was crowded with eight-oars, sixes and fours, several colleges being well represented: Queen's College and St John's from Oxford, Trinity and Caius (who carried a handsome silk flag with the U.B.C. colours) from Cambridge.

The umpires chosen were CHAS. B. WOOLASTON, Esq. for Oxford and J. C. SELWYN for Cambridge; and W. HARRISON, Esq. the Commodore of the Royal Thames Yacht Club, had accepted the office of referee. The Oxonians required to have two other umpires on Putney Bridge, and named — HOBHOUSE, Esq. on their part, in whose hands the Cantabs were content to leave that post, without naming another. Mr Edward Searle, having undertaken the office of starter, went to Westminster Bridge at half-past four o'clock.

The Oxonians rowed down in their pea-coats and therefore did not afford us a good opportunity for quietly observing their muscular powers. The Cantabs went down ready for work in their short-sleeved guernseys, and a finer boat's crew could not, we think, be selected. They were apparently a heavier crew than their opponents. They wore white guernseys and white straw hats with light blue ribbons, the steerer having a rosette of the same colour on his breast. The Oxonians wore dark blue guernseys with white stripes, dark straw hats with dark blue ribbons. Oxford won the toss, and chose the inside position towards the Middlesex shore

Precisely at 13 minutes before 5 the word was given to start, and both went away in gallant style, at a pace seldom equalled for rapidity. As far as Roberts's they were as nearly oar and oar as possible, and a severe struggle was anticipated; but at this point the Cambridge boat appeared to be creeping in advance, and though the Oxonians put forth every particle of strength they were unable to keep level with the Cantabs, who drew palpably ahead off the Bishop's Palace, and at the Horseferry were so far in advance that the steerer took them over into their opponents' water, so that he was enabled to go inside some lighters which were moored there. Never did men exert themselves more than the Oxford men to gain their lost ground, but their manly and strenuous efforts were of no use, for the Cantabs kept increasing their advantage, and at Vauxhall were several boats' lengths in advance; at the Red House they were eight or ten, and still more at Battersea Bridge, which they passed under in $18\frac{1}{2}$ minutes from

starting; and at 18 minutes past five they shot
through Putney Bridge, one minute and forty-five
seconds ahead, amidst the almost deafening shouts
from hundreds of spectators, and roaring of cannon
from Avis's. The great distance that the Oxonians
were behind was due in a great measure to their
being steered too close in shore at Broom Houses,
when they had to jam the tide in coming out to go
under Putney Bridge.

Bell's Life says:

The Oxford was certainly a very fine crew, and
pulled well; and in the latter part of the match, when
their hopeless distance astern might very well have
damped their ardour, they kept at work in a most
plucky manner, though it was evident that several
of the crew were greatly exhausted. Their style is
not to our liking. The Cambridge men pulled like a
piece of mechanism, so beautifully did they work together. Their stroke was really terrific; one of the
severest we ever saw. It was as long as the men could
stretch forward, and at the same time tremendously
swift: only one of their men appeared at any time
to have had enough, and that was between Battersea
Bridge and Wandsworth, where he seemed a little
"baked;" but it was evident afterwards that he was only
shirking his work a little, for when the coxswain called
"to pick her up fore and aft through Putney Bridge"
he did his duty most manfully, and they sent her
through with a spirit as though they had just started.
We should be doing an injustice did we not mention
our opinion, that the Cambridge owed much of their
distance ahead to the steering of Mr Egan, which was
the admiration of every waterman and amateur on the
river.

The crowds who came to witness the race were
immense. Several steamers accompanied the boats,

but there does not appear to have been any complaint as to their behaviour.

At the dinner, Mr Selwyn, in responding to the toast of "The Umpires," observed that the true way to make his office unnecessary was to allow no waterman to have anything to do with the matches, but to leave it all to gentlemen. He did not wish to say a word against watermen, but watermen's ways were not their ways, or watermen's notions their notions.

BIOGRAPHICAL NOTICES.

A. H. SHADWELL, graduated 1840, graduated at Eton and St John's College. Second Class Classic and Junior Optime; son of Vice-chancellor Shadwell, and late examining clerk in Chancery. He resigned the post some years ago and became an attorney. He has now retired from practice.

W. W. SMYTH, M.A., F.R.S., F.G.S., chief Inspector of Crown Mines; Lecturer in Mining and Mineralogy in the Royal School of Mines; sometime President of Geological Society.

J. ABERCROMBIE, Senior Optime and B.A., 1839; a physician in practice at Cheltenham.

A. PARIS, graduated 1840.

W. H. YATMAN, M.A., of Wellesburne, Warwick, graduated 1841; called to the Bar 1844; Magistrate for the counties of Warwick and Gloucester.

Sir W. B. BRETT, educated at Westminster and Caius Coll.; Senior Optime, 1840; called to the Bar at Lincoln's Inn, 1846; practised as Special Pleader on the Northern Circuit; unsuccessfully contested Rochdale 1865; M.P. for Helston 1866—68; succeeded the late Lord Justice Selwyn as Solicitor-General in Mr Disraeli's Government in February, 1868, when he was knighted; and was raised to the Bench as Lord Justice of Common Pleas in August, 1868.

C. T. PENROSE, Bell's Scholar; graduated 1839 as second in first class Classical Tripos, and Junior Optime; ordained 1842; head master of King Edward's School, Sherborne, 1845—50; curate of North Hykehame; author of *Eight Village Sermons; Private Orations of Demosthenes;* died 1867.

S. LEE, graduated 1840; ordained 1840; rector of Broughton with Bossington, diocese of Winchester, 1842.

B. COMPTON, M.A., Post-Master of Merton, 1st class Mathematics, 3rd Lit. Hum., B.A., 1841; ordained 1853; Fellow of Merton Coll., 1841; Master at Rugby, 1851—57; rector of Barford, near Warwick.

S. E. MABERLY, M.A., educated at Eton and Christ Church. A barrister; afterwards Curate of Mells, Somerset; died there 1848.

W. G. GARNETT, M.A., graduated 1841; Captain of the boats at Eton, 1837; of Bleasdale Tower, Garstang; late M.P. for Lancaster.

R. G. WALLS, graduated 1841; ordained 1842;

rector of Firsby with Great Steeping, diocese of Lincoln, 1844.

R. HOBHOUSE, M.A., graduated 1839; ordained 1841; rector of St Ive, Liskeard, 1844; author of *Ministerial Watchfulness* (a visitation sermon), 1848.

P. L. POWYS, M.A., educated at Eton and Balliol; now Powys-Lybbe, of Hardwicke, Berks.; Barrister on Oxford Circuit; late M.P. for Newport, Isle of Wight.

C. BEWICKE[1].

W. FOOKS[2].

Henley Regatta.

In the early part of the year the inhabitants of Henley seem to have become alive to the fact that they had a beautiful reach of water, and that it was a great reproach to them that it was not made available for the purposes of Rowing by the institution of a regatta. A meeting was called, resolutions were passed, and money subscribed in the usual way in which we manage such matters in England; the Universities promised to assist, both by money and by personal appearance, if that were possible, and everything was arranged so satisfactorily that 100 guineas was soon raised for the Grand Challenge Cup, which was to be rowed for

[1] Of this gentleman I can find no trace.
[2] The orthography of this gentleman's name is most doubtful. In the University Calendar it is spelt in two ways, Fookes and Fooks; and in the books of the Exeter Boat Club it is spelt in four different ways, one being Ffolkes.

annually by such amateur crews in eight-oar boats, as might be duly entered and qualified, and be held by the winner on the terms specified in the regulations then made. The qualification rule was as follows :—

That any crew composed of members of a college of either of the Universities of Oxford, Cambridge, or London, the schools of Eton and Westminster, the officers of the two Brigades of Household Troops, or of members of a club established at least one year previous to the time of entering, be considered eligible.

Every boat was to be steered by an amateur member of the club or clubs contending.

All fouling was forbidden.

The entrance money (fixed at £5 for that year) was to be applied to the general expenses of the regatta, and for the purchase of medals for the winning crew.

On the same day it was fixed to have a race for the Town Challenge Cup for amateurs in four-oared boats.

The honorary secretaries were Mr J. Nash and Mr C. Towsey.

Of the Grand Challenge Cup, *Bell's Life* says that it is "the most classic thing of the kind we have ever seen. The symbolical allusions are of the most perfect order, and in excellent keeping with the subject which they are intended to illustrate. From a rich and boldly chased foot springs a stem, composed of water lilies and bulrushes, on which the cup is supported. The form which the manufacturers have given to it is that of the celebrated Warwick Vase. One side is left blank for the inscription; the other is occupied with a recumbent figure of Old Father Thames, which is beautifully designed and chiselled. The handles, which also represent aquatic productions elegantly twined together, spring from heads typifying Thames and Isis; and the border, which surrounds the upper edge of the cup, completes a classic treatment throughout, by being formed of the flowers and plants which adorn the noble river on whose waters the wager is to be decided."

To those who are not conversant with the nature of the course at Henley, it may be necessary to remark that it is about a mile and a quarter in length; of this, as will be seen on referring to the map, about the first mile, that is, up to the Poplars, is nearly straight, though indented by a point below Remenham Lodge; but just above the Poplars the river bends sharply to the Berkshire side, and thus gives a great advantage to the boat having that station, which has not only a less distance to row over, being on the inside of the circle, but is also more out of the stream. The object of the boat on the Bucks side is, therefore, in all cases to go off first, if possible, and thereby obtain a sufficient lead at the commencement of the bend round the point, to take the other's water; while, if the boat on the Berks side can prevent this, the crew is almost always good enough to go in first, unless very deficient in stoutness or pluck.—*The Field*.

The following crews entered for the Grand Challenge Cup :—

Oxford—Brazenose College, " Child of Hale."
Cambridge—Trinity Boat Club, " Black Prince."
Oxford—Etonian Club.
Oxford—Exeter College.
Oxford—University Boat Club.
Oxford—Wadham College.

The Regatta was fixed to take place on Friday, June 14th. Some disappointment was felt that neither the Cambridge University Boat nor Leander had entered.

The O.U.B.C. and the Exeter boat did not start; the four remaining boats contended in heats. In the first heat the Etonian Club easily beat Brazenose; in the second, Trinity beat Wadham after a good race by about one length. The winners of the two trial heats contended in the final heat, which was a most exciting affair. Up to the Point they alternately had the lead, but to such a trifling extent that they may be considered to have been oar and oar. After this, however, Cambridge, who had the inside of the corner, got a decided lead, but their opponents were close upon them, and it was only after the most severe struggle that the " Black Prince " were finally hailed as victors. The Grand Challenge Cup therefore came to Cambridge first.

1840.

After having suffered two such severe defeats as those of 1836 and 1839, the rowing men at Oxford set to work to introduce more method into their system of forming the University Crew. For this purpose they formed the O.U.B.C., which differs materially in its constitution from the C.U.B.C. The latter consists of the members of the different college boat-clubs, and is governed by a committee consisting of the captains of all the boats which contend in the regular University eight-oared races. The effect of this is that each college club is represented in proportion to the number of racing boats it has, and so approximately to the number of its rowing members.

At Oxford the club consists of such members of the University as choose to subscribe, irrespective of their being members of their college club. The club is governed by the captains of the college clubs, so that each college has one, and only one, representative. Owing to the fact that there is less difference in size amongst the colleges at Oxford, this plan, which would be impracticable at Cambridge, works well there.

In the middle of February a challenge was received at Cambridge from Oxford, the terms being as follows :—

" To row an University match in eight-oared

boats from Westminster to Putney with the tide, none but undergraduates to row. The match to take place at Easter."

The Cambridge captains decided on accepting the challenge to row, but would not consent to the clause excluding bachelors.

Three gentlemen were elected to form a committee of management and to carry on the correspondence with Oxford. This latter part of their duties seems to have been somewhat onerous, as I find from the books that " at least a dozen letters passed between the committee and the captain of the Oxford crew before anything was settled."

After the question of bachelors was settled, there was considerable discussion concerning the day on which the race was to be rowed, and this point was not settled until sixteen days before the race actually took place. Besides, owing to various causes, 17 men were tried before the crew could be fixed upon.

The crew was not finally got together till very late, in fact their first practice was on Friday, April 10, the match was rowed on the 15th, and on Monday, the 13th, they rowed the distance in $28\frac{1}{4}$ minutes. This is apparently very fast; for the average of the times of doing it in the five Oxford and Cambridge races that were rowed over this course is 31′. 59″, and the shortest of them is 29′. 30″.

The names of the two crews are as follows:—

CAMBRIDGE.

1. ALFRED HUDSON SHADWELL[1] ...*Joh.*
2. WILLIAM MASSEY ....*1st Trin.*
3. SAM. BARNARD TAYLOR ....*1st Trin.*
4. JOHN M. RIDLEY ....*Jesus.*
5. GEORGE CHARLES UPPLEBY ......*Magd.*
6. FRANCIS CRANMER PENROSE ...*Magd.*
7. HEIGHWAY C. JONES.............*Magd.*
str. CHARLES M. VIALLS (capt.) ......*3rd Trin.*
cox. T. S. EGAN[1] ....*Caius.*

OXFORD.

1. JACOB G. MOUNTAIN ....*Mert.*
2. I. J. J. POCOCK............ ....*Mert.*
3. S. E. MABERLEY[1] ....*Ch. Ch.*
4. W. ROGERS ....*Ball.*
5. R. G. WALLS[1] ....*Braz.*
6. E. ROYDS ....*Braz.*
7. GODFREY MEYNELL ....*Braz.*
str. J. J. T. SOMERS COX (capt.)...*Braz.*
cox. W. B. GARNETT.................*Braz.*

The boats were started for the race by Mr EDWARD SEARLE, at half-past 1 on Wednesday, April 15. Oxford took the lead and held it till near the Red House, Battersea, where the Cambridge drew alongside, and passed them a little below Battersea-bridge; they were, however, unable to tail them, and won the race only by a boat's length and a half. The accounts of

[1] Were in the crew of 1839.

the time the race was rowed in were different. The best authenticated was from a stop-watch in Mr Harrison's boat (the Commodore of the Royal Thames Yacht Club, who acted as referee, according to which the time was $29\frac{1}{2}$ minutes. Mr C. J. Selwyn acted as umpire for Cambridge, and Mr Bewick for Oxford. Certain steamers which accompanied the match were very troublesome.

The account in the Oxford Books is not *materially* different: the Oxford were well ahead at Vauxhall-bridge; off the Red House the struggle was intensely exciting; but the Cambridge gradually drew ahead, and eventually won by $\frac{3}{4}$ths of a length.

Bell's Life says:

The starter was obliged to give the important word "off," at a time when several steamers were lying in the very track of the boats; and though the umpires and others repeatedly desired those in command of the steamers to move out of the way, they declined to do so. The Oxford boat was in motion in an instant, and dashed off with the lead at a startling pace. The Cantabs appeared as if they did not hear the word, for they hesitated before they dipped their oars, and then several of them missed the stroke. However, they soon got to work and proceeded after the Oxonians, who had obtained a very good lead. The steamers at the same time getting in motion, occasioned a swell, which was a great annoyance to both crews: so that all through Chelsea-reach the regularity of stroke was quite lost in both the boats. The Oxonians continued to increase their distance in advance to Vauxhall-bridge, and looked so much like winners, that the odds of seven to four, and in many instances two to one, on Cambridge now dropped to evens.

The Oxford boat was nearly three lengths ahead

at the Spread Eagle; but here the long and the strong pull began to tell, and it was soon observable that the space between them was lessening. The Cantabs were not long before they came up to their opponent's quarter, and, while in that position, an incident occurred which might have put an unpleasant end to the day's sport. Coombes, who was steering the *Dolphin*, called out to Mr Garnett to keep nearer in, in doing which Mr Garnett crossed the Cambridge boat, thereby violating, in a certain degree, the articles of the match[1]. He, however, gained but little by this proceeding, as Mr Egan, by keeping in his own course, forced him out again. We feel quite certain that he (Mr Garnett) had not the least intention to foul, nor perhaps was he aware at the moment that the other boat was so close upon him; and we only mention it to shew the impolicy, to say the least of it, of allowing watermen to row alongside, giving directions, and taking an active part in such matches.

At the Red House the struggle was intensely exciting, the Oxonians were laying out every particle of strength to prevent what appeared about to take place: but their efforts were unavailing; at every stroke the Cambridge men crept upon them till they were fairly oar and oar. After a most manly and determined struggle the Cantabs went ahead, and at length placed their antagonists astern of them, at about one-third of the distance between the Red House and Battersea-bridge. Off the church the *Primrose* steamer steered right across the bows of the Cambridge so close that the coxswain had to put the rudder hard over to clear the worst of her swell. Another steamer also passed through Battersea-bridge so nearly before them, and made so great a swell amongst the piles of that awkward erection, that the leading boat was nearly swamped,

---

[1] The Oxford Book gives the Articles of the Match as follows:
That none should row but Undergraduates, and Bachelors who had raced in the College races.
That the course should be from Westminster Bridge to Putney Bridge, with the tide, on the 15th of April. That no fouling or *crossing* be allowed.

and the Oxford fared but little better. When they came to the straight piece of water up to Putney-bridge the Oxonians made a last struggle, and both boats went along with renewed speed, amid the cheers and vociferations of the spectators. The Oxonians were right in the wake of the Cantabs, not a boat's length astern; and so closely and severely was the contest kept up the remaining distance, that the Cantabs only passed under the centre arch of the bridge three quarters of a boat's length in advance of the gallant crew of the sister University.

BIOGRAPHICAL NOTICES. (CAMBRIDGE.)

W. MASSEY, a country gentleman living in Cheshire.

S. B. TAYLOR, M.A., graduated 1838; Vicar of Kingswood, Ewell, Surrey.

J. M. RIDLEY, M.A., son of John Ridley, Esq., of Park-end, Northumberland. Scholar of Jesus Coll. Graduated as Senior Optime in 1841, and was called to the bar at Lincoln's Inn, 1844. Now living as a country gentleman at Walwick Hall, Hexham.

C. G. UPPLEBY, a country gentleman. Deputy Lieutenant for Lincolnshire, and Colonel of Volunteers.

F. C. PENROSE, M.A., youngest brother of C. T. Penrose (see p. 64), Scholar of Magd. Coll., graduated 1842 as Senior Optime; son of the late Rev. J. Penrose, Vicar of Langton, near Wragby, Lincoln; architect to St Paul's Cathedral. Mrs Penrose, whose maiden name was Strickland, was the author of Mrs Markham's *History of England.*

H. C. JONES, called to the bar at Lincoln's Inn, 24 Nov. 1845.

C. M. VIALLS, a country gentleman living in Berkshire.

BIOGRAPHICAL NOTICES. (OXFORD.)

J. G. MOUNTAIN, M.A., educated at Eton and Merton; graduated 1841, 2nd Class Lit. Hum.; Principal of St John's Coll., Newfoundland, died there 1856.

I. J. J. POCOCK, M.A., educated at Eton and Merton Coll. where he obtained a Postmastership; graduated 1842 2nd Class Lit. Hum., called to the bar at the Inner Temple, Nov. 19th 1847. Conveyancer. Resides at Bridge Lodge, Maidenhead.

W. ROGERS, M.A., educated at Eton and Balliol Coll., graduated 1842, ordained 1842. Perpetual Curate of St Thomas, Charterhouse, 1844—1863. Prebend of St Pancras in St Paul's Cathedral, 1862. Rector of St Botolph's, Bishopsgate, 1863. Chaplain in Ordinary to the Queen. Author of *A Letter to Lord John Russell on the Educational Prospects of St Thomas, Charterhouse.*

E. ROYDS, graduated 1842. Ordained 1844. Rector of Brereton, Cheshire, 1845.

G. MEYNELL. Called to the bar at Middle Temple, Nov. 1845.

J. J. T. S. COCKS, ordained 1845; Rector of Cheviocke, Cornwall, 1845; vacated his living 1855; died 1867—8.

W. B. GARNETT, graduated 1840, ordained 1841. Preacher of Bunbury, 1853.

The dinner went off as usual with the greatest *éclat*. Mr C. J. Selwyn in returning thanks for the Umpires, after commenting on the bad behaviour of the steam-boat captains, congratulated the members of the Universities on the gentlemanly and generous spirit in which this match had been conducted. The principles which they always maintained were,—first, that gentlemen should steer; second (which follows from the first), that fouling should be abolished; and last, not least, that victory should be its own reward. These principles were now established, and this was a triumph in which all present might share, and was one prouder and more lasting than that which had just been gained by the Cambridge crew, for, if the time should come, and he trusted it never would, when the University crews should cease to be the first of the amateur crews of England, still they would have done enough to entitle them to the gratitude and respect of all the admirers of aquatic sports.

I have thus fully given Mr Selwyn's speech, because in 1839 there was a correspondence in *Bell's Life*, which gives us a very clear idea of the improvement that has taken place since that time in the tone prevalent among amateurs of the art of Rowing.

In the Number published Sept. 15, 1839, a challenge was inserted by a member of the Leander and London Scullers' Club, to row a fair scullers' wager from Westminster to Putney, for £20 a side.

This challenge was accepted by a member of the Dolphin Club, who however declined to have any *money on*, alleging that it was not invariably the practice to have matches for money, and instancing the matches between Cambridge and Leander in 1837-8. The following letter, remarkable enough according to our ideas now-a-days, then appeared:

SIR—I cannot consent to row the gentlemen of the Dolphin Club for "nothing at all;" and although it is true that the matches with members of the University, being *in statu pupillari* have been rowed for the honour of victory alone because they were forbidden from rowing for money, yet.....I do not remember any match of the least public character that has taken place but for some stake. I cannot but think that the public interest in the river as well as the spirit of rowing would soon cease if all the contests were for honour only; at all events, I am certain that watermen do not wish us to arrive at this state, nor can I, either for their sake or my own, agree to set so poor an example. I shall, however, be most happy to meet the gentlemen of the Dolphin Club on my terms.

Sir, your most obedient,
A Member of the Leander and Scullers' Club.

Sept. 27, 1839.

This letter most naturally drew forth replies from the Universities, in the first place showing how wide of facts the Leander man was in stating that there was any prohibition of University men from rowing for money: finally, one says, " At neither of the Universities is it considered essential to the 'character of a match' or to 'the spirit of Rowing' that a gentlemanly amusement should be converted to a source of profit."

In reply, the Leander man said that his information had been derived from University men, who had declined to row for money on the ground that "they could not." He further remarked, that though University men would not row for money, they would row for money's worth in the shape of cups when given by others (!).

It is hardly necessary to point out that to compare Rowing for a Challenge Cup, which is only held as a badge of victory until it can be wrested from the holder by superior force and skill, with "Rowing for lucre," is about as ridiculous as to speak of Lord Carrington on his neat turn out on the way to Windsor in the same breath with the full-blown dignity of the driver of a twopenny 'bus. Besides which the Universities had not been illiberal in subscribing to the funds of Henley Regatta.

The Leander gentleman, however, goes on to say that he would, in the case of a University man, row for a cup.

One of the University correspondents, appa-

rently a Cambridge man, then wrote as follows:—
"I must repeat my assertion that the University crews have never been otherwise prevented from rowing for money than by their own sense of propriety. I freely admit that they 'cannot' and 'dare not' do so; for if they did they could never again appear on the Isis or Cam, but must retire to some other place to practise their new handicraft and count their honourable gains......... An English gentleman may stake his money on his yacht or his race-horse, or any game in which chance is involved; and in such cases the stake may be necessary to excite an interest in the event, but will he habitually prostitute his own powers of body or mind for 'lucre' in public matches? will he condescend to derive an income from rowing, from cricket, or from chess?"

The correspondence closes with a letter from the Leander man, in which he says, "Your two correspondents of last week would lead us to infer that he who rows for money is no gentleman, while some may consider that he who makes a public match without some stake is no small fool. To others I leave the alternative, which for myself I decline next season, and only hope that, should both classes appear on the river, their combined exertions may do as much to keep up the spirit of Rowing as some who have gone before them." I think we may say that this hope has been more than fulfilled. Since that time Rowing, Rowing-men, and Rowing-matches have become more and more matters of interest to the public: and Rowing has begun to rival Cricket as a *national* sport. Such a hold has it obtained that at our own University some seven thousand pounds sterling have been subscribed for the improvement of the river solely for rowing purposes, whereas in 1835 the Club quite despaired of raising two: and, more remarkable than all, the Conservators of the Thames have found themselves obliged to ask the Imperial Parliament for an extension of their powers in order to meet the exigencies of a boat-race[1]. Few, I think, will doubt that this interest in amateur Rowing, and more especially in the University Boat Race, is mainly due to the unbounded confidence which is universally felt that matches between gentlemen are always rowed on their merits. So long as this confidence exists will Rowing continue to hold its place among national sports; so long as Rowing continues to be what it is to the Universities, will this confidence remain. But if ever (and may the time never come!), if ever boating men at the University look upon Rowing in any other light than as a recreation and as an art, in which excellence is to be sought solely for its own sake, if ever the spirit of covetousness enter into their pursuit of it, then both Rowing will have passed into the same category as the Turf, the high aim of those who, through evil

[1] This was done chiefly, I believe, on account of the complaints made of the behaviour of steamers on the occasions of races between Cambridge and Oxford.

report and good report, brought it to its present standing as a University recreation, will have been frustrated, and, what is more lamentable, the Universities will have succumbed to the evil tendencies that are at work in the nation at large.

Henley Regatta.

Leander won the Grand Challenge, beating University College, Oxford, and Trinity Boat Club, Cambridge.

1841.

In the middle of March a challenge was received from Mr Menzies, the Oxford secretary, "proposing that the *annual* race between the Universities should take place at the middle of June." As it would have been almost impossible for the Cambridge crew to have kept together so long after the end of term, the Oxford men readily consented to have the match at Easter, as usual.

The Cambridge crew began to practise regularly on Wednesday, March 17, but did not get finally settled until the 27th, from which day till the race they practised regularly, with the exception of one day, when No. 7 was laid up by an accident. The distance from lock to lock was never done in less than 22 minutes.

The race this year was fixed for Wednesday, April 14. The Cantabs accordingly "went up to London in a drag and four on Friday, April 2." What strikes one most forcibly in reading the accounts of what University crews used to do in former days is the much greater amount of hard work they did than we do now.

For instance, the ordinary practice of the University crew at Cambridge in 1868 was as follows: We started either from Searle's or the Railway Bridge. In the former case we generally had two easies before the bridge, one at S corner, the other at the Horse Ferry at Chesterton. That abomination of a Railway Bridge necessitated a third, and occasionally we stopped at Grassy corner. In the other case the boat was sent down to the bridge and we rowed down to Clayhythe: besides the necessary stoppage at Baitsbite Sluice we sometimes had an easy at Grassy, and generally one in the middle of the Clayhythe course. The rowing home was somewhat harder; but even so, this does not seem sufficiently hard work to test whether a man is capable of enduring the severe struggle over the Putney course, which is more than 4 miles long; nor is it likely to render such a one fit to undergo the severe trial of the University race: more especially when we remember what Mr Maclaren has said in his book on 'Training,' viz. "that muscular power plays quite a secondary part in rowing; respiratory power makes the first claim, and makes it more exactingly than in any other mode of physical exertion in which men can be engaged." It seems obvious then that a crew training for the Putney course ought above all things to be accustomed to row hard for long distances.

Another thing too has struck me very forcibly with regard to the practice of training. It is the custom to give men pedestrian exercise to supplement the rowing. This of course is right; but I think that in the first place there is not enough of it, and secondly, that it is often done at the wrong end of the day.

With regard to the first point I would refer those of my readers who take an interest in the matter to Mr Maclaren's book, pp. 49—56; with regard to the second, it seems to me that running should come before (not immediately before) the rowing, not after it. During rowing the legs get stiff and the flexor muscles are exceedingly liable to cramp; in which state it is impossible to run; walking is certainly suitable for them then, but what running is done should be in the morning. I am sure that at the present day we are at Cambridge far behind our predecessors in our attention to pedestrian exercise.

At Putney again it is usual for the crews to row over the course six or seven times, at most, including in that number the actual race; the remaining time is spent in comparatively short pieces, say from Putney to Chiswick and back, or paddling to Mortlake and rowing back in two or three spells.

Whereas formerly the practice seems to have

been, when at Cambridge, to row at full racing speed the whole distance from lock to lock (*i.e.* about 3½ miles) every day, without any of the easying off at corners to which Mr Denman so justly took exception at the Cam Improvement Meeting at St James's Hall, in 1868;—when at Putney, to row over the racing-course every day at full speed.

By this means those who had the choosing of the crew were able to detect the weak points, each man's stamina being tested long before the crew had to leave for the Thames.

Whereas now anxious friends who are left behind are never free from the apprehension of hearing at any time that some one has "shut up in training." And, after the race, in the ensuing term one will come up and say in a confidential whisper "How did five stand the work? Did he shut up at all? was not two worked out before the race?" with sundry other like queries. Now I maintain that all such questions ought to be entirely out of place. In the interests of the Boat Club and in justice also to the men themselves every possibility of suspicion about a man's being able to 'last' ought to be entirely done away with.

If this be done, I venture to say that we shall hear no more of Mr Skey's warnings, and no more of parental prohibitions.

But to return to the crew of 1841. They went to London on the second of April, and seem to have rowed over the course every day up to the race. They were usually accompanied by and raced with the following crew of the Cambridge Subscription Room (London), who generally gave them very hard work, and, on the occasion when No. 7 was unable to row, beat them by 50 or 60 yards.

Subscription Rooms Crew.

1	W. N. NICHOLSON	*1st Trin.*
2	A. H. SHADWELL	*St John's.*
3	W. A. CROSS	*1st Trin.*
4	T. A. ANSON	*Jesus.*
5	C. J. SELWYN [1]	*Old* [2] *2nd Trin.*
6	W. M. JONES	*Caius.*
7	J. ABERCROMBIE	*Caius.*
8	W. B. BRETT	*Caius.*
COX.	T. S. EGAN	*Caius.*

The following interesting particulars respecting the crews are taken from *Bell's Life*:—

"The Cambridge had the advantage in weight (if advantage it may be called); the Cambridge crew weighing 101 st. 11 lbs., that of the Oxford 99 st. 7 lbs.

"Amongst the Oxonians there were four of the hands who rowed in the match of last season, viz. Messrs. Cocks, Meynell, Royds, and Mountain. The first three rowed their present respective oars of 8, 7, and 6; whilst Mr Mountain, who this year pulled No. 3, formerly handled No. 1. In the Cambridge crew Nos. 8, 6, 4 filled respectively

---

[1] The late lamented Lord Justice of Appeal, the brother of the Bishop of Lichfield.
[2] This word I don't understand, but it is in the Book, and I have left it.

their old places of 1840. Nos. 5 and 1 (Messrs Cobbold and Croker) were to have rowed in their present places in that year, but the former was prevented from so doing by a family affliction, and the latter by illness. It was erroneously stated that an alteration had been made in No. 4, such a thing never having been contemplated; Mr Jones, of Magdalene, who rowed No. 7 last year, was to have taken No. 3 this, but he also, unfortunately, from family motives, could not row, and Mr Ritchie, a most efficient substitute, was then placed in his stead. Among the Oxford crew three gentlemen are Etonians, three Westminsters, two Rugby men, and one Shrewsbury, and all along the captains of the Oxford crews have been Westminsters, viz. Massey, Bewicke, and Cocks. In the Cambridge boat the captain also is a Westminster man, No. 6 Winchester, Nos. 5 and 2 Shrewsbury, and the rest were at no public school. We have observed that private schoolmen often make the best oarsmen when taught at Cambridge, because they go straight to work, without any prejudice, and have no bad tricks to unlearn. It had been agreed that only one umpire should be appointed, but subsequently it was deemed advisable to conform to the usual practice, and Mr T. S. Egan, of Caius College, Cambridge, and Mr Walls, of Brazenose, Oxford, were appointed umpires; Mr Antrobus, M.P. for East Surrey, a great lover of aquatic sports, and formerly a winner of the Colquhoun or Cambridge silver sculls, officiated as referee.

"Both boats were built by Messrs Searle, and were exactly alike in length (52 ft. 7 in.), breadth, weight, and model, the only difference being that the Oxonians had their boat carvel built, viz. the edges of the planks being so brought together as to rest on one another, thus giving a perfectly smooth surface outside; whilst the Cambridge boat was constructed on the old clinker-built plan,—*i.e.* with the planks overlapping each other. The general appearance of the crews was such as to justify the confidence of the backers of either party; they all looked in capital condition and full of spirits, and eager for the contest. It had been generally supposed, from the pulling of the crews, that Oxford would get the lead at starting, even if they did not ultimately win, as they always *appeared* to make a better spurt at the first than their rivals, and a good deal of money was laid out on their being first through Vauxhall Bridge. At 10 m. past 6 o'clock, both boats having taken their stations, the greatest interest and anxiety prevailed, and the two crews bending to their oars waited the sound of Mr Searle's pistol, to whom had been delegated the task of starting them. Precisely at the above-named time the signal was given; and then it was that the Cantabs surprised their friends and their opponents at the same time, and showed them that they could start well if they liked. Lightning was scarcely quicker than their first stroke, and even the well-known rapidity of Mr Cocks's stroke could not prevent the Cantabs' boat taking the lead, which was increased by No. 6 of the Oxford missing his oar at the start."

The account of the race given below is from the Cambridge books.

"The race was rowed on Wednesday, April 14.

"The two crews took their stations under Westminster-bridge exactly at 6 o'clock in the afternoon. The Cambridge, who had won the toss, took the first arch from the centre on the Surrey side, and the Oxford the next arch on the same side. The steerers held lines from each of the piers, so that the boats lay straight in the full tideway.

"The start took place at 10 minutes past 6. The Cambridge got a beautiful start, the Oxford perhaps not quite so good: we began almost immediately to draw upon them and before Lambeth were clear, at Vauxhall bridge two or three lengths a head, which we kept increasing till near Battersea where the Oxford made a vigorous push but did not recover any of their lost ground, and we entered Battersea bridge six or seven boats' lengths ahead; we then came up with the Cambridge Subscription Rooms crew and had a good race with them till about half way between the two bridges, when they were unfortunately fouled. All this time we were tailing the Oxford boat, and finally after a good spurt in to Putney bridge were a minute ahead, which seemed to be about 300 yards. The time was 32 minutes, but the tide was very small and there was a stiff head-wind. On the Tuesday week before, starting at about 150 yards below Westminster bridge, the distance was done in 27 min."

The names of the crews were as follows:

Cambridge.

			st.	lbs.
1	W. Croker	Caius	9	12
2	Hon. L. Denman	Magd.	10	12
3	H. C. Jones[1]	Magd.	11	10
4	J. M. Ridley[1]	Jesus	12	7
5	R. H. Cobbold	Pet.	12	4
6	F. C. Penrose[1]	Magd.	12	0
7	Hon. G. Denman	1st Trin.	10	7
str.	C. M. Vialls[1]	3rd Trin.	11	7
cox.	J. M. Croker	Caius	10	8

Oxford.

			st.	lbs.
1	Richard Bethell	Exeter	10	6
2	Ed. Vaughan Richards	Ch. Ch.	11	2
3	J. G. Mountain[1]	Mert.	10	9
4	E. Royds[1]	Braz.	11	13
5	H. Wm. Hodgson	Ball.	11	10
6	Wm. Lea	Braz.	11	7
7	G. Meynell[1]	Braz.	11	11
str.	J. J. T. S. Cocks[1]	Braz.	11	3
cox.	Charles B. Woolaston	Exeter	9	2

Messrs Egan of Caius and Walls of B.N.C. were umpires, and Mr Antrobus of St John's, Cambridge, referee.

Both boats were built by Searle, and were 52 ft. 7 in. in length, and Cambridge were the winners by 1 m. 4 sec., rowing the distance from Westminster to Putney in 32½ minutes.

The last two paragraphs together with the

---
[1] Rowed in 1840.

names and weights of the crew is all the mention made of the race in the Oxford books.

The crews dined together at Putney after the race at Batchelor's instead of Avis's, at the express desire of the Oxford men. Both boats were built by Searle; the Oxford boat after the carvel principle, but ours was clinker built.

BIOGRAPHICAL NOTICES. (CAMBRIDGE.)

W. CROKER. Graduated 1839 as ninth wrangler; afterwards fellow of Caius College. Died in 1841 of consumption, accelerated doubtless by rowing, probably also by hard reading.

HON. L. W. DENMAN, M.A. Third Class Classical Tripos and 8th in the Poll, 1844; ordained 1844; formerly rector of Washington, Durham, 1848—1861; rector of Willian, dio. of Rochester.

R. H. COBBOLD, M.A. Graduated 1843; Senior Optime and 2nd Class Classic. Ordained 1844; formerly venerable Archdeacon of Ningpo, Victoria, 1856—58; vicar of Field Dalling, Norfolk, 1858—9; rector of Brosely with Limley, Salop. Author: *Questions on the Collects.*—*The Chinese at home.*—*England's reception of Denmark's daughter* (*A Sermon*).

HON. G. DENMAN, M.A., M.P., Q.C. Graduated as senior classic in 1842, called to the bar at Lincoln's Inn, Nov. 24, 1846, M.P. for Exeter. Mr DENMAN for many years presided at the annual Dinner which used to be given to the University crews by the Thames Subscription Club after the boat race.

J. M. CROKER, M.A. Graduated in 1840 as 8th wrangler; afterwards fellow and Tutor of Caius College; ordained 1846; rector of Lavenham, Suffolk, diocese of Ely, 1855.

BIOGRAPHICAL NOTICES. (OXFORD.)

BETHELL. Educated at Eton and Exeter Coll. In 1864 was farming in New Zealand. Son of the late Vice-Provost of Eton.

E. V. RICHARDS, Q.C. Student of Ch. Ch.; 2 Class Math. and Phys., 1843; called to the Bar at the Inner Temple, 1847; Oxf. Circ.

H. W. HODGSON. Graduated 1844; ordained 1844. Vicar of Ashwell, diocese of Rochester, 1851.

W. LEA, M.A. 2 Class Lit. Hum. 1841, B.A. 1842, ordained 1843; vicar of St Peter's, Droitwich, 1849; honorary canon of Worcester Cathedral, 1858.

C. B. WOOLASTON. Graduated 4th Cl. Math. and Phy. 1838; ordained 1842; vicar of Felpham, diocese of Chichester, 1842.

Henley Regatta.

Seven boats entered for the Grand Challenge Cup, but only four started. Leander, it will be remembered, were the holders. In the trial heat the Cambridge Subscription Rooms (London) beat Trinity College (Oxford) and the St John Cross Club (Oxford). This last-mentioned club consisted of members of different Oxford colleges, but I do not know what its constitution was or in what it differed from the O.U.B.C. *Bell's Life* calls it a University College Club, but there were a Magdalene man, two Oriel men, and one St John's man in it. The race was a very close one, and resulted in favour of the Cambridge crew. The final heat was rowed the next day between the two following crews:

C. S. R.

			st.	lbs.
1	Hon. G. Denman	1st Trin.	10	8
2	A. H. Shadwell	Ly. Margt.	10	9
3	W. A. Cross	1st Trin.	10	6
4	T. A. Anson	Jesus	12	8
5	W. H. Yatman	Caius	10	10
6	W. M. Jones	Caius	11	10
7	C. M. Vialls	3rd Trin.	11	9
str.	W. B. Brett	Caius	11	10
cox.	T. S. Egan	Caius	9	6

Leander.

1	Shepheard	10	2
2	Layton	10	11
3	W. Julius	11	6
4	Romayne	11	8
5	Sherrard[1]	12	3
6	Wallace	11	7
7	Wood	10	12
str.	Dalgleish	11	2
cox.	H. Gibson	10	0

[1] One of the best oarsmen of the Club came down and took Mr Sherrard's place.

Cambridge won the toss and took the Berkshire shore. The race unfortunately terminated in a foul, which was given in favour of Cambridge. The Leander challenged Cambridge to row either for a thousand or five-hundred pounds, or even for "love," but the Cambridge declined, as it was the second occasion on which the races between the two clubs had terminated in the same unsatisfactory way.

For the New Cup for four-oared boats manned by Amateurs, which was this year instituted under the name of the Stewards' Cup, there were three entries—The St George's Club, The Oxford Club (London), The Cambridge Subscription Rooms (London). The Oxonians won, beating the Cambridge by more than a boat's length, the St George's being several lengths in the rear.

1842.

Towards the close of the year '41 a challenge was received from Mr Menzies the secretary of the O.U.B.C. proposing that there should be an inter-University race from Westminster to Putney on the last week of June or the first of July. In appointing a committee to correspond with Oxford the captains expressed an opinion that Easter should be insisted on as the time of the race; a good deal of correspondence passed between the committee and Mr Menzies without arriving at any satisfactory result.

When it became evident that matters could not be arranged so as to suit both parties, Mr Ridley of Jesus, who was captain of the University, suggested that a challenge should be sent "to the Leander Club, proposing a match without allowing that we either lost the disputed race of 1838 or that we had anything to do with the race in which the Cambridge Subscription Rooms were beaten last August[1]."

Mr G. Denman, who was secretary, seconded the motion, stating his conviction that the letter could easily be written without compromising the dignity of the University Boat Club. To this motion the captains agreed, and the following is the copy of the secretary's letter:

"SIR—It was decided at a captains' meeting yesterday that a letter should be written to your Club with the view of bringing about a match.

"We have long been hoping that you would send us a challenge, but it is now so long since our last race, that we think we are justified in waiving the etiquette usual in such cases, and proposing that we row an eight-oared match, on the same terms as those on which you raced the Cambridge Subscription Rooms last August, on

[1] This match was rowed on Aug. 7th 1841, and Leander won by 1 min. 10 sec.

any day between Monday, the 30th of May, and Monday, the 6th of June, inclusive.

"I remain, Sir,

"Yours obediently,

"G. DENMAN, *Sec. of the U.B.C.*"

In reply to the above challenge, Mr Dalgleish, secretary of the Leander, wrote to the following effect, which shows that Mr Denman had fully redeemed his promise not to compromise the dignity of the club:—"The Leander had such a small number of members that they would be unable to get together an eight-oared crew that year, but would be happy, if the U.B.C. would consent, to row a race in four-oars instead. He hoped, however, that ere long they would be again able to meet their old competitors of the Cam in fuller force."

A meeting of the U.B.C having been summoned to consider Mr Dalgleish's letter, it was decided that they could not consent to row a four-oared race, but offered to row any eight-oared crew from any club or clubs whatsoever, if Mr Dalgleish or anyone else would make one up; and they further decided that a challenge to this effect should be inserted in *Bell's Life.*

At a subsequent meeting the secretary stated that,—having heard that the Oxford men were complaining bitterly of our conduct in giving a challenge to any eight-oared crew to remain open to the 6th of June, and yet refusing to accommodate

Oxford on the 10th,—he had written to Mr Menzies to enquire whether the 10th was the day he meant, as he (Mr M.) had never mentioned any day earlier than the 12th (a Sunday): in answer to which Mr Menzies had sent the following reply:

"DEAR SIR—I received your letter last night, &c.......we will be happy to meet you on Saturday, the 11th June, under the following restrictions, viz. that you do not row on London water before Wednesday, the 8th of June, the first day on which we can leave Oxford, and that none of your crew be bachelors of more than one term's standing."

After some discussion upon the above letter it was agreed that the challenge be accepted with the condition of not rowing in London before the eighth of June, but that the secretary also give them to understand that "although our present crew does not contain any bachelor of more than one term's standing, we cannot consent to make that a condition of the match."

This being settled, practising became the order of the day: but during the week ending Saturday, the 21st of May, it was not very first-rate, owing to the numerous suppers, dinners, and general conviviality which prevails the week after the May races; but from that time till the 6th of June they practised regularly. There were, however, numerous changes, as well in the men who constituted the crew, as in the oars which they severally manned;

and only two or three days before leaving for the Thames there were three important changes made, one new man being brought in, and two others having their places changed. The distance from lock to lock, which is about 3½ miles, was never done in less than 22′ 10″, the weeds presenting most determined obstacles to steady practising. On Tuesday, June 7, the crew proceeded to town in a drag and four, and took a quiet paddle to Waterloo Bridge to ease the rowlocks, &c.

The next day they rowed over the course from Westminster to Putney in 28′ 23″. The following are the names of the two crews:—

OXFORD.

			st.	lbs.
1	F. T. MACDOUGALL	Magd. H.	9	8
2	R. MENZIES	Univ.	11	3
3	ED. A. BREADON	Trin.	12	4
4	W. B. BREWSTER	St John's	12	10
5	G. DRINKWATER BOURNE	Oriel	13	12
6	J. C. COX	Trin.	11	8
7	G. E. HUGHES	Oriel	11	6
str.	F. N. MENZIES	Univ.	10	12
cox.	A. T. W. SHADWELL	Balliol	10	4
	Average		11	$9\frac{5}{8}$

CAMBRIDGE.

			st.	lbs.
1	F. E. TOWER	St John's	10	2
2	Hon. L. DENMAN[1]	Magd.	10	11
3	W. WATSON	Jesus	10	13
4	F. C. PENROSE[1]	Magd.	11	10

[1] Rowed in 1841.

			st.	lbs.
5	R. H. COBBOLD[1]	Pet.	12	6
6	J. ROYDS	Chr.	11	7
7	G. DENMAN[1]	Trin.	10	9
str.	J. M. RIDLEY[1]	Jes.	12	0
cox.	A. B. POLLOCK	Trin.	9	7
	Average		11	3¾

The Oxford won the toss, and took the first arch from the centre on the Surrey side. Cambridge took the next arch on the Surrey side.

At starting Oxford got a slight advantage, but this was soon regained. Cambridge was then beginning to draw rapidly ahead, when those abominations of boat-races, a steamer and a lighter, threw them out of their course, and thus let Oxford get a decided lead. From the Penitentiary to Wandsworth they were not once free from the swell of the steamers, so that the Oxford men, not being annoyed to so great an extent, drew gradually away. About a mile from Putney, Cambridge got clear of the steamers and recovered a good deal of their lost ground; but the race was then decided, and they passed under Putney Bridge three lengths astern of Oxford, now for the first time victorious on London water.

On referring to the account given in *Bell's Life*, I find that the time given is 30′ 45″, and that Oxford won by 13″. This would give time for about 10 strokes, supposing them to be rowing about 45 strokes per minute, which would be the pro-

[1] Rowed in 1841.

bable pace for finishing; and as it takes about three strokes to clear your length (with heavy in-rigged boats it would quite take that), we see that the two apparently independent accounts agree substantially.

After the race the crews and their friends dined together at "The Bells."

I have given the account of the race as I find it in the Cambridge books. In the Oxford book is pasted the account given in *Bell's Life*. The Oxford captain adds the following :—

"The *feelings* of 'Bell' seem to me very much to favour the Cantabs, so much so that the editor, being taxed with having written the account previous to the match, expecting Cambridge to win, confessed it. The main point, however, was gained by Oxford, viz., arriving at Putney Bridge first; which they did by the umpires' time in 30' 10", the Cantabs being about 5 or 6 boats' lengths astern. There had been considerable difficulty in arranging the match, as the Cantabs did not feel anxious to row at any time except at Easter. But after the match for this year was, as we thought, put an end to, the Cantabs challenged the world; on which Oxford took up the gauntlet, and was victorious, and thus at last gained those laurels which for four successive times she had failed in, this being the first time she ever came off victorious in the London water. Owing to the circumstances mentioned above, the Oxford men had only 3 weeks and 2 days to train in, and during a part of that time the college races were going on three days a week. This caused our training to be as *severe* as it was quick; sundry bets had been made by Cantabs that their boat would be first under all the bridges; but, alas for their exchequers!! Oxford went under Vauxhall 1 boat length ahead, through Battersea 4, and through Putney 6. I cannot finish this sketch of the race without expressing my gratitude to the crew who backed me so well not only in the race but during all the training: and the best wish I can express for my successors in office is that they may have the luck to find 7 other men as staunch and true.

"Hurrah for Oxford.
"FLETCHER NORTON MENZIES,
"Captn. of Oxford boat, 1842."

The Oxford crew was trained by E. W. Mackintosh of University; now of Raymore, Inverness. He represents the Inverness burghs in Parliament.

BIOGRAPHICAL NOTICES. (OXFORD.)

F. T. MACDOUGALL, D.D., graduated 1844. King's College, London, Gold Medallist for General Medical Proficiency, 1837. Sometime Fellow of the Royal College of Surgeons, and Demonstrator of Anatomy at King's College, London. Missionary to Borneo. Consecrated first Bishop of Labuan, 1853, where he laboured until 1867, when he resigned his bishopric and accepted the vicarage of Salford, Godmanchester, near Huntingdon.

Sir R. MENZIES of Menzies, Bart., Castle Menzies, Aberfeldy, N.B.

E. A. BREEDON, M.A., graduated 1843. Entered the Royal Horse Guards Blue, and after serving in them some time retired, and now resides on his property at Pangbourne.

W. B. BREWSTER, son of the Irish Lord Chancellor Brewster. Saw much service at the Cape with the 1st batt. Rifle Brigade, of which he was Capt. and Adj. Afterwards Col. of the Inns of Court Volunteers. Died 7th July, 1864; the only one of the crew who is not now alive.

G. D. BOURNE, M.A., graduated 1842 (? 1844). Ordained 1845. Rector of Weston-sub-Edge, diocese of Gloucester and Bristol, 1846.

J. C. COX. Entered holy orders. Until last year chaplain to the British Embassy in Paris. Now vicar of Felstead, Essex.

G. E. HUGHES, D.C.L. Called to the bar at Doctors' Commons, 1850. Now resides on his property at Offley Place, Luton.

F. N. MENZIES, served in the Post Office and War Office, London, for $5\frac{1}{2}$ years. Then took to farming in Perthshire, and is now secretary to the Highland and Agricultural Society of Scotland, No. 3, George IV. Bridge, Edinburgh.

A. T. W. SHADWELL, M.A., graduated 2nd Class Lit. Hum. 1843. Ordained 1844. Rector of Langton, near Malton, Yks. 1850.

BIOGRAPHICAL NOTICES. (CAMBRIDGE.)

F. E. TOWER, M.A., graduated 1843. Ordained 1844. Son of the late C. T. Tower, Esq., Weald Hall, Essex. Educated at Harrow. Rector of Elmsthorpe with Earls Shilton, Leicestershire, Diocese of Peterborough.

W. WATSON, died in 1847.

J. ROYDS, son of Clement Royds, Esq., of Greenhill, Rochdale, Lancashire, a banker, was born in 1818, died from heart disease about 1854. Cousin of E. Royds, see p. 75.

A. B. POLLOCK, M.A., graduated 1845. Called to the bar at the Middle Temple 1846.

Henley Regatta.

It had been decided, says the Cambridge Secretary, that unless we beat Oxford we should not go to Henley, but under the circumstances it was thought that we ought to go in order to satisfy ourselves as to which was the best crew.

The only change made in the boat was that of replacing Penrose, who could not stay, by Vialls, 3rd Trinity. The crew so constituted practised at Henley on Monday, June 13.

The next day was that fixed for the Grand Challenge.

The boats entered were:
    The two University crews,
    The two Subscription Rooms,

The King's College, London,
The Oriel and Etonian boats of Oxford, being eight in all. The Oriel, having two men in the University crew, scratched.

On drawing for competitors and stations, the two boats drawn for the first heat were the two University crews, and grand sport was anticipated from the fact that in practice they had done the course within a second or two of each other. The time given was 8′. 48″.

The *Holders* this year were the Cambridge Subscription Rooms, and it would appear that it had been privately arranged that, in event of the Cambridge University boat being beaten in the trial heats, certain members of that crew should row in the Subscription Rooms crew in the final race. To this course the Oxford men objected; and to the great disappointment of all, who were expecting a fine race between the Universities, Mr Menzies withdrew his crew.

This of course caused a great deal of discussion and confusion, and very general disappointment. The public missed seeing a good race, and the Cambridge men were naturally annoyed at not having an opportunity of retrieving their lost laurels.

Bell's Life states that after the Oxford boat was withdrawn, as Mr Menzies was leaving the Committee Room, the Cambridge men challenged the Oxford to row a friendly heat, which Mr Menzies declined.

After much discussion the Etonian and Oxford Rooms crews started to go down to the post, but were caught in a tremendous thunderstorm, which filled their boats with water.

The King's College and Cambridge University were therefore started at about 5 o'clock. "This race," says the chronicler, "of course was soon decided by the Cambridge boat going ahead and taking the inside from their opponents and winning as they pleased by a couple of lengths."

The Etonian and Oxford Rooms then rowed their race, the former pulling in the Oriel boat, the head of the river at Oxford (built by Hall of Oxford). The "Rooms" won easily by about a boat's length.

Cambridge then started with the Rooms: the latter had won the toss and took the inside; the race was one of the hardest ever seen, for they led " for at least three quarters of the distance, but could never leave us at all, and we came in with our stern only four or five yards, at the most, before theirs. Their crew was the same which a few days before had beaten the Oxford University crew from Putney to Westminster." (Cambridge book.)

Bell's Life says that Cambridge won by about a yard, and that the time was 8'. 45".

Having won the heats it remained for the C.U.B.C. to race the holders, viz. the Cambridge Subscription Rooms. It was generally expected that the condition and practice of the former would give them the victory; the C.S.R. having only pulled together once before, and that the same morning. However the Rooms had the best of it throughout, though it was a hard race and they were barely clear of the U.B.C. at the finish. The latter were none the better for their desperate race the day before with the Oxford Rooms.

The names of the winning crew were as follows:

1	W. H. YATMAN	*Caius.*
2	A. SHADWELL	*John's.*
3	G. C. UPPLEBY	*Magd.*
4	J. G. LONDSDALE	*1st Trin.*
5	A. M. RITCHIE	*1st Trin.*
6	W. M. JONES	*Caius.*
7	C. J. SELWYN	*2nd Trin.*
str.	J. BERESFORD	*Pet.*
cox.	T. S. EGAN	*Caius.*

The winning crew had the advantage of the inside station.

The Cambridge crew was steered by J. Pollock of Trinity (*Bell's Life* says Caius) College, in the final heat, but Egan steered them in the trial heats.

1843.

In Feb. 1843 the secretary of the C.U.B.C. received a communication from Mr Shadwell, of Balliol College, Oxon., explaining that the Oxford men could not possibly get up a crew for Easter, and proposing to meet at Henley, from Mill End Lock to Henley Bridge, at Whitsuntide. This proposal was declined by a unanimous vote of the Cambridge captains.

In consequence of this there was no race between the Universities this year.

It was in this year that one of the most noble feats of rowing on record was achieved, which, though it had not really anything to do with the contests between the two Universities, has nevertheless been so often confounded with them, that it may be well to explain the whole matter thoroughly.

I have several times had occasion to mention the Cambridge and Oxford Subscription Rooms crews in connection with the chronicle of the inter-University Boat-races. These belonged to two London Clubs, one composed entirely of Cambridge men, the other of Oxford men. The crews were generally composed of University men who had ceased to reside, though occasionally resident members of the University rowed with them. The reader will remember that in 1842 the O.U.B.C. withdrew from the contest for the Grand Challenge, because they objected by anticipation to men who were going to row in the C.U.B.C. boat being allowed, in case of defeat, to row in the Cambridge Subscription Rooms'.

Thus it will be seen that the two Cambridge clubs were quite distinct, whilst at the same time there was a very close bond of union between them. This had been a good deal strengthened in the spring of this year (1843), as I find on reference to the books. The "Rooms" proposed (and the U.B.C. accepted the offer) that by an annual payment from each college club at Cambridge, the whole of the members of that club should be members of the "Rooms" so long as they resided in Cambridge.

This made it *possible* for any member of the C.U.B.C. to be put into the Cambridge Rooms' crew: but, of course, to the vast majority of men resident at the University the inconvenience of practising with a crew in London would be an almost insuperable difficulty. Thus, the distinction between the two clubs was as clear as ever to persons acquainted with the facts, but it was not unnatural that the public generally should not be able to distinguish between a University crew of one year and a crew whose composition was very similar the next year, but which could not in any true sense be said to represent the U.B.C.

Hoping that the reader now clearly understands the meaning of the words "Subscription Rooms' Crew," I proceed with the narrative.

The scene of action was Henley, the time the summer of 1843, the occasion was the final race for the Grand Challenge.

It will be remembered that, the year before, the "Cambridge Rooms" had remained holders of the Grand Challenge Cup. In 1843 the O.U.B.C.

sent a crew to contend for it, and beat the rest of the challengers. Mr Menzies, of University College, was again stroke, but between the third and final heats was taken so seriously ill as to be unable to row. It was proposed that a substitute should be allowed to row for him, but to this the Cambridge Subscription Rooms objected, as Oxford had not entered a spare man according to the regulations. When this point was decided in favour of the holders, the Oxford men, with a courage to which it is hard to accord adequate praise, determined to row with only seven oars. The Subscription Rooms naturally felt themselves placed in a very awkward situation by this most unexpected decision, and asked the Committee whether they were obliged to row against a crew with only seven oars. To this Lord Camoys answered that, if they did not, the cup would certainly be adjudged to the Oxford crew. This settled the matter, and the race began, and was won in the most gallant manner by the Oxford crew, who came in nearly a length ahead.

The Oxford crew was one of the heaviest on record. It will be seen that the average of the seven men who rowed is somewhat over 12 st. 1 lb. In the final heat Hughes rowed stroke, and Lowndes 7; bow being left out.

Oxford Crew.

			st.	lbs.
1	R. Lowndes	Ch. Ch.	11	2[1]
2	R. Menzies	Univ.	11	3
3	E. Royds	B.N.C.	12	0
4	W. B. Brewster	St John's	13	0
5	G. D. Bourne	Oriel	13	12
6	J. C. Cox	Trin.	11	12
7	G. E. Hughes	Oriel	11	11
str.	F. N. Menzies	Univ.	10	13
cox.	A. T. W. Shadwell	Ball.	10	8
	Average		11	13⅝

Camb. Subscription Rooms' Crew.

1	W. H. Yatman	Caius.
2	A. H. Shadwell	John's.
3	G. Mann	Caius.
4	J. M. Ridley	Jesus.
5	R. H. Cobbold	Pet.
6	W. M. Jones	Caius.
7	L. Denman	Magd.
str.	C. Vialls	3rd Trin.
cox.	T. S. Egan	Caius.

I extract the following from the Oxford Books:

"On Wednesday, June 28, the Oxford University Crew arrived at the scene of action, and

---

[1] These weights are copied from an article in *London Society*; but I am unable to give those of the losing crew.

in the evening practised over the water: the river was very full, and the stream was much greater than at any previous regatta. The First Trinity crew was out also: they had had a good deal of practice in London, and its effects were perceptible in their high feathering, &c.

"They spurted over the first quarter of a mile at their best pace and then stopped; the time was 1 m. 22 sec. Our crew rowed the whole distance, and took exactly the same time to the same gate at which they stopped: this frightened them not a little. The time over the whole course was 8 m. 29 sec. by the enemy's watches, which was a most wonderful pace. Fletcher Menzies was not well at leaving Oxford, and the excitement of driving the crew over and of rowing made him worse. The race with the Etonians took nothing out of the crew, and that with the Black Prince was the most hollow affair imaginable. *Bell* calls it *half*, but it was at least a beating of a *full* dozen boats' lengths......Fletcher Menzies suffered a good deal on Thursday night, but was cooler and better on Friday morning.

"The holders of the cup, the Cam. Subn. Rooms Crew, arrived on Thursday, and in the evening rowed over the course. Their boat was a bad one, and the crew not properly got together. Their stroke, however, Vialls, rowed in the most superb style: but he was destined to pay amply for his previous victories over Oxford University crews. Their time was 9 m. 3 sec., which quite decided those who had any doubts as to our superiority. They, however, were still confident...On Friday afternoon our gallant captain seemed rather better, though still feeling sick and faint. He was kept out of the sun and well wrapped up, and though we were very anxious about him we did not doubt his ability to give us his stroke, which was all that was necessary to polish the Cantabs."

The Rev. Arthur Shadwell, who steered the seven-oared crew, has kindly furnished me with the following particulars concerning the race and the circumstances attending on it:—

"When the deciding heat for the Grand Challenge Cup was about to come off, Mr Fletcher Menzies, captain and stroke oar of the Oxford University crew, fainted while stepping into his boat. A deputation from that crew immediately proceeded across the river to inform the holders of the cup, the Cambridge Subscription Rooms crew, of this accident: they found them taking their places to row down to the course. They asked if an eighth man might be allowed them to fill the captain's place. No one was specially proposed to be his substitute, but the rules of the regatta, which had been drawn up in accordance with a remonstrance made by Oxford in the preceding year, did not allow anyone to be substituted for a man who had already rowed in a heat: it must be the same crew in its entirety throughout the races. The Cambridge Rooms, indeed, were not willing to grant the petition, but neither was it in their power to grant it. The Oxford men then asked for a delay to enable them to make arrangements: some of the opposite crew were unwilling at first to grant this, but their objections were overruled, and it was finally arranged that the competitors should meet in an hour's time. Oxford then shifted their No. 7 to 8, and their bow man to No. 7, and taking up their station close under the lee of the Oxfordshire bank, to be out of the wind, then blowing fresh, were enabled to hold with their opponents from the very first, and then gradually drawing ahead crossed over with a clear lead to the Berkshire bank, and won by two lengths between the two boats. Such is the account of this the most remarkable race on record. The truth was that the winning crew was not only composed of the heaviest and finest material ever brought together in an eight-oar, but they had been gradually forming with incessant care from the October term preceding, and had been handled in their practice as though they were preparing for a race on the London long course. No less pains had been bestowed upon their boat itself, which was truly worthy to carry them[1]. Its subsequent history is remarkable. A few days after the Henley match it defeated the Leander club: in the next

---

[1] She was built by the late Isaac King of Oxford; but the whole of the floor was modelled by Mr F. N. Menzies, by whom also a great part of the boat was actually built.

summer it beat both Cambridge University and the Leander; and after lasting for years as a kind of sacred model, it was dismembered to form souvenirs of every kind, oars, rudders, and snuff-boxes; till at last the portion containing the coxswain's thwart was converted into a presidential chair of state for the University Boat Club barge twenty-five years after its launch."

The following inscriptions are cut on the shields ornamenting the President's chair presented to the Club by Mr Alderman Randall.

Hanc quam spectas
sedem ipsam gubernatoris
in sellam transformatam
Carinæ
in quâ apud Henlegam Tamesianam
anno MDCCCXLIII
septem Remorum
victoria reportata est;
quibus honoribus
In Scholis, in Senatu, in Foro, in Ecclesiâ,
Artibus, armis,
Ludis campestribus vel aquaticis,
ubique alumni potiti sunt,
horum care et jucunde memor,
Gratiarum haud oblitus,
Academiæ Oxoniensis Remigum Consortio
Civitatis non ignobilis
Oxoniæ civis
D. D.
Thomas Randall
MDCCCLXVII.

8

SEPTEM.

I. ....
II.   Robertus Menzies e coll. Univ.
III. Edvardus Royds e coll. Æn. Nas.
IV.   Gulielmus B. Brewster e coll. D. Jo. Bapt.
V.   Georgius D. Bourne e coll. Oriel.
VI.   Joannes Carolus Cox e coll. Trin.
VII. Ricardus Lowndes ex æde Christi,
                                  olim I.
VIII. Georgius Edvardus Hughes e coll. Oriel,
                                  olim VII,
vice Fletcher Norton Menzies e coll. Univ. qui inter sodales remigii facile princeps, febri furenti ipsâ horâ certaminis parumper succubuerat.

Arturus Thomas W. Shadwell e coll. Ball.
Gubernator.
Eneas Gulielmus Mackintosh e coll. Univ.
Magister.
January 29, 1868.

After the finish of the Henley Regatta, so glorious for Oxford, so disastrous for their opponents, the crew went to London and practised at Putney for the Thames Regatta.

This Regatta was established this year "at the instance of a few gentlemen zealous in the cause that they had espoused, at a time when the great increase of steamboats on the river had almost deprived the watermen of their occupation; and by diminishing the number of both amateur clubs and rowers, had taken away the principal means of support of an industrious class of mechanics employed in boat building. As soon as the project was announced, many noblemen and gentlemen residing on the banks of the Thames, the Universities of Oxford and Cambridge, the principal London boat clubs, the most distinguished amateurs on the river, cordially responded to the appeal, and H.R.H. Prince Albert kindly consented to become the patron of the Regatta and to contribute towards its support. In this the Prince was seconded by the Dukes of Northumberland and Buccleuch, the Earl of Ripon, Lords Castlereagh and Grimston, and that steady patronizer of the river Thames *whether in or out of it*, Sir Launcelot Shadwell Vice-Chancellor of England[1]," all of whom supported the undertaking by purse and good wishes.

For eight-oared boats a splendid Gold Challenge Cup was offered, with the tempting condition that if any club won it three years in succession, it should become the property of the club.

There were besides many other races of different kinds both for watermen and amateurs.

For this Grand Challenge Cup the Oxford crew entered. Mr H. E. C. Stapylton was put bow to fill up the deficiency caused by the illness of Mr Menzies.

The other boats entered were the Leander and the Cambridge Subscription Rooms.

---

[1] *Bell's Life*, June 29, 1845.

The Saturday before the Regatta the O.U.B. did the course from the bottom of Chiswick Eyot to Putney Bridge, a distance of 2 m. 3 fur., in 12 min. 30 sec.

On Monday the Regatta commenced. The Grand Challenge was to have been rowed on the flood-tide; but, owing to the previous racing being late, the race had to be rowed with the ebb. Buoys had been fixed to start from, but had moved from their place owing to the ebb having commenced. For this reason the boats were not evenly placed at starting, and as the Leander men would not obey the umpire, the start was effected in a manner very disadvantageous for Oxford.

The race appears to have been a series of fouls from beginning to end, the Leander coxswain being chiefly in fault; the Oxford men however rowed in a most plucky and determined manner and eventually came in first, Leander being second, having been continually bumped for the last three-quarters of a mile by Cambridge, whose coxswain throughout "steered with the greatest forbearance and the most consummate skill." Cambridge appealed against the Leander, but as the umpire's boat had been left behind, he saw nothing of the race, and the committee decided that the race must be settled as the boats came in.

1844.

In the fall of 1843 and the beginning of 1844, there had been some correspondence on the subject of a race between the Universities, and from the correspondence up to February one would judge that both parties were agreed upon the Easter vacation as the time. The last letter given in the Cambridge books is one from A. Shadwell of Ball. Coll. Oxon. in which he expressed his willingness to have the race about that time, but on account of the state of the tides suggested that the race should be from Barker's Rails above Mortlake to Putney Bridge. No reason is given for the match being broken off.

Though however there was no match between the Universities the crews met at the Thames Regatta.

The Cambridge men seem to have had very great difficulty in getting a crew together: and when one was fixed upon, untoward circumstances caused changes to be made so late on, that the crew which pulled in the race had never been in a boat together before.

The crews entered were the O.U.B.C. (holders), the C.U.B.C. and the Leander. The names of the crews were:

OXFORD.

First Station.   st. lbs.

1	W. C. STAPYLTON	...*Merton*	10	8
2	W. SPOTTISWOODE	...*Balliol*	10	6
3	W. H. MILMAN	...*Ch. Ch.*	11	0
4	H. MORGAN	...*Ch. Ch.*	12	11
5	W. BUCKLE	...*Oriel*	13	11
6	W. J. DRY	...*Wadham*	11	5
7	F. M. WILSON	...*Ch. Ch.*	12	8
8	F. E. TUKE	...*B.N.C.*	11	9
COX.	A. T. W. SHADWELL	*Ball.*......	10	8
	Average		11	8¾

LEANDER.

Second Station.

1	SOANES	9	3
2	PEACOCK	10	6
3	LEE	12	0
4	HODDING	11	6
5	JULIUS	12	0
6	BUMPSTEAD	12	0
7	JEFFERIES	9	4
8	DALGLIESH	10	6
COX.	SHEPHEARD	10	0
	Average	10	11⅞

CAMBRIDGE.

Third Station.

			st.	lbs.
1	T. RAVEN	Magd.	8	13
2	T. VENABLES	Jesus.	10	2
3	G. MANN	Caius.	10	7
4	W. P. CLOVES	1st Trin.	11	11
5	H. BROOKES	Trin.	11	7
6	J. RICHARDSON	1st Trin.	11	12
7	W. N. NICHOLSON[1]	Trin.	10	3
8	F. M. ARNOLD	Caius.	11	11
cox.	T. S. EGAN[1]	Caius.	10	0
	Average		10	11¾

"When they got to their stations the tide was still just flowing, but very slack, so as scarcely to stretch the line in the coxswain's hands. [The start was a very even one, and a neck-and-neck race ensued for some time.] The Leander coxswain, knowing between what two enemies [Egan and Shadwell] he was placed, was so alarmed at a demonstration of coming to close quarters on the part of Tom Egan, that he sheered right across towards the Oxford boat; luckily there was room enough, and the Oxford men prevented any further danger by coming right out with the lead, and taking up the straight course for the bridge. [Off the Vice-Chancellor's they got clear, and after that the other two crews kept gradually dropping further and further behind, Oxford winning by *four* lengths, Cambridge coming in *six* lengths ahead of Leander.]

[1] Cambridge Subscription Rooms.

"After having beaten both Cambridge and Leander at London the Oxford, with a crew somewhat differently constituted, went to Henley and won both the Grand Challenge and the Stewards', beating the Oxford Subscription Rooms for the latter, and the Caius College, Cambridge, for the former."—*Oxford Book.*

The crews in this were as follows:—

OXFORD.

			st.	lbs.
1	W. C. STAPYLTON	*Merton*	10	8
2	W. SPOTTISWOODE	*Ball.*	10	6
3	H. E. C. STAPYLTON	*Univ.*	10	10
4	J. SPANKIE	*Merton*	11	4
5	F. M. WILSON	*Ch. Ch.*	12	8
6	F. E. TUKE	*B.N.C.*	11	9
7	J. W. CONANT	*St John's*	12	5
8	H. MORGAN	*Ch. Ch.*	12	7
COX.	A. SHADWELL	*Ball.*	10	0
	Average		11	7⅛

CAIUS.

1	T. A. CARMICHAEL	10	0
2	T. T. WHITE	9	4
3	G. MANN	10	7
4	F. M. ARNOLD	11	12
5	H. W. LABORDE	11	10
6	A. C. FORBES	10	10
7	T. RAVEN	8	12
8	T. T. DOVE	10	3
COX.	T. S. EGAN	10	0
	Average	9	9¾

The crews for the Stewards' Cup were

O.U.B.C.

			st.	lbs.
1	W. C. STAPYLTON	*Merton*	11	8
2	W. J. DRY	*Wadham*	11	5
3	F. M. WILSON	*Ch. Ch.*	12	8
4	F. E. TUKE	*B.N.C.*	11	9
COX.	G. B. LEWIS	*Oriel*	10	0
	Average		11	11

OXFORD CLUB (LONDON).

		st.	lbs.
1	M. HAGGARD	9	12
2	J. WELCH	11	0
3	G. MEYNELL	11	3
4	H. LAMBERT	11	1
COX.	H. CHURCHILL	9	8
	Average	10	11

The time of the race for the G.C.C. was 8′. 22″, the shortest then on record. The Caius men rowed pluckily, but our men were too strong for them, and the stroke too quick.

F. E. TUKE.
N. HUGHES D'ARTH.

1845.

So early as the middle of November 1844, the Cambridge captains empowered the Secretary to write to Oxford with a view of re-establishing the

University race at Easter. The O.U.B.C. Committee seemed willing, but declined to make any definite arrangement till the Lent Term.

In that term the Oxonians proposed to change the course from below to above Putney Bridge. Their chief reasons for suggesting this were that the state of the navigation and traffic below Putney made it inconvenient for practising, and rendered the chances of a fair race very small.

This view the Cambridge men fully concurred in; and it was eventually settled to row from Putney Bridge to Mortlake Church on Saturday, March 15.

The following is taken from the Cambridge book :—

On Mr Brooks resigning his office as captain of the U.B.C. Mr Wilder of Magdalene was elected as his successor; but, he having fallen ill, Mr Brooks was re-elected. Unfortunately the same cause obliged him to resign again, and Mr Richardson of 1st Trinity was appointed his successor. As soon as the Lent Term races were over two crews went into practice, but made little advance owing to the illness of certain of the crew.

The crew practised for the most part twice a day, and in spite of stiff head-winds did the distance from lock to lock on several occasions in 21 minutes.

The race had been fixed for Saturday, March 15th, and the course was to be above Putney. It was unanimously resolved by the captains of the C.U.B.C. that steps should be taken to have the race put on an annual footing.

The Cambridge men went up to town on the Wednesday before the race, but the Oxonians did not arrive till Friday.

The first day the time taken (in the boat) from Putney bridge to Hammersmith was 8 minutes, and over the course to about ¾ths of a mile beyond Mortlake Church was 21′ 55″. The time to Hammersmith bridge on Thursday was 9 minutes, and on Friday and in the race 9½, the days having been less and less favourable.

The Oxford men went over the course on Friday: they seemed to start well but did not keep it up far; the Cambridge men were very confident, and they had plenty of backers at evens. Indeed the betting on Saturday morning was 5 to 4 on Cambridge. A fortnight before it had been 3 to 1 on Oxford. W. H. Harrison Esq., Commodore of the Royal Thames Yacht Club, again consented to act as umpire.

The account of the race given below is a comparison of *Bell's Life* and the Cambridge book.

The time fixed for the start was half-past five, and Cambridge having won the toss took the Middlesex side. It was however six o'clock before the crews (Oxford by the bye being rather dilatory) took their stations one on each side of the next arch but one to the middle arch of Putney bridge. Searle started them by word of mouth.

The crews were:—

CAMBRIDGE.

			st.	lbs.
1	GERARD MANN	............*Caius*...	10	7
2	W. HARKNESS	...............*John's*...	10	0
3	W. S. LOCKHART	.........*Christ's*...	11	3
4	W. P. CLOVES	............*1st Trin.*...	12	0
5	F. M. ARNOLD	...............*Caius*...	12	0
6	R. HARKNESS	...............*John's*...	11	0
7	J. RICHARDSON	.........*1st Trin.*...	12	0
str.	C. G. HILL	.........*2nd Trin.*...	10	11
cox.	H. MUNSTER	............*1st Trin.*...	9	2
		Average	11	2⅝

OXFORD.

			st.	lbs.
1	M. HAGGARD	............*Ch. Ch.*...	10	3
2	W. C. STAPYLTON	.........*Merton*...	10	12
3	W. H. MILMAN	............*Ch. Ch.*...	11	0
4	H. LEWIS	...............*Pembroke*...	11	7
5	W. BUCKLE	..................*Oriel*...	13	12
6	F. C. ROYDS	............*Pembroke*...	11	5
7	F. M. WILSON	............*Ch. Ch.*...	12	3
str.	F. E. TUKE	...............*B.N.C.*...	12	2
cox.	F. J. RICHARDS	.........*Exeter*...	10	10
		Average	11	9

Cambridge got a slight lead, but about the third stroke the swell of a steamer waiting for the race threw the bow-side oars into confusion and completely unshipped No. 7's oar; in consequence of this accident the Oxford drew a few yards ahead (4 or 4½), but the Cambridge men kept very cool and steady, and gradually pulled up the lost distance; a fine race ensued till Finch's cricket ground, when Cambridge put on a fine spurt and gained seven or eight feet, and gradually went away in advance, and by the end of the Bishop of London's Walk had drawn clear. The cheers of their friends were tremendous, and the coxswain became so excited that, whilst waving his hat about in a most unphilosophic manner, he dropped it in the river and lost it as he well deserved. The steering was not good in either boat on rounding the Waterworks corner, both boats hugging the shore too closely. The Oxonians were at Hammersmith Bridge 3 lengths in the rear and, despite the most plucky exertions, still lost ground, and came in eight or ten boat lengths behind their opponents. The Cambridge book says $\frac{1}{2}$ a minute or about 160 yards. The day or rather night was of the most inclement possible, and the water very rough.

Bell says, the Cambridge crew had far better general style and more freedom throughout than the gentlemen of the other University.

The Cambridge crew rowed in a boat built by Logan and belonging to Second Trinity Boat Club. Searle built them an "outrigger," 60 feet long and "only 2 ft. 10 in. wide," so says *Bell's Life*. It was laid down the Tuesday week before the race and launched in eight days. They were however unable to use it on account of the bad weather. *Bell* "feels certain that the 'outrigger' will be brought into active service during the summer."

The Oxford men rowed in a boat built by King of Oxford, and a more perfect model it was generally admitted could not have been turned out.

According to the Oxford Books, the account of the challenge and race given in *Bell* is "*unusually true.*" The Cambridge men came up to town on Wednesday, and stayed at the "Bells;" practising over the course every day, and taking the utmost pains with their training. (It is perhaps worthy of note that two of their crew were "teetotalers".) Rumours had reached Oxford that the Cambridge was a *mild crew*, and that victory was almost certain seemed the general impression in the University; odds being freely given on our crew, not only by our men but by Cambridge men.

"At last the fatal day arrived. We came up to town on the Friday morning, and rowed over the course about half-past five, preceded by a made-up crew with Shadwell *coxswain*, to show us the best line to take. Our time, as the tide was rather slack, was 23 minutes, and as Shadwell observed "tidy." We dined afterwards and slept in town—arriving again at Putney on the following day about one o'clock. At two we made our last training meal on mutton chops and sherry, and remained at the "Bells" during the afternoon, as is usual "in a funk." At a quarter before six we walked down to our boat, rowed her through the bridge, and after an interval of 5 minutes or so rowed up to our station, "the Surrey side," as we lost the toss for choice of station.

"The word 'off' being given by Mr Searle, jun., we dashed off with a slight lead, which we bettered for some distance. About Finch's however the Cambridge boat came up to us, and though we pulled 'all we knew' began gradually to gain on us, at last being *so unpolite* as to get clear ahead of us and dispense with our company. The cold was now intense, and several of our men complained that they could with difficulty hold their oars, much less their way with the Cambridge boat. However at Hammersmith Bridge we began to row up to them, and faint hopes were raised that they *were done.*

"This however did not seem correct, for after passing the bridge they kept on gaining, though slowly, in spite of several long and strong spurts which we put on—coming in winners by *about eight lengths.* Alas! alas! On turning round we found that the Oxford Rooms' boat did not make its appearance, to which we had entrusted our jackets &c., and a more bitter, cold and miserable row never could have been experienced than we had down to Putney against a head wind, strong tide and floating ice. Right glad we were to arrive at Mrs Avis', and many a long pull and strong pull did we take at the warm beer after our freezing. In the evening we dined with the Cambridge men, and mustered in all 46.

FRANCIS EDWARD TUKE."

BIOGRAPHICAL NOTICES.

G. MANN. Graduated as first Junior Optime, 1845; was ordained soon after he left Cambridge, and died Oct. 1855, aged 33, of fever he caught whilst visiting one of his parishioners.

W. HARKNESS. Graduated 1846; curate of Kingsdon, Taunton; vicar of Winscombe, Somerset, 1859; died in 1863, of consumption. He had received as a boy a severe blow from a cricket-ball, which was supposed to have laid the foundation of the disease which ended his life.

W. S. LOCKHART. Took no degree. Died many years ago.

W. P. CLOVES. Graduated 1846. Died Sept. 25, 1849, of constitutional consumption, which had already carried off all the other members of his family of the same generation.

F. M. ARNOLD, M.A. Graduated as wrangler in 1848; late schol. of Caius College, ordained 1848; late Senior Fellow of St Nicholas College, Shoreham, Sussex; living at Kingston on Thames; Major of the 2nd Surrey Volunteers.

R. HARKNESS, M.A. Graduated 1848, ordained 1849; perpetual curate of Trinity, North Malvern, 1855—62; rector of Sternfield, diocese of Norwich, 1862.

J. RICHARDSON, M.A. Graduated 1844 as Senior

Optime; rector of Sandy, diocese of Ely, 1858; rowed in 1st Trinity first boat as a freshman, and head of the river three years.

C. G. HILL. Graduated 1846; ordained 1848; curate of Great Stanmore, Middlesex; formerly curate of Stanmore, Middlesex, 1848—58.

H. MUNSTER. Called to the bar May 1848; and in practice as a special pleader on the home circuit; now M.P. for Mallow.

M. HAGGARD, student of Christ Church; curate of St Paul's, Bedminster; resigned 1853; died of decline 1854.

W. C. STAPYLTON, M.A. Graduated 1847; ordained 1849; elected fellow of Merton College, by which he was presented to the vicarage of Malden with Chessington in the diocese of Winchester, 1850.

W. H. MILMAN, M.A. Graduated 1847; ordained 1849; rector of St Augustine's with St Faith's, city and diocese of London, 1857; librarian of Sion College, 1857; Minor Canon of St Paul's Cathedral, 1859; formerly curate of Christ Church, Hoxton, London.

H. LEWIS. Graduated 1846.

W. BUCKLE. In holy orders; curate of Stretton Grandison, Ledbury.

F. C. ROYDS, M.A. Graduated 1847; ordained 1850; rector of Coddington, diocese of Chester, 1855.

F. M. WILSON, M.A. Graduated 1847; of Stow Langtoft, Bury St Edmund's; magistrate for

Suffolk; lord of the manor of Stow Langtoft.

F. E. TUKE, M.A. Graduated 1846; ordained 1848; perpetual curate of Wye, diocese of Canterbury, 1858.

F. J. RICHARDS[1].

In the following summer term it was decided to enter a U.B.C. boat for the Grand Challenge Cup at Henley, and the Committee appointed to choose the crew were also empowered to enter a boat for the Stewards' Cup and for the Gold Cup at the Thames Regatta.

Henley Regatta came off on the 6th and 7th of June. A four-oar of the C.U.B.C. was entered but did not show. The only boats entered for the Grand Challenge were those of the two University clubs.

The crews were:

CAMBRIDGE.

1	G. MANN	*Caius.*
2	W. HARKNESS	*John's.*
3	W. S. LOCKHART	*Magd.*
4	W. P. CLOVES	1*st Trin.*
5	F. L. HOPKINS	1*st Trin.*
6	H. J. POTTS	2*nd Trin.*
7	F. M. ARNOLD	*Caius.*
str.	C. G. HILL	2*nd Trin.*
cox.	H. MUNSTER	1*st Trin.*

[1] Of this gentleman I can find no trace.

OXFORD.

			st.	lbs.
1	W. C. STAPYLTON	Merton	10	6
2	W. SPOTTISWOODE	Balliol	10	11
3	W. H. MILMAN	Ch.Ch.	10	10
4	W. BUCKLE	Oriel	13	6
5	E. A. BREEDON	Trin.	12	5
6	E. H. PENFOLD	John's	11	10
7	J. W. CONANT	John's	11	13
str.	F. M. WILSON	Ch.Ch.	12	11
cox.	T. RICHARDS	Trin.	10	4
	Average of crew		11	$10\tfrac{3}{4}$

Cambridge having won the toss took the Oxfordshire side; the start was well effected (by word) in spite of the boisterous weather; for the first quarter of a mile there was not any very great difference, but then Cambridge began to draw ahead so fast that when about $\tfrac{3}{4}$ths of the way from the starting point they were easily able to cross and, by taking their opponents' water, to make the race certain. The time was slow, owing to the weather and to the winners' taking it pretty easily at the last.

The O.U.B.C. won the Stewards' Cup after a most exciting race with the St George's Club. The race was so close that the two umpires differed in their opinions as to which crew won. But it was finally given to the O.U.B.C.

The Oxford Books say that the eight-oared crew suffered from most adverse fortune; losing within a very short time of the race Mr G. Hughes, who rowed stroke to the gallant seven-oar, and within a few days afterwards Mr Tuke, who had strained himself so severely as to be put *hors de combat*.

The new eight-oared race was won by the St George's from 1st Trinity and St John's; and the prize to pair oars was won by Messrs Arnold and Mann (Nos. 7 and 1 of the C.U.B.C. crew).

At the Thames Regatta, which was held on Tuesday, Wednesday and Thursday, 24th, 25th and 26th of June, the Cambridge Subscription Rooms won the Gold Challenge Cup against the O.U.B.C., the Neptune and St George's clubs. The O.U.B.C. four however carried off the palm again from the St George's crew with whom they had had the exciting and much disputed contest at Henley.

All the Rooms crew with the exception of A. Shadwell were resident members of the University. Mr Mann, who was to have rowed 2, was taken ill during (or after) the final heat for the pairs, and W. S. Lockhart filled the vacancy.

The " Rooms" crew were :—

 1   CORNELIUS RIPPINGALL ......*St John's.*
 2   ALFRED HUDSON SHADWELL...*St John's.*
 3   W. S. LOCKHART ....*Magd.*
 4   WILLIAM PICKERING CLOVES   1*st Trin.*
 5   EDMOND WILDER ....*Magd.*
 6   FREDERICK LYON HOPKINS ...1*st Trin.*
 7   FREDERIC MONTAGUE ARNOLD *Caius.*
 str. CHARLES GRAY HILL ....2*nd Trin.*
 cox. THOMAS SELBY EGAN ....*Caius.*

This was therefore the third defeat sustained by Oxford this year.

1846.

In February 1846 a challenge was received from Oxford proposing a match at Easter about the same time as the year before. The challenge was of course accepted, and the Rowing Committee were empowered to decide on the *style of the ship* that the race should be rowed in. The meaning of this clause was that they should decide whether the race should be rowed in the outrigged boat or whether they should keep to the old style of boat. It will be remembered that an outrigger had been built for the crew the year before, but they were unable to use it.

The Cambridge Book says:—

"The race was fixed for Friday the third of April, from Putney Bridge to Mortlake Church.

"The University crew began practising on Tuesday, March 24. The distance from lock to lock was rowed in 20 min. 45 sec., there being a slight stern wind and no stream; some delay was occasioned by shipping oars at the Railway Bridge.

"The crew rowed in an outrigger built by Searle, 60 ft. in length, 2 ft. 8 in. in breadth.

"The crew went to town on the Tuesday morning before the race, and rowed over the course from Putney to Mortlake in the afternoon.

"On Wednesday they had a race with a Watermen's crew, got clear of them at the Crab Tree, and came in at Mortlake six or seven lengths ahead. The Watermen's crew was:—

1	F. PHELPS.	5	MAYNARD.
2	GOODRUM.	6	LETT.
3	T. COOMBES.	7	NEWELL.
4	J. PHELPS.	8	R. COOMBES.

"The time was, to Hammersmith Bridge 8 min. 23 sec., to Mortlake Church 22 min.

"The Oxford crew went to town on Monday, and had a row that day.

"In consequence of the tide, it was found necessary to row down from Mortlake to Putney, and 11 o'clock was fixed for the start.

"C. J. Selwyn, Esq., was appointed umpire. Mr Searle as usual started. Friday morning was fortunately very fine, and the little wind there was with the tide. At 10 min. past 11 a.m. both crews came to the starting-post, and had no sooner taken their stations than Mr Searle gave the signal. Oxford had the lead for the first five or six strokes. After that we drew a little ahead, and at Chiswick our No. 7's oar was clear of their No. 2's. But here our station (the Middlesex), which had been of advantage to us in the start, began to tell against us; we were in shallow water and had the outside of the corner[1]. Consequently Oxford regained

[1] One would suppose that as they had the outside they would be in deep water; but at the corner above Chiswick Eyot there used to be, and (for anything I know to the con-

part of their lost ground, and brought the bow of their boat opposite our No. 1. About this period the oars were overlapping, so that a foul was apprehended. At Hammersmith Bridge Cambridge had drawn half a boat's length ahead, so that their oars were again clear, but Oxford put on a desperate spurt and came up as before. But this was their final effort; for, in pulling with unparalleled pluck and resolution, they had taken it all out of themselves; so that after three miles the superior strength of Cambridge began to tell, and at the Crab Tree the latter went by them with comparative ease, coming in 12 strokes or about three lengths ahead. The race was the hardest and fastest ever rowed, the distance being four miles one furlong, and time 21 min. 5 sec. The crews dined together as usual at Avis' at 6 o'clock, and kept up the party to a late hour."

The only mention of the race in the Oxford Books is:—

"As 'Bell's' account of the race is quite correct nothing need be added to it. The result was such as I hope rather to encourage our men to another effort than to make them despair. I earnestly recommend future captains to look to the building of their boats, and see that they have sufficient strength, as that is of infinitely more importance than mere lightness.

W. H. MILMAN, *President*."

trary) is now, a shoal, so that the outside boat would in reality be in shallow water.

Bell's Life says that the Oxford crew was trained by Noulton, the Cambridge by the Champion Sculler Coombes. Many persons expressed an opinion that it was better that amateur crews should not be trained by watermen, however respectable and clever, as they undoubtedly were on this occasion; the objections to which course were clearly and forcibly pointed out in a pamphlet on "Steering," published in 1845 at Oxford, the joint production, as *Bell* supposes, of an Oxonian and Cantab, great proficients in the art of which they treat. I believe I am right in stating that these were Messrs Egan and Shadwell.

The Oxford boat was expressly built for this match by King of Oxford; she was outrigger, $58\frac{1}{2}$ ft. long, and was of admirable construction; very low in the water forwards, but rising to every stroke "like a duck." The Cambridge boat however did not give such great satisfaction.

The race was fixed for 11 o'clock, and started from Mortlake. The great distance of the starting place from London caused a great scantiness of spectators. "Instead of having a host of cutters to receive them as usual, the crack Leander eight was the only boat afloat at Mortlake worth recording which had rowed up to witness the start."

Both boats were afloat about the same time, and "we[1] never saw two finer crews than they appeared, as they leisurely rowed to take their stations

---

[1] *Bell's Life.*

at two buoys moored off the Malt House, the Oxford on the Surrey, the Cambridge on the Middlesex side of the river: the wind being aft made little difference to either." Very little betting was done, but Cambridge were the favourites at 5 or 6 to 4. The tide was about half ebb at the time of the start, which was as usual admirably effected by Mr E. Searle.

The account of the race in *Bell's Life* is almost exactly the same as that I have given above. Though there was hardly anybody to witness the start at Mortlake, there was one of the largest crowds ever seen at Putney, who hailed the winners with the most hearty and long-continued cheering.

"Both crews were very much exhausted at the finish; it was evident they had both worked their hardest, and, in fact, it could not be otherwise, for the race may be said to have been a succession of 'bursts' throughout, and both boats deserve the highest praise. The winners rowed the distance in twenty-one minutes and five seconds, which was a great improvement on their several trials. Thus ended one of the finest, most game, and best contested matches ever seen on the river Thames."

The names of the men were:—

CAMBRIDGE.

		st.	lbs.
1	GEORGE FRANCIS MURDOCH *L. Marg.*	10	2
2	GEORGE FREDERICK HOLROYD 1*st Trin.*	11	1
3	STEPHEN THOMAS CLISSOLD 3*rd Trin.*	12	0
4	WILLIAM PICKERING CLOVES 1*st Trin.*	12	12
5	EDMOND WILDER ....*Magdalene*	13	2
6	ROBERT HARKNESS[1] ......*Lady Marg.*	11	6
7	ED. PARKER WOLSTENHOLME 1*st Trin.*	11	1
str.	CHARLES GRAY HILL[1] ...2*nd Trinity*	11	1
cox.	T. B. LLOYD ....*Lady Marg.*	9	8
	Average	11	8⅝

OXFORD.

		st.	lbs.
1	H. S. POLEHAMPTON ...*Pemb.*	10	9
2	E. C. BURTON............*Ch. Ch.* ...	11	0
3	W. U. HEYGATE.........*Merton* ...	11	8
4	E. H. PENFOLD ....*St John's*...	11	8
5	JOHN W. CONANT ......*St John's*...	12	4
6	F. C. ROYDS[1] ............*B.N.C.* ...	11	9
7	W. C. STAPYLTON[1] ......*Merton* ...	10	12
str.	W. H. MILMAN[1] ....*Ch. Ch.* ...	11	0
cox.	C. J. SOANES ....*St John's*...	9	13
	Average	11	5⅝

S. VINCENT, 1st Trin., was to have pulled bow, but was unable to row.

[1] These were members of the crew of 1845.

BIOGRAPHICAL NOTICES.

G. F. MURDOCH, graduated 1847; educated at Winchester and Trinity; died of gastric fever some years ago.

G. F. HOLROYD, M.A., graduated 1846 as Wrangler and Second Class Classic; magistrate for Northampton and Lieutenant of Northampton Militia. Hatton Hall, Wellingborough.

S. T. CLISSOLD, educated at Eton and Trinity; graduated 1848; called to the Bar at Inner Temple 1850, afterwards resident magistrate and commissioner of the gold fields, Ballarat, Victoria, now living on his property at Wrentham, Suffolk.

E. WILDER, educated at Eton and Magdalene, afterwards in Colonial Office.

E. P. WOLSTENHOLME, M.A., graduated as 30th Wrangler and Third Class Classic 1847; called to the Bar at Lincoln's Inn 1850. Eq. dr. and conv.

T. B. LLOYD, M.A., graduated 1846; ordained 1848; Perpetual Curate of St Mary's, Shrewsbury, 1854.

H. S. POLEHAMPTON, M.A., Late Fellow of Pembroke College, Oxford, and Chaplain to the H.E.I.C., Bengal. In 1858 was published "Memoir, Letters, and Diary of the late H. S. Polehampton, Chaplain at Lucknow."

E. C. BURTON, M.A., graduated 1849; alive 1869.

W. U. HEYGATE, M.A., graduated 1847; called to the Bar at Lincoln's Inn, Nov. 1850. Eq. dr. and conv. Midland circuit; alive in 1869.

E. H. PENFOLD[1].

Rev. J. W. CONANT, lives at Surbiton, Surrey; son of the late police magistrate at Marlborough street.

C. J. SOANES, graduated 1847.

This year it was found impossible to get up a University crew for the Henley and Thames Regattas. The 1st Trinity boat club however sent in an eight for the Grand Challenge and Ladies'. At this time the Ladies' Cup was open to *all* crews, like the Grand C.C. The race for the Ladies' was first. That for the G.C.C. was rowed same day. In the former race they were beaten by the Thames Club (London) by two lengths, Eton and Westminster (Oxford) being third. For the Ladies' there were three entries,

>1st Trinity (Cambridge),
>Eton and Westminster (Oxford),
>Thames Club (London).

The Thames Club had a fresh man, Mr Peacock, at No. 3.

The "Eton and Westminster" was virtually the Oxford University crew, but was so named because all the men happened to be either Eton or Westminster.

1st Trinity won a desperate race with the Thames Club by a yard; "Eton and Westminster" tailed off.

At the Thames Regatta 1st Trinity were again beaten for the Grand Cup, by the Thames Club;

---

[1] Of this gentleman I can find no trace.

but carried off the Four-oar Cup, beating the O.U.B.C. by two lengths, and seven other boats.

The crews were as follows:—

First Trinity.[1]	O.U.B.C.
1 S. Vincent.	1 W. C. Stapylton.
2 G. F. Holroyd.	2 F. M. Wilson.
3 E. P. Wolstenholme.	3 J. W. Conant.
4 W. P. Cloves.	4 W. H. Milman.
cox. H. T. Holland.	cox. Mark Haggard.

1847.

In the beginning of the year a challenge was received from Oxford proposing a race, but making a condition that the crews should not be trained by watermen. In accordance with a resolution of the captains, the Secretary wrote to Mr Stapylton objecting to the condition, on the grounds that we should be at a disadvantage in the summer when contending against London crews if we were not coached by a waterman. However, the day after, he got a second letter from Mr Stapylton, withdrawing the challenge because of the opposition of certain College authorities to a race at that time, and on account of the severe illness of two of their intended crew. He however stated that they would be happy to meet us in the summer.

---

[1] This crew rowed in a one-streaked outrigger by Searle.

It was decided to enter a crew for the G.C.C. at the Henley and Thames Regattas, but the latter was fixed for such a late date that it was found impossible to get up a crew. Henley was fixed for the 17th and 18th of June.

The crew for the G.C.C. at Henley was trained by R. Coombes; two or three men were prevented by illness, almost at the last moment, from rowing, and on the 14th it was found necessary to take two fresh men into the boat. In addition to this they found on their arriving on the Thames that the boat which Searle had built for them partook more of the nature of a box than a ship; and they were obliged to row in the Trinity boat, which was much too small for them.

The entries were:

Thames Club, London (holders).

O.U.B.C.

			st.	lbs.
1	E. G. MOON	*Magd.*	10	4
2	M. HAGGARD	*Ch. Ch.*	10	6
3	J. OLDHAM	*B.N.C.*	11	7
4	F. C. ROYDS	*B.N.C.*	11	10
5	E. G. C. GRIFFITHS	*Worc.*	12	6
6	W. KING	*Oriel*	11	0
7	G. R. WINTER	*B.N.C.*	11	3
str.	E. C. BURTON	*Ch. Ch.*	11	0
cox.	C. J. SOANES	*St John's*	9	10
	Average		11	2¾

C.U.B.C.

			st.	lbs.
1	W. Maule	1st Trin.	9	12
2	T. Gisborne	L. Marg.	10	10
3	E. P. Wolstenholme	1st Trin.	10	10
4	A. Garfit	1st Trin.	12	8
5	C. A. Nicholson	1st Trin.	13	5
6	R. Harkness	St John's	11	4
7	S. Vincent	1st Trin.	10	10
str.	F. Jackson	St John's	11	0
cox.	G. F. Murdoch	St John's	10	3
	Average		11	3⅞

The trial heat between the two U.B.C. crews was fixed for the 1st day. Cambridge having won the toss took the inside station. Both got a good start, but immediately after Oxford gained a slight lead which they continued steadily to improve, and just below the Poplars they took their opponents' water, ultimately winning by two and a half boats' lengths.

On the following day they beat the holders by 3 boats' lengths, and thus became winners. The time over the course was the shortest ever known, 7′ 56″.

The B.N.C. crew of Oxford won the Ladies' plate from the Trinity (Cambridge) boat by about ¾ boat's length.

The Diamond Sculls were won by W. Maule 1st Trinity, who beat three others, including Moon of Magd. Coll. Oxon., the winner of last year (1846).

The Oxford captain was as fortunate this year as his predecessor had been unlucky in 1845. He says:

"After the College races were concluded we set about forming our crew, having three weeks or little more to do it in, but we were so fortunate in our selection that not a man was changed afterwards: nor could it be doubted but that the eight men chosen were the best our University could produce to maintain her honour and add to her rowing celebrity." The crew was composed of men from six Colleges: stroke, six, and two were Westminster men, seven was from Eton, four and three from Rugby, bow and coxswain from the London river. The Thames club were a very fine crew, and were backed in London at 7 and 6 to 4 against the field. The Cambridge were the heaviest crew, the Oxford the lightest. "The speed of our boat was immense; the time and swing perfect, and such was the regularity that in the distance she looked like a boat propelled by a single pair of oars." After the two Universities had taken one practice on the Henley water the betting was 6 to 4 on Oxford for the trial heat, the winners of which were to contend with the holders, "The Thames Club." The Oxford went clean away and won by "four good lengths, or three lengths clear." The same afternoon the Thames crew practised on the course in a "beautiful boat

of Searle's build, which carried them magnificently.
They went well and started like lightning: there
was no mistake about their being a splendid crew.
They struck no little awe into the minds of our
men, but we retired to bed determined to do our
utmost with them on the morrow." The Thames
won the toss and took the tow-path side. "They
outstarted us, and led the way over the first two
hundred yards by half a length; we then drew on
them, got even, picked up the boat fore and aft at
a given signal (a railway whistle carried by the
coxswain), and in a few more strokes cleared the
boat and continued gaining up to the post, winning
by *four* good lengths. *Bell* says the distance was
done in *eight minutes*, but it is beyond doubt that
the real time of this extraordinary race was 7 min.
54 sec., faster by nearly half a minute than the
distance had ever been rowed previously, while
what wind there was was against the boats, though
that was very little...The Thames Regatta this
year was held late in the summer, consequently no
University men rowed there, but it is satisfactory
to us that both the Thames eight and the St
George's four were the conquerors in the two
greatest prizes there—the two crews we had so
comfortably beaten at Henley.

EDMUND CHARLES BURTON,

Nov. 14*th*, 1847.   *President."*

1848.

In the beginning of this year (March 15), at a meeting of the captains, Mr Maule explained that it was generally understood that the Oxford University were willing to row us at Easter, but considered that, in consequence of our unfortunate defeat at Henley last year, we ought to send the challenge.

The Secretary was thereupon empowered to write a challenge, and the usual preparations for the race were at once commenced. A voluntary subscription was also opened among members of the University to defray the expenses of training, which had hitherto always fallen upon the crew.

There is no other mention whatever in the C.U.B.C. books about the correspondence with Oxford, nor is it even stated why no race took place.

This year there was a very unpleasant controversy about the Henley and Thames Regattas. Originally both were fixed for the 6th and 7th of July. This truly absurd arrangement was of course objected to by everybody who really cared to see good sport. The Cambridge term ended early, the Oxford late. The latter were holders of nearly all the prizes at Henley, and it was thus manifestly unfair to fix Henley at a time when they could not contend. Again Cambridge considered it unfair to them that both Regattas should be fixed at a time when it was impossible for them to get a crew together. If both Regattas were held at the same time there would be little chance of real racing; for the London Rowing Clubs would have all one Regatta to themselves and Oxford all the other. It was suggested on the part of Cambridge that Henley should be held early in June, so that they and London would be able to compete at it, and Oxford and London at the Thames National in July. The stewards of both Regattas however refused to accede to any of the proposals which were made with a view to the convenience of Cambridge; and the result was that no Cambridge crews were able to enter. Mr Bagshawe of 3rd Trinity entered for the Diamond Sculls and won them, beating Mr Wilberforce of Oxford.

The C.U.B.C., feeling that a want of proper regard to their interests had been shown, withdrew their subscription of £25 to each Regatta, but considering it their duty to support rowing generally, voted a donation of £10 to each.

The O.U.B.C. carried off the G.C.C. with the following crew, the Thames Club being the only challenger.

		st.	lbs.
1	W. G. Rich	10	11
2	M. Haggard	10	4[1]
3	E. J. Sykes	11	0
4	F. C. Royds	11	11
5	G. R. Winter	11	6
6	A. Mansfield	11	10
7	W. H. Milman	11	0[1]
str.	E. C. Burton	11	0[1]
cox.	C. J. Soanes	10	0[1]

Christ Church won the Stewards' and the pairs, Messrs Milman and Haggard being the successful competitors for the latter prize. "The sculls alone were not secured by Oxford. These were won by Mr Bagshawe of Trinity College, Cambridge.

G. R. Winter, *President.*"

1849.

In February a challenge arrived from Oxford proposing a race at Easter, and suggesting that the matches should be alternately at Easter and Midsummer.

"The challenge was accepted *unconditionally.*"

The Lent races were finished on March 10, and the University crew began practising on Tuesday the 13th, under the superintendence of Robert

---

[1] These weights are doubtful.

Coombes of London. The crew was made up as follows:

1	HUGH PROBY	*2nd Trinity.*
2	W. JONES	*2nd Trinity.*
3	A. D. RUTZEN	*3rd Trinity.*
4	C. J. HOLDEN	*3rd Trinity.*
5	WM. LEONARD GILL BAGSHAWE	*3rd Trinity.*
6	WM. HENRY WADDINGTON	*2nd Trinity.*
7	VAUX	*2nd Trinity,*
	afterwards HODGSON	*1st Trinity.*
str.	J. C. WRAY	*2nd Trinity.*
cox.	F. BLOMFIELD	*3rd Trinity.*

The weather was very fine for practising, though the water was very low; and on Saturday the crew performed the distance from Searle's to Baitsbite in 19½ minutes. On Monday the University boat (a one-streaked out-rigger, 62 ft. 9 in. long, 2 ft. 2 in. wide, constructed by Searle) came down to Cambridge. During the ensuing week the crew practised daily from lock to lock, but the weather being cold and windy the time was never very good—scarcely ever under 22 minutes. The crew being pretty well got together by Saturday, started for Putney on Monday March 26, the race being fixed for Thursday the 29th. They went over the ground the same day, and had a race with a picked watermen's crew on Tuesday, which they beat by 8 or 10 boats' lengths, the two boats having been neck and neck the first 2 miles of the course.

The Oxford crew began practising on the 6th

of March, and were trained by a well-known amateur. Their boat was built by Hall of Oxford; it was the larger of the two, having a bigger floor and being flatter.

The following are the names and weights of the crews; it will be noticed that all the Cambridge crew were Trinity men.

CAMBRIDGE.

			st.	lbs.
1	H. PROBY	2nd Trin....	9	13
2	W. J. H. JONES	2nd Trin.	10	13
3	ALBERT DE RUTZEN	3rd Trin....	11	8
4	J. C. HOLDEN	3rd Trin....	11	8
5	W. L. G. BAGSHAWE	3rd Trin....	11	10
6	W. H. WADDINGTON	2nd Trin....	11	10
7	W. C. HODGSON	1st Trin. ...	11	2
str.	J. COPLEY WRAY	2nd Trin....	10	12
cox.	GEORGE BOOTH	1st Trin....	10	7
	Average of crew		11	2½

OXFORD.

1	D. WAUCHOPE	*Wadham*	10	4
2	J. W. CHITTY	*Balliol*	11	2
3	H. H. TREMAYNE	*Ch. Ch.*	11	5
4	E. C. BURTON[1]	*Ch. Ch.*	11	0
5	CHAS. HOLDEN STEWARD	*Oriel*	12	0
6	A. MANSFIELD	*Ch. Ch.*	11	8
7	J. J. SYKES	*Worc.*	11	0
str.	W. G. RICH	*Ch. Ch.*	10	0
cox.	C. SOANES[1]	*St John's*	10	8
	Average of crew		11	0⅝

[1] Were in the crew of 1846.

Blomfield was to have steered the Cambridge boat, but met with a slight accident which obliged him to give up the rudder lines to G. Booth.

The following account of the race is compiled from two accounts which appeared at the time in *Bell's Life* and the *Times* newspaper, which from internal evidence appear to have come from the same pen.

The weather was extremely inauspicious, the rain pouring down in torrents at the time appointed for the start. Four or five steamboats crowded with passengers, together with numerous craft of all descriptions, floated on the river awaiting the appearance of the crews. Many old oarsmen were of course present to view the contest, among whom were noticed Messrs Wilder, Menzies, Vincent, Egan, the Earls of Verulam and Kilmorey, the latter rowing stroke of his four-oared cutter, the Vice-Chancellor of England, and many well-known barristers, for instance Hon. G. Denman and Mr Thos. Chitty.

As soon as the pelting shower had cleared off, Putney bridge was lined with carriages, and hundreds of horsemen, with a sprinkling of ladies, crowded the towing path with the intention of keeping level with the race.

About half an hour before the time fixed for the start a consultation was held between the two crews and their friends as to the advisability of altering the winning post from Mortlake to Barnes Bridge. The chief reason alleged for doing so was that the arches of the bridge were too narrow to admit of two boats going through together. But the Cambridge men, trusting to their training, refused to have the course shortened. Cambridge won the toss and chose the Middlesex shore.

An even start having been effected, Oxford soon began to draw ahead, and when they arrived opposite the Star and Garter they were half a length to the good and were gaining at every stroke. This continued for the first half-mile, Cambridge hugging the Middlesex shore a good deal too closely. They however kept resolutely working at it, and the increased exertions on their part called forth corresponding efforts on the side of their opponents. So they went at it with might and main until they reached Hammersmith, where it became evident that the killing pace was beginning to tell on the Oxford men. After passing the bridge the Oxford coxswain steered his boat too near the Surrey bank, which gave the Cambridge men a considerable advantage. Immediately after passing Hammersmith the Cantabs began to gain steadily, and on passing Chiswick Eyot were level with them. No words can express the excitement evinced by the crowds on the banks while the crews remained in this relative position for some few moments. But when the Cambridge began to draw ahead, in the same manner as Oxford had previously passed them, the shrieks from the steamers were almost beyond description. As soon as they were clear they began to draw rapidly ahead, and though the Oxford men were determined to show fight to the last, the Cambridge boat shot Barnes Bridge several lengths ahead, and eventually came in about 60 sec. in advance. Great praise was due to the winning crew for the pains they had taken in training, for they were in most excellent condition, and had evidently profited to the greatest possible extent by Coombes' instruction. Oxford however did not come so *fit* to the post, though many preferred their style of rowing to that of Cambridge.

It was said that a good deal was due to the superiority of the Cambridge ship, which seems to have "oiled" well through the water, while the Oxford boat at each stroke "lifted" at the stern and "hung fire" on the feather.

The account of the race given in our books is substantially the same. They attribute the victory chiefly to their excellent training, and remark that the Oxford stroke was much too fast for a long course, and that the Oxford boat wanted the "steady swing" which the Cambridge men had.

From Oxford books I copy the following remarks on the Easter match 1849.

"Another disastrous Easter match is here recorded, in which the fairest hopes were destined to be blasted. To speak of the merits of the crew were unnecessary, otherwise than to give the opinions of Messrs Shadwell of Oxford and Egan of Cambridge.

" They said we ' had shown to those who could

appreciate it *a most brilliant specimen of perfect rowing.'*

" The causes of our defeat were partial want of condition, a bad boat (built by Hall), and bad steering. We led from the moment of starting to Chiswick Eyot; but here our coxswain took us over the back-water on the Surrey side, and without any apparent diminution in our efforts, the boat seemed to stop almost dead, the Cantabs came up in the midstream and tide, and passed like a shot. The race was then at an end.

W. G. RICH, President O.U.B.C."

The following is what Mr Egan said of the two crews, as I find it quoted in a letter to *Bell's Life* by Mr Shadwell:—

"The Oxford crew were beaten through want of condition, but as long as their physical powers of endurance lasted they maintained a gallant lead. At Chiswick Eyot they shut up and Cambridge went by. Nothing could be more praiseworthy than the unflinching pluck and superb condition of the latter, while nothing is more to be regretted than the want of it in the former. *The rowing was perfection*, and that alone, in spite of their boat, which did not carry them, and buried bodily amidships at every stroke, bore them along in triumph for at least two miles. This is doubtless a correct account of the race, while I suppose by people generally the result will be laid to a different cause, viz. the better rowing of Cambridge, and the generalship of Bob Coombes. But I am satisfied."

In October of this same year a challenge was received from Oxford to row at Christmas. This was promptly accepted. Mr Holden of 3rd Trinity was elected Captain in the room of Mr Bagshawe, who resigned the office because he thought he would be unable to row again.

BIOGRAPHICAL NOTICES.

H. PROBY, drowned in Australia.

W. J. H. JONES, died in India.

A. DE RUTZEN, called to the Bar at Inner Temple, April 1857; South Wales Circuit, Gloucester and Glamorganshire Sessions.

J. C. HOLDEN, died within a few years of leaving College.

W. L. G. BAGSHAWE, late of Wormill Hall, Derbyshire, was murdered by poachers in his river, the Wye, July 24, 1854.

W. H. WADDINGTON, graduated 1849, as second in the first class Classical Tripos and third Senior Optime. He was bracketed for the Chancellor's Medal.

W. C. HODGSON, M.A., graduated 1850; ordained 1851; Vicar of Watton, diocese of Norwich, 1861.

G. BOOTH, lives on his property near Dublin.

D. WAUCHOPE, M.A., 1848; ordained 1849; Curate of Stour, Dorset, 1849—63; Chaplain to the 10th, 11th, and 12th Dorset Rifle Volunteers

1860—64; Rector of Church Lawford with King's Newnham, diocese of Worcester, 1863.

J. W. CHITTY, M.A., graduated 1851; called to the bar at Lincoln's Inn, April 1856; Equity draughtsman and conveyancer. Mr Chitty has ever since the year 1857 acted as umpire in the University race.

H. H. TREMAYNE[1].

CH. H. STEWARD, M.A., graduated 1851. In holy orders. Living at Copthorne, Pershore, Worcestershire.

A. MANSFIELD, M.A., graduated and ordained 1850. Perpetual Curate of Shirehampton, diocese of Gloucester and Bristol.

J. J. SYKES[1].

W. G. RICH, student of Ch. Ch.; graduated 1851.

After numerous trials the following crew was chosen to row against Oxford, and began to practise regularly on Monday, Nov. 26.

1. A. Baldry; 2. J. H. Jones; 3. A. de Rutzen; 4. C. J. Holden; 5. W. L. Bagshawe; 6. H. J. Miller; 7. Substitute. Str. H. Pellew.

Mr Wray had kindly consented to row stroke again, but was unable to come to Cambridge before the end of the week. R. Coombes was engaged to train the crew. Little was done during the first week, as the regular crew could not be got together; but on Monday, December 3rd, practising began in good earnest. After some discussion on the

---

[1] Of these gentlemen I can find no trace.

respective merits of Mr Jones and Mr Pellew, the latter was chosen to row 2; Mr Wray having taken the place of stroke, and Mr Hodgson of 1st Trinity being put 7.

The weather on the whole was favourable for practice. The times of the crew at Cambridge are as follows.

Monday, Dec. 3rd. Wind high, S.E., unfavourable in many reaches. Stream very strong. 21 min.

Tuesday, Dec. 4th. Wind N.W., very light. Stream rapid, altogether a most favourable day. 19 min. 46 sec.

Wednesday, Dec. 5th. Wind S.W., rather high, stream not much more rapid than usual. 21 min. 40 sec.

Thursday, Dec. 6th. Calm. Stream rapid. 20 min. 5 sec.

Friday, Dec. 7th. Wind high from E.S.E., dead ahead in most of the reaches, the last reach not very rough. Stream very slack. 22 min. 2 sec.

Saturday, Dec. 8th. Wind moderate. Stream tolerably rapid. 20 min. 39 sec.

After a week at Cambridge the crew went up to Putney on Monday, 10th, and on that day had a row in the new boat built by Searle. The time from the "Ship" at Mortlake to Putney bridge was 22 min. 20 sec.; the tide having turned about an hour and running down rather strongly. The practising was seriously interrupted by Mr De Rutzen being obliged to return to Cambridge on Tuesday to attend College examinations. He was not able to get back to Putney until Friday morning, and in the meanwhile his place was filled by a waterman. On Wednesday we raced with a picked crew of watermen, a man named Leach (who by the bye shut up after rowing a very short distance) taking Mr De Rutzen's place. As usual the watermen were easily beaten. On Friday a few starts and a quiet paddle were the order of the day.

The following account of the race is taken from *Bell's Life.*

"... Their (the Oxonians') defeat of last Easter served but to instigate them to a repetition of exertion, and eager for the fray, to throw down the gauntlet for a race out of the ordinary course. This challenge was immediately accepted; and each party ran over the list of available men to select a befitting crew, and never were there men upon whom the aquatic reputation of the body could better be placed than in the present instance; they were all that the most fastidious trainer could require, with unquenchable spirit and courage to boot.

"A fortnight's sharp work knocked off the rust, if any existed after the College races, and they came to town early this week, bright as stars, and courageous as lions. The Cantabs went to work first; they took up their quarters at Avis', the Bell Tavern, Putney, and began their performances on Monday morning with a turn down from the goal at Mortlake to the starting-place of the match,

Putney Bridge. The time, in which we are assured this trial was done, occupied only 22 minutes, but they had the advantage of a great deal of landwater falling in and strengthening the tide under them, which in itself was but indifferent. Tuesday and Wednesday found them again at their labour, and on the latter day the few spectators who had assembled were gratified with a fine bustling race between them and a crew of watermen. The result was the defeat of the watermen in this trial by something like three lengths.

"Up to this time no opportunity had been given of comparing the respective merits of the two crews; but on the following day (Thursday) the Oxonians, who were located at the Star and Garter, Putney, gave so strong a proof of what they were competent to do as to induce those who had previously thought the Cantabs invincible to abstain from speculating at odds. Nor did the Cantabs themselves look upon them with anything short of the greatest respect, although they never for a moment lost one iota of confidence in their own superiority. As far as the Oxonians' feelings in these matters were concerned, it may be reasonably inferred that their impression was that no University crew that came from Cambridge could be deemed less than formidable, at any rate as far as their experience had gone upon the London river.

"Betting was strictly even, as far as good judges were concerned, and these availed themselves in some few instances of the slight odds offered by friends or strong partizans on either side. Speculation, as far as the wide-awake class who ordinarily endeavour to make a harvest on these occasions went, was lost in conjecture; and up to the day of racing things kept at a very sober turn."

The following is a list of the crews:

OXFORD.

			st.	lbs.
1	J. J. HORNBY	B.N.C.	11	8
2	W. HOUGHTON	B.N.C.	11	2
3	JAMES WODEHOUSE	Exon.	11	7
4	J. W. CHITTY[1]	Balliol	11	9
5	J. AITKEN	Exon.	12	1
6	C. H. STEWARD[1]	Oriel	12	2
7	J. J. SYKES[1]	Worcester	10	2
str.	W. G. RICH[1]	Ch. Ch.	11	2
cox.	RICHARD WM. COTTON	Ch. Ch.	9	0
	Average of crew		11	5⅞

CAMBRIDGE.

			st.	lbs.
1	A. T. BALDRY	1st Trin.	10	10
2	H. P. PELLEW	3rd Trin.	11	0
3	A. R. DE RUTZEN[1]	3rd Trin.	11	8
4	J. C. HOLDEN[1]	3rd Trin.	11	11
5	W. L. G. BAGSHAWE[1]	3rd Trin.	12	0
6	H. J. MILLER	3rd Trin.	12	0
7	W. C. HODGSON[1]	1st Trin.	11	3
str.	J. C. WRAY[1]	Clare Hall	11	0
cox.	GEORGE BOOTH[1]	Trin.	10	12
	Average of crew		11	5¾

[1] Were in the crew of Easter 1849.

"In the above it will be seen that the working hands in each boat were, upon the aggregate, level in weight. The wet weather of the previous day continued, with the addition of a very heavy wind. Nothing indeed but the greatness of the attraction could have induced such an immense number of persons to have braved the pitiless pelting they were doomed to endure. The circumstance of there being a high wind was deemed advantageous to the Cantabs, as their style of rowing was held to be more suitable to stormy weather than the lofty action of the Oxford crew, the wind in some portions of the match amounting to a "dead noser." This impression led to an alteration in the state of the betting, Cambridge being favourites at the start at 6 to 5.

"At twenty minutes to three the Cambridge men were afloat, and were warmly greeted by their friends. Their style of rowing was long, powerful, and scientific. In a few minutes afterwards the Oxonians followed towards the starting place, and though their style was widely different from that of their opponents, as being round and very lofty[1], it was evidently great, and had the effect of getting way upon their boat in firstrate style.

"The appearance of the men was extremely bright and good: they had evidently been trained

---

[1] This phrase "lofty rowing" is very vague, and I am in doubt whether it means merely a high feather throughout, or a feather in which the oar is elevated high over the water just before beginning the stroke.

with the utmost care and attention, while their boats (both from the firm of Searle and Sons), were masterpieces of art. Splash boards had been run round their gunwales in consequence of the roughness of the weather.

"The Oxford had the choice of station and took, injudiciously to our taste, the Middlesex shore, Cambridge being on the Surrey side at the next arch, Mr E. Searle superintending the start. At a quarter to three the Cambridge, on the signal being given, clipped the water with their oars like lightning, and jumped off with a good start, which they had increased on their arrival at Messrs Searle's so much as to have drawn their rudder just clear of their opponent's bows. For the next half mile they continued in almost precisely the same positions, with perhaps an increase of half a length on the part of the Cantabs; but on nearing the point just below the Crab Tree on the Surrey shore, the Oxford men began to manifest a marked improvement in speed, and showed symptoms of overhauling their opponents.

"At this point of the race the excitement on all sides was most extraordinary, and those who had three minutes before laid 3 and 4 to 1 on Cambridge began to show signs of uneasiness, while the partisans of each shouted terms of encouragement to the rival crews. The pace up to this had been most extraordinary, and it had become a question which could muster up strength enough to secure a victory. [What follows shows that the writer of this article ought to have stated that the Cambridge men had already taken the Oxford men's water, which they did at Craven point, and that they now tried to recross over into that which had now come to be the water of the Oxford men to the end of the race.] Off the Crab Tree the Cantabs began to cross towards the Surrey shore to make for Hammersmith Bridge; but in consequence of the Oxford men overhauling them and nearing them so much at each stroke, the Cambridge steerer could not possibly cross them without a foul; consequently he bored his antagonist. But the Oxford steerer was determined not to be put out of his position or course, and as the Cambridge boat was partially athwart their adversaries' course, the Oxford boat as a consequence struck their stern, and ran up to the first portion of the ironwork or outrigger. The Oxonians were of course brought to a standstill by this, and the Cantabs got away something like three lengths before the adverse party could well get to work, and the Cantabs passed close under the Surrey side under the Suspension Bridge with another length added. From this point up to the Railway Bridge the steering was anything but good, while the pace of the Oxonians was so fierce that they gradually lessened the distance between the boats, and arrived at Barker's Rails, Mortlake, with their nose almost amidships with the Cambridge boat.

"On the arrival of the boats at Mortlake Mr Fellowes of the Leander Club, who had been appointed umpire, at once decided in favour of the Oxford men on the ground of the foul, and his decision was not in any way questioned by their opponents. What might have been the result but for the foul, of course we cannot pretend to determine, but at that time the Oxonians were going hand-over-hand at a pace that looked amazingly like passing their opponents.

"The time occupied in the race was stated variously from 25 min. 7 sec. to 25 min. 12 sec."

There is another account in *Bell's Life* which describes the foul thus: "In wending their way to the other side of the river the Oxford boat 'bumped' that of Cambridge, and amidst a terrific yell of 'Foul, foul' the Oxonians raised their oars on end and then recommenced rowing."

The umpire's decision was founded on Rule IX. of the Regulations for Boat Racing, which is, "It shall be held that a boat's own water is the straight or true course from the station assigned to it at starting; but if two boats are racing and one fairly takes the other's water by a clear lead, it shall be entitled to keep the water so taken to the end of the course; and if the two boats afterwards come into contact, while the leading boat remains in the water so taken, the boat whose water has been so taken shall be deemed to have committed a foul; but if they come into contact by the leading boat's departing from the water so taken, the leading boat shall be deemed to have committed a foul."

After giving an account of the race which differs

but very slightly from the one I have given, the Cambridge Secretary says;—"The *foul* was, however, given in favour of Oxford, who was accordingly declared to have won the race. The decision was made under Rule IX. of the 'Regulations for Boat Racing' drawn up by the delegates from the two Universities and London a short time since, and according to that rule was quite just.

"It is much to be regretted that a foul should have taken place, as, besides rendering the race an imperfect test of the merits of the respective crews, it very much disturbed the harmony and good feeling which should exist between members of the rival Universities in such contests.......

CHAS. BAGOT,
Sec. U.B.C."

The occurrence of a "foul" in the University boat race is happily so rare a thing that it caused no little stir, and a long and (on the part of one or two writers) very abusive anonymous correspondence resulted, in which one *irrepressible* who signed himself "Cantab" used such language as made it apparent that he was no gentleman, and he was only finally silenced by being told that no one could suppose him to be a member of the University; and that no more of his letters would be inserted.

The Oxford captain writes,

"To Mr Arthur Shadwell the University of Oxford is deeply indebted, not only for the present flourishing state of the O.U.B.C., but more especially for her victory on this occasion. Under his directions was the crew trained, and through his frequently taking the rudder lines their style and trueness of rowing was attained. For the first ten days the crew paddled to Sandford—during the next fortnight the run was extended to Nuneham and back, no stopping—and for the last three weeks the row was to Abingdon corner and back to Sandford, no stopping, where the crew got out and walked or ran home, the boat being brought home by watermen; also during the last three weeks the distance was rowed at full speed, time 20 min. 50 sec. (from 1st corner below Sandford Lock to Abingdon corner); previous to this *steady and careful slow rowing* was adopted. On their return home the crew dined *together* at the Maidenhead Inn. This method of practising a crew is *infallible*, and no set of *painstaking* oarsmen can fail to *win* under such a preparation[1].

Bell has given as usual a favourable account for Cambridge. He describes the *foul* as a bump, whereas it was a most inexcusable *foul* arising from an error in judgment on the part of the Cambridge cox., who tried to cross, not having a clear lead. Nor does *Bell* mention that while Oxford stopped Cambridge continued rowing, thereby getting a clear lead of three lengths, and at the finish the Oxford bows were up to the Cambridge stroke."

---

[1] The italics are the President's own.

Speaking of the Cambridge crew, he says:—

"Their style of rowing was very different to that of their Easter crew, much quicker, not so far back, but somewhat short. The Oxford crew rowed a slower stroke than at Easter .... The Cantab. crew expressed themselves quite satisfied of the superiority of the Oxford.

W. G. RICH,
President O.U.B.C."

BIOGRAPHICAL NOTICES. (OXFORD.)

J. J. HORNBY, D.D., graduated 1849; ordained 1854; elected Fellow of Brazenose; Principal of Bp. Cosin's Hall, Durham; Vice-Principal and Tutor of University College, Durham; Head Master of Eton College.

W. HOUGHTON, M.A., graduated 1850; ordained 1852; Hulme's Exhibitioner at Brazenose; Rector of Preston on the Wildmoors, Salop, diocese of Lichfield; Author of *Natural History*, Articles in Dr Smith's *Dictionary of the Bible*, and various papers in literary and scientific journals.

J. WODEHOUSE, graduated 1851.

J. AITKEN, M.A., graduated 1851; ordained 1852; Curate of Woodmansterne 1852—54, of Beddington 1854—59, of Woodmansterne 1859.

R. W. COTTON. Student of Christ Church.

BIOGRAPHICAL NOTICES. (CAMBRIDGE.)

A. T. BALDRY, graduated 1851. Living at Torquay.

H. PELLEW, graduated 1850. Only son of the late Dean of Norwich. Educated at Eton and Trinity

College. Married in America, and has since returned to England.

H. J. MILLER. Second son of the late Sir T. C. Miller, Bart. Educated at Eton and Trinity Coll. Lord of the Manor of Anstey, Hants.

J. C. WRAY, graduated from Trinity, 1849, as 10th Wrangler. Elected Fellow of Clare the same year. Called to the Bar 1853, does not practise. Major in Lancashire militia. Chairman of the Univ. Life Assur. Society.

1850.

Cambridge challenged to row at Easter, but Oxford did not accept, being determined not to row another Easter match without an agreement from Cambridge to meet in the following summer or at Christmas. There were two proposals in the Oxford letter declining the challenge, to which the Cambridge men would not consent. The one was to row the match at Christmas the next few years, and the other was to give up the practice of employing watermen as trainers. The O.U.B.C. walked over for the Grand Challenge and Stewards' cups at Henley, and for the Four-oared race at the Thames Regatta. Messrs Chitty and Hornby won the Pairs at Henley, and walked over for them at the Thames.

1851.

During the October term 1850 there was a long correspondence between the two clubs about the time of rowing. The Oxford men *challenged* the Cambridge to row at Christmas that year, but the latter could not get a crew up then on account of the degree examination.

The Cambridge men proposed to row in June 1851, at Easter 1852 and so on, each club alternately taking the inconvenient time of year. This the Oxford men refused to accede to, though it appears to have been reasonable enough, and was a repetition of their proposal of 1846.

The Cambridge men then decided to challenge Oxford to row in June 1851. And here occurred a mistake which led to a great deal of trouble afterwards. The late much lamented Mr Charles Hudson, who met with his death by the fatal accident on the Matterhorn a few years ago, was at this time Secretary. He appears to have proposed the match for the end of the Easter term, thinking that that was synchronous with June. The challenge was accepted on these terms. At the end of the Lent term however Mr Hudson resigned the secretaryship and Mr Cowie was elected in his stead. The officers of the C.U.B.C. found themselves engaged to row a race with Oxford in July, at a time when it seemed impossible to have a crew together. They had to make choice of three courses; first to row a race without any crew at all worthy to represent the University, second to break off the match, third to have the time altered.

Now, as a question of strict right and wrong, they were doubtless bound, if the O.U.B.C demanded it, to row at the time that had been agreed on by their Secretary, for the two Secretaries were the only channel of communication between the two clubs. But they doubtless considered, and not unreasonably, that the University boat race was supposed to be a trial of strength between the two Universities as regards rowing, and presupposed that each club was duly represented. They therefore first tried to have the time of the race altered, so that they might have a decent crew. It so happened that each of the Universities had entered for the Grand Challenge Cup at Henley. Our men therefore suggested that as the Oxford men could go to Henley, they could also give them a long race at Putney about the same time; or if the Oxford College and University authorities would not allow that, on any water to which the Oxford men had access. As however this failed, they chose the second rather than the first alternative, and wrote to say that they were very sorry a mistake had arisen, but explained that it was impossible for them to bring a University crew to Putney in July. This course is certainly not the one that would be adopted now-a-days at Cambridge; and most people, I think, would say that the more courageous course would have been to abide by the arrangement that they had made through the Secretary, however disastrous would have been the result. The committee however thought, I suppose, that as it was through their negligence that the mistake arose, it was better that the individual members of the committee should bear the brunt of the hard words used about them, than that the whole club should suffer a defeat by being inadequately represented. Both courses have much to be said for them : I am sure that, if the same case occurred now, the course followed would be the opposite of the one that was taken in 1851. I think that the club would not allow the officers to act so, but that, while censuring them, it would accept any liability that had been incurred by them, and that some, or perhaps many, Alexanders would cut the Gordian knot, just as it will be seen was the case in 1860. In this, as in all other dealings between man and man, *quicquid honestum utile.* On the other hand I think that the Oxford men hardly acted in a generous spirit, in refusing to row a long race at about the same time as the Henley Regatta. One thing, however, seems perfectly clear, that the Cambridge men did not in any degree shirk a contest with Oxford in which they had a chance of getting a crew which could fairly represent the University.

..Although as we have seen the Cambridge crew could not be kept together till July so as to have a " Long " race, the two Universities met at Henley in the race for the Grand Challenge Cup. They were the only two boats which were entered. The crews were as follows :

"Long" race, and one grievance always begets the desire for another. On the other hand, the Cambridge men thought that the Oxonians ought to have given them a day for the "Long" race about the time of Henley instead of waiting till after term time. This however it was impossible for the Oxford men to have proposed, because if the Oxford Dons had got wind of it, they would have put a stop to it at once, so that the means adopted would have been futile to bring about the desired object.

The Oxonians, however, did when at Henley offer to row the Cambridge men both the race for the G.C.C. over again, and also to row at Putney on any of the three days succeeding the regatta. This proposal however the Cambridge men could not accept, because some individual members of the crew had made engagements to leave Henley immediately after the race for the Grand Challenge, and could not possibly have gone to row at Putney at the proposed time.

I think no good could possibly be done by reprinting the correspondence, and it would probably be distasteful to the writers, but I cannot help inserting one letter from an anonymous writer, who made a happy suggestion, which however seems not to have been acted upon; though after all that had been said and written, the two Universities met on the most amicable terms, as will be seen, at Easter 1852.

"Mr Editor,—There can be, I should imagine,

but one opinion as to Mr Chitty's letter in this week's *Bell*. It is evident that in saying he is pained to see the turn your University correspondence has been taking, he speaks sincerely, and the moderation of his language we should do well to imitate for the future. Perhaps had he denied himself the luxury of a little irony, not quite to the point, in a former letter, and not been quite so ready to adorn the sister University with the white feather from the outset, there might not have existed so much necessity for his present observations.

* * * * *

"There has certainly been enough mismanagement on the part of Cambridge to try the patience of anyone; but there was really no sort of desire to shirk the race on the long course, but quite the reverse. In conclusion I would suggest that as many of the leading aquatic members of the two Universities as happen to be in town simultaneously at the time when University men "most do congregate" there—be it in October or at Christmas—should dine together sociably, drown all their animosities in the flowing bowl, and settle the preliminaries of a race to come off at the earliest time convenient to both parties."

1852.

It will have been noticed that from the very commencement there was always a struggle between the two Universities as to the time at which the race should take place. The Oxford men always raised objections to an Easter match, the Cambridge men to the Midsummer. I think it will be interesting to see what both sides had to say on the subject. From the Oxford books I copy the following *précis* of the correspondence on the subject, in which Mr Chitty, though writing for the benefit of his successors merely, has shown that impartiality and moderation of expression which always characterise him.

A challenge had been sent from Cambridge, couched in the usual terms, in December 1851, but could not be answered till the next term.

"Our answer," says Mr Chitty, "was to this effect. We would row at Easter, their time, if they would grant us some fair equivalent. We proposed that we should have the right of fixing the time for the next race, but under the following conditions favourable to them:

"1. That we give six weeks' notice at least.

"2. That they be not bound to appear more than 14 days if in the summer, and 7 days if in the winter, after their vacation commenced.

"3. That the whole agreement terminate at the expiration of the year.

"Yet we did not insist on this proposition, but expressed our willingness to listen to any other that they might suggest.

"To this they replied with general statements. 'They never refuse our challenge, therefore no reason to attempt to bind them by an agreement as in the present instance.

"'They would be giving up the right of challenging us till Easter 1853.

"'They labour under greater, incomparably greater disadvantages in rowing at Christmas than we do at Easter.'

"In answer we showed:

"(1) That they had actually refused all our challenges but one to row at Christmas—all they could say was that they never refused our challenges when it was *convenient* for them to accept them[1].

"(2) They would not be surrendering the right of challenging us before Easter '53—we would make an express stipulation to the contrary.

"(3) Their objections to Christmas lay in the near approach of their degrees[2]. Against this one we set three: 1, our degrees; 2, moderation according to the new statute; 3, that as our college races do not take place till the summer[3], we have not the advantage of selecting men from crews in practice.

---

[1] I do not understand how at any time it could have been *convenient* to have the race at Christmas; and it certainly was not in 1849, for one of the men had to leave the crew at Putney in order to attend College Examinations.

[2] At this time all the Degree Examinations, whether Honour or Πόλλ., took place about Christmas.

[3] At this time there were first division races at Cambridge in the Lent Term.

"The effect of this to us is that we lose four men if we row at Easter.

"We endeavoured to impress upon them the necessity of both parties making some concessions, if another Oxford and Cambridge match was ever to take place. We would yield the first point, if they would make us some return. 'The question which we wish to press upon your consideration is whether or not you intend to grant any equivalent for what even you yourselves admit to be a concession?'

"To this direct question they made no answer. They wished for a simple answer to their original challenge. Though we considered we might very fairly throw this over, yet we came to the determination of accepting it.

"We were induced to do so, partly from our fair prospects of success; we had the materials of a good crew, and Mr Thos. S. Egan had kindly promised us his services; partly from the general wish that there should be a race, to which we desired that Oxford should oppose no unnecessary obstacles, partly from regard to our successors, who may now refuse peremptorily to row again at the Cambridge time, unless they find it to their advantage to do so. We called the attention of the Cambridge men to this fact in one of our last letters. 'We shall advise our successors not to row again at a time which will be so inconvenient to them, until you shall have first made the same concession as we are making now.'

"As it may be useful to those who follow to understand distinctly the position in which they stand as regards the C.U.B.C., I considered it advisable to make this brief abstract of the correspondence.

"J. W. CHITTY, *Balliol*,
"*President O.U.B.C.*"

Mr Chitty appears either to have forgotten or to have been unaware of the fact that in 1850 the Cambridge men renewed the proposal of Oxford to row alternate years at Easter and Midsummer, and that Oxford refused to accede to this arrangement, alleging that it did not afford equal advantages to both Universities.

This year is remarkable for two things.

It was the first occasion on which Oxford won an Easter match, and the first on which either University received aid in "coaching" from a member of the other University.

In this year the well-known talents of Mr T. S. Egan were exercised in bringing to perfection the Oxford crew, and the results must have been exceedingly gratifying: for this crew attained such a high degree of excellence that it has been handed down to posterity as a model; and I have been several times told by an old President of the O.U.B.C. that it was a tradition at Oxford some 10 years later that "Chitty's crew was so nearly perfect that the best judges could find no greater fault in it than that 'bow' turned his elbows out a little too much."

The Cambridge men began training under the superintendence of Robert Coombes on Monday, March 8th, the race being fixed for Saturday, April 3rd. Owing to the long continuance of drought, the river could hardly be said to have any water in it, and the wind being north-east almost all the time the crew was practising, their "time" was by no means good. The last week the crew rowed at Cambridge there was considerable improvement.

The following are their "times" from lock to lock:—

		m.		*s.*	
Monday, March 22nd,	21	„	7	First day in new boat, wind S.W. but very slight.
Tuesday „	23rd,	21	„	14	No wind.
Wednesday „	24th,	22	„	15	Wind N.E., not very strong.
Thursday „	25th,	23	„	0	Wind high from N.N.W.
Friday „	26th,	21	„	15	Wind very light N.W.
Saturday „	27th,	20	„	50	Very calm and favourable.

On the 26th, Mr Shaw of John's, who was rowing 7, being indisposed, Mr Macnaghten of 1st Trinity rowed in his place. Coombes being afraid of a return of his malady advised the captain to keep Mr Macnaghten in the crew, which was accordingly done. The majority of the crew were aware of the expediency of this alteration, though sorry for Mr Shaw's disappointment, that gentleman having trained and exerted himself to the utmost for nearly three weeks. On Monday the crew left for Putney. They rowed over the course in the evening and did the distance in very fair time, there being a very slack tide. The Oxford crew arrived at Putney on the Saturday previous in the finest possible condition, and rowing together like clockwork. This was universally allowed to be owing to the pains which that experienced trainer Mr T. S. Egan (formerly of Caius College, Cambridge) took with the crew.

On Wednesday the Cambridge crew had a race with a picked watermen's, which the amateurs of course won by two or three hundred yards. Great excitement now prevailed with respect to the ensuing race. The "times" of each crew were taken every day, and Cambridge appeared to have a slight advantage in pace: the result of the race proved either the fallibility of timetaking, or that the Oxford crew having had work enough did not do their utmost during the last week.

The following account of the race is taken from *Bell's Life:*

"At a quarter to two the crews, whose names are subjoined, took their stations, Oxford being on the Middlesex side of the centre arch of Putney Bridge, and the Cantabs (who had won the toss) on the Surrey side.

OXFORD.

			st.	lbs.
1	O. K. PRESCOTT	B.N.C.	10	0
2	R. GREENALL	B.N.C.	10	12
3	PHILIP HENRY NIND	Ch. Ch.	11	2
4	REGINALD JOHN BULLER	Ball.	12	4
5	HENRY DENNE	Univ.	12	8
6	W. HOUGHTON[1]	B.N.C.	11	8
7	W. O. MEADE KING	Pembroke	11	11
str.	J. W. CHITTY[1]	Ball.	11	7
cox.	R. W. COTTON[1]	Ch. Ch.	9	2
	Average		11	6½

CAMBRIDGE.

			st.	lbs.
1	E. MACNAGHTEN	1st Trin.	11	0
2	H. BRANDT	1st Trin.	11	5
3	H. E. TUCKEY	Lady Marg.	11	3
4	H. B. FOORD	1st Trin.	12	6
5	E. HAWLEY	Sidney	12	5
6	W. S. LONGMORE	Sidney	11	4
7	W. A. NORRIS	3rd Trin.	11	9
str.	FREDERICK WM. JOHNSON	3rd Trin.	11	8
cox.	C. H. CROSSE	Caius	9	7
	Average		11	8½

"Charles Selwyn, Esq. was umpire, and Mr Searle as usual started the crews.

"The signal was given at 45 m. 50 sec. past one, and immediately off both went at an astonishing pace for some hundred yards, when Oxford ob-

---

[1] Were in crew of December, 1849.

tained a slight advantage, which they kept improving to the point. From this part of the river there was the divergence consequent on the different doctrines held by the two Universities as to the course to be taken—a difference which, it will be recollected, on the last occasion ended in a foul. The question in dispute is, whether the boats should here begin to shape their course for the centre arch of Hammersmith bridge, or go over to Surrey, with a view of passing under the arch on that side, or, in other words, going between the land and the pier. It was owing to this that it was considered desirable that the crews should occupy the positions which they eventually did, as it would allow each party to steer according to their own fancy, Cambridge under the 'generalship' of R. Coombes steering for the Surrey, Oxford for the centre arch. As to which is right, the reader may refer to a letter by 'Palinurus' (who, I believe, is A. Shadwell), which appeared a short time before the race.

"On nearing Hammersmith bridge Cambridge appeared to shorten the distance between them, and it was hoped that by their method of steering they would come out level: but it was not so, for Oxford on reaching Chiswick Eyot were well ahead and improving their distance at every stroke. The race may be considered to have been over at this point, for the Oxford party had settled quietly and steadily down to their work, and were going ahead in right good earnest. The Cantabs most manfully endeavoured to lessen the gap between them but without effect, for at the Railway Bridge they were at least four or five lengths in the rear. 'All was lost now;' and it would be useless to say more than that the Oxford coxswain doffed his cap, twirled it over his head, gave a cheer to his crew, and then safely, and we may say admirably, steered them on to victory, which they gained by at least six boat lengths.

"We cannot conclude without noticing two very untoward accidents, that might have been attended with very serious results. The swell caused by the steamers just before reaching Barnes Bridge was so terrific as to upset a four-oared outrigger and immerse Messrs Wolstenholme, Bagot, Vincent and Co. No sooner was this done than a similar fate befel the Leander eight-oared cutter, which, though not an outrigger, was soon under water. Among the crew was the venerable Mr Layton, and with him Messrs Nicholas Cocks and Wray, names well known in the annals of the University Boat Races. These were soon *nantes in gurgite vasto* with Jem Parish their cox., whose position was anything but pleasant, as he could not 'swim a yard.' And here we must not omit to record an act of rare generosity and courage. The boat went down headforemost, so that the men rowing aft could not see the danger, though the coxswain could, and the latter said to Mr Harrison, who was rowing stroke, 'Give me your oar, sir, to hang on by, for I can't swim;' upon which Mr Harrison generously tossed him the oar, saying 'Nor can I:'—a piece of magnanimity which speaks for itself. One of the crew, who seemed more like a water rat than a man, sat quietly up to his middle in water on the bottom of the boat, after she was turned upside down, ordering the numerous boats around him to pick up their unlucky coxswain; which done, he still kept his throne, and directed the rescue of the oars and clothes; and even when they were collected, he still 'stuck to the ship,' and was rewarded for his trouble by bringing her to land uninjured."

The following is the letter referred to:—

"Mr Editor: Since the great event of the aquatic year is about to come off in a few days according to precedent as the first fruits of the season, we may express our anxious hope that it will not be marred on the day of trial by any untoward incident. But we must do something more than express hopes, we must try and be beforehand with the danger of this match being marred as the last was, by that ugly, and to University men, most unwonted and unwelcome phenomenon, a foul. For this purpose I shall go back to the match of Christmas, 1849, and investigate what then took place. A vast deal of correspondence ensued on that match, but no true exposition of the facts appeared in your epistolary columns. Now what did take place is very easily told, and when told is very easily seen to have been the true cause of the foul. Four days before the race the Cambridge coxswain went over the course, accompanied by two gentlemen, who, if anyone, must know what the true course over that water is. The bearings were carefully pointed out, and the coxswain expressed himself deliberately convinced by his own senses of the necessity of taking the course indicated. But a coxswain is not always *sui compos*. It seemed that the real coxswain of the Cambridge boat was not Mr —— of —— College, but the illustrious R. Coombes. It was he who was invisibly to guide the yoke lines upon the race day; he issued his *fiat*, or his *caveat*, for the Cambridge boat not to pass through the centre arch of Hammersmith Bridge, and the coxswain was accordingly forbidden by his own crew on any account to take the centre arch. Now, sir, centripetal and centrifugal forces combined retain the heavenly bodies in their orbits, and preserve the harmony of the spheres; but they unhappily will not combine in steering two eight-oars. 'Fugio' is hostile to 'peto,' and 'peto' is death to 'fugio.' So it proved: the Oxford coxswain was attached to seeking the centre as much as he of Cambridge was instructed to avoid it. At the moment when it became necessary for the latter to begin to fulfil the fatal dictum of Coombes, and to *cross* the water to Surrey, the Oxford boat had overtaken the Cambridge boat, and could not let it pass athwart its bows without running into it, it being evident that a vessel upon the Middlesex side must cross the path of another in the mid-course in order to attain the desired and beloved (of watermen) Surrey side. Hence a foul match and endless discontent. Now what is to happen next Saturday? Suppose Cambridge starts upon the Middlesex hand, and keeps way with its opponent up to the Crab Tree, and then feels a strong centrifugal attachment to Surrey. Oxford, better instructed, keeps a centre course, and cannot go out of its way, because ground in a race is too precious to lose. Then there must be a foul, for the Thames is not wide enough for the simultaneous exercise of two such antagonistic forces and principles of steering. If I were steering an eight-oar over that course, I know that no consideration should induce me to make a double curve instead of a single one, however much I may love the green pastures of Surrey. When I am once in that course which the experience of years, and repeated close observation, as well as the highest authority, assure me to be the only imaginably true one, to that course I would adhere, any or all watermen's judgments notwithstanding. I suppose we may know our business as well as they theirs; and I suppose we may know our own water as well as they theirs. And I say that coxswainship is our business, not theirs; it is gentlemen's business, not watermen's; it has, by some of them, been made a study of; they steer eight-oared matches, watermen do not. And as to the water, I beg especial attention to the fact, not, perhaps, generally remembered, that the Putney and Mortlake course is not like that of Westminster and Putney, the hereditary domain of watermen, but that they have, with the tide of boating, emigrated to it of very late years. It was not likely that that course should be known for the purpose of boat racing, *i.e.*, for taking the shortest and truest line, till boat racing began upon it. When was that? In 1843 first a great race was transferred from London to suburban water, and Eton and Westminster contended over it. In the same year the Thames Regatta began. Now, if we began first to study that water at that time, we see no reason why our judgment is not equally good with that of those who never studied it before. You may depend upon it that when a gentleman, bred to the water, gives his earnest attention to the true course to be pursued on a river with which he has, from all his habits, been well acquainted, he is, at least, as likely to be right as other persons who are not called upon to exercise the particular craft of coxswainship at any time, and to whom the water in question is professionally new. In conclusion, I say, if we are to have no more danger of fouls in our greatest of all contests, let the University crews be guided in their course by those who alone have the capacity, as well as the right, to pilot them.

"PALINURUS."

The following is from the Oxford Books:

"As this is the first Oxford crew that has ever won a match at *Easter*—though too much stress must not be laid on this point, Oxford having proved victorious in several long races at other seasons—and as it was universally acknowledged to be superior to its opponents in speed, last and style, and further was pronounced by many excellent judges to be almost a model of perfection, it may be as well to subjoin some particulars of its career.

"In the October term, after the old set had passed away, there suddenly appeared an extraordinary dearth of good men. There remained but three who had ever held an oar in a University crew, only two of whom had experienced a *long race:* nor were there any rising oarsmen as yet known to fame. Under these circumstances a diligent search was commenced and numbers were tried, a crew being steered down by the captain at least once a week. There was indeed no immediate prospect of a race, and many, looking at the chances of success, thought this a subject of congratulation for the University. A challenge, however, was received just before the Christmas vacation, but Oxford was not wholly unprepared: she knew where to look for men. Accordingly at the commencement of the next term the body of the crew was formed, there remaining but one or two vacancies. Eventually the filling up of bowman's place gave the greatest trouble, Mr Cherle retiring about three weeks before the match, and Barker who succeeded him being likewise compelled to resign after a few days: when at length Mr Prescott solved the difficulty by consenting to row. With this exception the crew was completed

8 weeks at least before the race, at which period it commenced easy but careful practice.

"This brought men gradually to the severer training, which began 5 weeks before the day appointed for the match, and was carried throughout with the greatest regularity and uniformity. The slow paddling was always considered of the highest importance; as the men were not then strained in their exertions, individual imperfections could be more easily removed, and more attention paid to the general swing and time and to the tone of the stroke. The daily work consisted of a paddle to Sandford, the spurt thence to Abingdon lasher, a paddle back to Sandford, and a run home to Oxford. The crew generally breakfasted together, and always dined together.

"The honesty, perseverance and steady temper of the men throughout were most remarkable. About the middle of training the usual symptoms of weakness appeared; and several expedients were consequently devised to lighten the work without losing the row over the course—such as a conveyance from or to Sandford, and sometimes the curtailing the paddle back merely to Nuneham. The whole was carried on under the immediate superintendence of Mr Egan, to whose care and diligence, supported as they were by great experience and a perfect knowledge of the art, the University owes a large debt of gratitude.

"These details may be tedious and uninteresting, but they may serve to show that a young crew may turn out as good as an old; that the many obstacles which are encountered in the course of training may all be surmounted by good temper and perseverance; and finally, that regular practice and regular habits united to steadiness and pluck are the chief requisites for success, whereas carelessness and irregularity and bad management, though the men individually be firstrate, can never form a firstrate crew, but are sure to end in disgrace and defeat—in a word, that the method invented or perfected by Messrs Egan and Shadwell may still be pronounced *infallible.*

"J. W. CHITTY,
"*President.*"

I think it well to insert the following letter from Mr Egan, which appeared in *Bell's Life* soon after the race.

"MR EDITOR,—Seeing that my work is still incomplete in that there are those who have not been able to comprehend my motives, it is my desire to explain the position I have taken. I say to *explain*, not exculpate myself; for principles are involved which, if not rightly understood, should be declared. I am a Cambridge man, and have trained a victorious Oxford crew. Those arts which once led Cambridge to victory have now contributed to the success of Oxford, and to Cambridge men should be made known the cause of this apparent change of allegiance. Now the principle which has guided me is not, in truth, at all novel; I have long entertained it myself, and others to whom, as to myself, the fortunes of rowing have been entrusted, share it equally with me. Our feeling, then, has always been, that our favourite science, rowing, ought to be the first object of our love; that the great object to be pursued, the chief end of these great contests, is to exhibit to the world rowing in perfection; whatever, therefore, tended to lower style in rowing, or to diminish aught of the beauty and polish of the perfect eight-oar, was to be resisted and condemned. Hence it follows that if, at any time, one's own University departed from its old, tried, and acknowledged principles of gentlemen's rowing, and took up another system prejudicial to the interests of rowing, one's higher and nearer allegiance to rowing itself should over-rule the secondary duty and subordinate tie by which one was bound to his University. And now, having the opportunity afforded me, I make public statement of my belief—and my experience in rowing, especially in training crews, entitles me to make it—that the Universities did neither wisely nor well in ever allowing watermen to touch the yoke-lines of their match-boats. My conviction is, that rowing has suffered from their interference; and, to speak more definitely, eight-oar rowing necessarily declines from its high perfection in the hands of a waterman. I never saw a crew trained by one which exhibited that entire uniformity, and machine-like regularity of performance, for which the practised eye looks at once in a University crew, and which is the glory and delight of the oarsman. We ought to be able to point to our match crews, and challenge the world to produce anything so uniform in motion, so polished in form, at once so speedy and so graceful, as one of those picked eights of the gentle blood of England. I speak not of mere lack of bodily training, endurance of fatigue etc., but of those higher excellencies which we have a right to look for in these crews, those highest beauties which we used to see year by year developed in them. Holding this belief, therefore, and being strengthened in my convictions by every successive appearance of the system in practice, I have felt that injury was done to rowing, whether by Cambridge or Oxford was not the question; injury was done, it ought and must be checked as far as possible. That school of rowing which reverted back to the principle of gentlemen's rowing was the one to be supported, whether at Oxford or Cambridge. To support that would be to bear public testimony to the merit of that school, and to make its crew victorious would add another proof to the many foregoing that the old hereditary way of training crews was the good, the right, the true, and the certainly successful way. I have no wish to lay unnecessary blame on the present race of rowing men at Cambridge. They have but followed in the broad path of ill the footsteps of those their predecessors who first blindly wandered from the true road; they did not know their errors, being educated therein, and the only way left to convince them was the one I have chosen, and chosen happily, if a right use be made of it.

> 'Qui semel adspexit, quantum dimissa petitis praestent, mature redeat, repetatque relicta.'

Let them remember that I have not been contending for Oxford, but for ROWING; not with Oxford against Cambridge, but with the spirit and genius of the victorious past against the poorer innovations of later years; not against the honour of Cambridge, but for the honour of that system which long gave Cambridge the proud right to proclaim to the world on her banner,—

> 'Iside et Thamesi triumphatis Anglia in certamen provocata Granta victrix.'

Yours, &c.,
THOMAS SELBY EGAN."

BIOGRAPHICAL NOTICES.

O. K. PRESCOTT, M.A., graduated 1851; ordained 1853; curate of Southwell, Notts., 1853—56; perpetual curate of St John's, Dukinfield, Cheshire, 1856—60; curate of North Wraxall, 1861.

R. GREENALL, M.A., graduated 1852; ordained 1853; perpetual curate of St Thomas, Eccleston, 1858; curate of Grappenhall, Lancashire.

P. H. NIND, son of Rev. P. H. Nind, Woodcote. Emigrated to Vancouver's Land. Has returned to England.

R. BULLER[1].

---

[1] Of this gentleman I can find no trace.

R. H. DENNE, M.A., graduated 1856.

W. O. MEADE KING, second son of R. K. Meade King, Esq. of Walford House, Somerset. Farmed in Canada for some years.

E. MACNAGHTEN, University Scholar; graduated 1852; bracketed First in the Classical Tripos, and Senior Optime in the Mathematical; second Chancellor's Medallist; Fellow of Trinity.

H. BRANDT, graduated and ordained 1852; rector of Burrow, diocese of Peterborough.

H. E. TUCKEY, graduated 1852.

H. B. FOORD, graduated 1852; is dead.

E. HAWLEY, M.A., graduated and ordained 1854; minister of Shireoaks Chapel, Worksop, diocese of Lincoln.

W. S. LONGMORE took orders, and died in March 1855 of consumption.

W. A. NORRIS, M.A., graduated and ordained 1854; curate of Langley, diocese of Worcester, 1854—57, Feliskirk, Yorkshire, 1857—60; rector of Oaksey, diocese of Gloucester and Bristol, 1860.

F. W. JOHNSON, Minister of St John's, Great Yarmouth, where he died of consumption, aged 28.

C. H. CROSSE, graduated 1851; ordained 1854; formerly curate of Stow with Quy; now engaged in preparing candidates for University examinations.

Henley, 1852.

"The entrance list this year was less brilliant than the last, owing to the almost total absence of

Cambridge boats, the time fixed—25th and 26th of June—being too late for them.

"The O.U.B.C., holding the Grand Challenge Cup, would have " walked over," but at the request of the stewards, and for the gratification of the spectators, the club raised two eights and made a race for it: the winners to be called " The O.U.B.C.," the losers the " Oxford Aquatic Club."

[The strokes of the two boats were Greenall and King. After an excellent race Greenall won by about a clear length.]

"The O.U.B.C. won the Stewards' Cup, beating the Argonauts and Thames Club. The crew was

    1   GREENALL.
    2   BARKER.
    3   NIND.
  str. KING.
  cox. BALGUY.

"The Argonauts led at starting, but we ultimately got ahead and won by two or three lengths. We are again indebted to Mr Egan for preparing us for this race, and for introducing one of Clasper's boats into Oxford, which was certainly one of the fastest and lightest "fours" ever turned out.

"Messrs Nind and Barker, of Christ Church, won the Silver Goblets easily. Four other crews started.

"Mr Macnaghten, of 3rd Trinity, Cambridge, won the Diamond Sculls, beating Mr Peacock, the holder, by six lengths." *Oxford Book.*

1853.

Henley Regatta.

Early in the May term Cambridge, for the first time, excepting the proposal to row at Easter and Midsummer in alternate years, sent a challenge to Oxford to row a race over the Putney course at Midsummer. In answer to this challenge the committee of the O.U.B.C. pointed out, "that if the Universities rowed a race at Putney in June it would materially interfere with the Henley Regatta, which had already shown sufficient inclination to decline. How brilliant the Regatta might be made by the co-operation of the two clubs, as the time fixed for this year suited each so well. That it was impossible to have the long race as well as a contest for the Grand Challenge."

The Regatta took place on the 10th and 11th of June.

Mr Chitty was the gentleman who superintended the forming and training of the Oxford crew; and he seems to have been very unfortunate in his men, as there was never a time throughout the period of training when all were well, and even on the day of the race No. 5 was taking medicine.

There are no particulars whatever given of the Cambridge men's training, and the only account of the race is the one given in *Bell's Life*, which is as follows:—

"The Grand Challenge came off after the district

Scullers' race. The names of the men who rowed in the two crews were as follows:

OXFORD.

			st.	lbs.
1	W. F. SHORT	*New Coll...*	10	8
2	P. H. MOORE	*B.N.C.*	9	12
3	W. KING	*Merton*	11	11
4	R. J. BULLER	*Balliol*	12	0
5	H. DENNE	*Univ.*	12	10
6	P. H. NIND	*Ch. Ch.*	10	12
7	O. K. PRESCOTT	*Merton*	10	3
8	W. O. MEADE KING	*Pemb.*	11	7
COX.	T. H. MARSHALL	*Exon.*	10	1

CAMBRIDGE.

			st.	lbs.
1	G. B. FORSTER	*St John's*	10	10
2	S. V. STEPHENSON	*Caius*	10	8
3	A. BRANWELL	*Trin.*	10	12
4	E. HAWLEY	*Sidney*	12	1
5	E. COURAGE	*Trin.*	11	12
6	H. TOMKINSON	*Trin.*	10	9
7	H. BLAKE	*Corpus*	10	11
8	E. MACNAGHTEN	*Trin.*	10	6
COX.	E. FRESHFIELD		8	6

"All eyes were now turned with intense interest towards the bridge, to catch the first glimpse of the rival crews, the flower of the Universities; and when they shot forth from the arch slowly and grandly, with the measured sweep which none but highly trained and polished eights can ever attain, the breathless silence of the vast multitude was a plain index of its admiration.

"Oxford went forth first, closely followed by the umpire, Cambridge some little distance astern; and the sight of these three wondrous crews, as they rowed down to the island, was to the eye of the oarsman as great a treat as any afforded by the Regatta; but it is hardly possible to convey to our readers in language any, even the faintest, idea of the splendour of the great struggle which ensued— a splendour conferred upon it not only by the almost dead-heat nature of the result, but what is still more worthy of reward, and still more redounding to the credit and honour of those engaged, by the great perfection of the rowing in both boats. Never perhaps since our memory serves have we had the pleasing task of speaking in such unqualified terms of praise of two rival crews. On the part of Oxford indeed we looked for great and good things when we saw the names of five of those who formed the magnificent crew of Easter 1852, and knew that the indefatigable exertions of Mr Chitty, the then stroke oar, had been for some time past bestowed in bringing them to proper form; but all were astonished at the great change and manifest improvement which the last 12 months had wrought at Cambridge, and many were they who were heard to exclaim, 'Why, this is *Oxford* rowing!' That their crew was composed of younger men than Oxford—some we should say almost too young—and in many cases of weaker men, serves but to show how much may be done by great care and attention, and what miracles may be performed when men obtain an uniform swing and do their work *together*. There was but one thing with them on the wrong side of the good, and we notice it with the regret of the impartial historian, whose business it is not to clothe all things in the colour of the rose.

"We cannot help thinking that that fatal *eighteen inches* might have been saved had not their No. 4 so often directed his attention to what the Oxford boat was doing, an error the more inexcusable, as, being the captain of the University, it was his duty to make his conduct an example to the rest.

"Oxford having won the toss took up its position on the Berkshire shore, leaving Cambridge the outside, a considerable disadvantage on this day, as the wind was blowing tolerably fresh from the N.E., and there was more stream than is usual on Regatta days, owing to the locks not having been stopped. On the umpire giving the word 'off!' both dashed away with a magnificent burst, Cambridge having a trifle the advantage; this with a few slight changes they improved before the 'Poplar' to something like the length of their bows. On reaching 'corner,' so often decisive to evenly contested races, the Oxford boat was steered a little out, and the Cambridge coxswain, apparently to avoid all possibility of a touch of the oars, steered out also, and at this moment the lead of some twenty feet was reduced to three or four. The terrific shout of the Oxonians on the bank told that there was a chance. A signal whistle was heard, even above the shouts, and the finest spurt that ever was seen by man finished the race with the nose of the Oxford boat *eighteen inches* in advance. None knew which was master in this noble strife, neither crews nor umpire could decide, and all eyes were turned to the Stewards' stand. In a few minutes the board was exhibited with *Oxford*, and the great event was finished. The cheering which greeted the victors was of course as tumultuous and prolonged as it was deserved, but in after time a man may relate with pride, and none shall be offended, that he rowed that day for CAMBRIDGE.

"The distance was accomplished in 8 min. 3 sec.

UMPIRE'S CREW.

1 M'KINNEY. 2 NEWELL. 3 DOUBLEDEE. 4 MESSENGER. 5 POCOCK. 6 PHELPS. 7 COLE. 8 COOMBES."

I believe that the account in *Bell* contains a very unjust censure upon Mr Hawley, as will be seen from the following statement of the case, with the gist of which I have been favoured by Mr Hawley himself.

At the point the Cambridge were so far ahead that Mr Freshfield, the coxswain, thought he had room to take the Oxford men's water: but Mr

Marshall, seeing his tactics, called on his crew for a last effort—their only chance—and their spurt caused the Oxford bow oars to overlap the Cambridge stroke oars, and Mr Hawley's oar (No. 4) was knocked clean out of the rowlock, while No. 2 lost two strokes. Mr Hawley naturally looked to his oar to get it back again. The consequence was the Cambridge coxswain had to steer right out to mid stream to clear the Oxford boat, and thus lost a good deal of ground, while the Oxford men quietly pursued their own course round the corner. The others, however, stuck to it, and eventually in the short distance between the corner and the winning-post had recovered so much of their lost ground as to only lose by 18 inches.

Had the course been any appreciable distance, 10 or 20 yards, longer, they would have passed the post easy winners.

Such is the account Mr Hawley himself gives, and it was corroborated by No 2 Mr Stephenson. The only point open to doubt is whether his oar was knocked out of its rowlock by one of the Oxford oars or by something in the river; but that his oar was unshipped there appears to be no doubt; and his character as an oarsman and captain was so fully vindicated that a very handsome and costly silver vase was presented to him, on his resigning his captaincy as a testimonial from the rowing men of Cambridge.

" Mr Chitty (says the Oxford president) did all in his power to form the best crew that could be picked in Oxford for this race, and when formed to eradicate individual imperfections, and establish a uniform swing throughout the boat. Mr Arthur Shadwell also gave us a few days just before the race. But we seemed doomed to misfortune throughout the time we ought to have been practising regularly with the *whole* crew: immediately on one man recovering from illness another got disabled, and so we went on till ten days before the race, and even on the day of the race No. 5 (who had been unwell throughout the training) was taking medicine. However, 'all's well that ends well,' and we managed to add one more to the list of Oxford's eight-oared victories."

Oxford also won the Stewards' Cup, beating the Argonauts. The O.U. crew was

1	K. PRESCOTT	*Merton.*
2	P. H. NIND	*Ch. Ch.*
3	W. MEADE KING	*Pembroke.*
str.	J. W. CHITTY	*Exeter.*
cox.	PETCH	*Trin. Coll.*

1854.

On the 26th of Nov. 1853, as degrees were coming on, Mr Hawley resigned the captaincy of the U.B.C., and there being none of the members of the last two crews specially eligible as his successor, Mr. T. S. Egan of Caius was requested to undertake the office as a temporary arrangement.

On Feb. 11, 1854, it was decided that a challenge should be sent to Oxford.

Mr Egan now had the sole management of the crew, which was this year rendered a most arduous task by circumstances of a most untoward nature.

The Lent term races finished on Wednesday the first of March, and on the next day the University boat went down. The following Monday the crew was as follows:

		st.	lbs.
1	H. R. M. JONES	10	4
2	S. V. STEPHENSON	10	13
3	H. SNOW	11	8
4	H. E. FAIRRIE	12	12
5	E. COURAGE	12	11
6	H. F. JOHNSON	11	8
7	H. BLAKE	11	7
str.	S. NAIRNE	11	1

The next day Courage was obliged to go down, and the crew was frequently altered, owing to numerous misfortunes, as will be seen by the names which appear on the day of the race.

Times of rowing from Cambridge lock to Baitsbite:

March 24th 24′ 30″. Tornado ahead.
  „ 25th 22′ 10″.
  „ 27th 20′ 50′. Long stoppage at Railway Bridge.
  „ 28th From Bottisham Lock to Upware. 3¼ miles with crew as in race, 20′;

		strongish stream and stiffish wind N.W.
March	29th	From Camb. to Baitsbite, 21' 30".
„	30th	21' 15", with uncomfortable wind though favourable, S.W.
„	31st	22' 15".
April	1st	From Chiswick Eyot through Putney Bridge, 12' 50", which is very long.
„	3rd	Putney to Hammersmith ...... 9' 26".
„	„	Chiswick Eyot .... 12' 24".
„	„	Mortlake .... 23' 0".
„	5th	Putney to Mortlake .... 22' 37".

The above gives some idea of what was done at Cambridge. In the mean time at Oxford, active measures had begun much earlier. Even before the challenge was sent from Cambridge, the Oxford President had not been idle, and had got a fair set of men ready by Feb. 20th. Mr A. Shadwell the old Oxford coxswain, a contemporary of Mr Egan's, then came up to take charge of the crew for awhile and to make things ship-shape.

The consequence of these energetic proceedings was that by the time the Cambridge men were just beginning to look about them, Oxford had their crew almost settled, and so were enabled to begin hard training on March 6th, giving them 5 good working weeks before the race.

Their crew then stood:

1 SHORT. 2 HOOKE. 3 HAYTON. 4 BLUNDELL.
5 HOOPER. 6 NIND. 7 MELLISH. str. KING.
Average 11 9½

Shadwell stayed for about 8 or 9 days, and then left the crew to the management of Mr Meade King the President and stroke, who received valuable aid from Mr Chitty. Their log from the time of going into training is given as follows by Mr Meade King (President).

March 6th Chitty steered to the Lasher (Abingdon). Left him at the Railway Bridge. Time from first gate below Sandford to Lasher $22\frac{1}{2}$ min. All dined at the Cross.

„ 7th To the Lasher—strong head wind: time 24 min.

„ 8th We went to Sandford; ran round the meadow after.

„ 9th To Iffley twice. I ran up the second time, Prescott rowing stroke. Agreed to dispense with No. 3, wrote to him accordingly, and sent to town for Cadiz.

„ 10th Cadiz arrives and rows 7; Mellish rowing 3: rest as before. We did not go below Iffley.

„ 11th To Abingdon. Strong wind. Time 24′ 27″.

„ 13th To Iffley. Wind very high.

„ 14th To Abingdon. Windy. Time 23′ 50″.

„ 15th To Abingdon. Very Windy. Time 25′ 55″.

„ 16th Changed Cadiz and Mellish. Chitty

		steered to Abingdon in a hurricane. Time 24' 20".
March	17th	Chitty steered. Hot and calm. To Abingdon. Time 23'. Dismissed Cadiz.
„	18th	To Sandford. Chitty steered. Pinckney rowing vice Cadiz. [Pinckney had been rowing in Feb., but had discovered that he had "got a heart, &c."]
„	20th	To Abingdon. Wind across and fair. Time 22' 30".
„	21st	To Abingdon. No wind; water very low. Time 22' 25".
„	22nd	To Sandford.
„	23rd	To Abingdon. Time 22'.
„	24th	To Abingdon. Scratch crew waiting for us at Nuneham. Time 21' 54".
„	25th	To Iffley in new boat.
„	27th	To Abingdon. Water very low. Head wind last mile. Time 23' 50".
„	28th	To Abingdon. Windy. Time 22' 57".
„	29th	Tried a new boat of King's. Approved of her and sent her to Putney. I had a bad foot and did not row. All went to Eton.
„	30th	Off to Putney. Rowed over the course against tide and wind. Shipped much water. Watch stopped.
„	31st	To Mortlake. Tide turned before we got there. Much wind. Time 23' 14".

April 1st   To Mortlake. Windy. Time 23'. Chitty steered.

"   3rd   To Mortlake. Rowing very bad. Time 23' 13".

"   4th   To Mortlake. Chitty steered.

"   5th   From Mortlake to Putney. Time 22' 47".

"   6th   Rowed against watermen, beat the same by any distance. Time 22' 45".

"   7th   Rowed up to the Crab Tree and back.

Bell's Life gives the following account of the race:

"... It is not our place to enter minutely into all the vicissitudes which sometimes wait upon the formation of an University crew (tho' the mishaps which attended Cambridge this year were allowed to be unusually many), but it is but justice to those who came forward when called upon at the eleventh hour, so late as within a week from the time at which the crew left Cambridge, to make mention of the very adverse circumstances under which they rowed, and which makes what they did entitled to so much the greater praise.

Neither Mr Courage nor Mr Wright had practised with the crew more than five days, having been substituted for others whom illness or other causes prevented from rowing.

On Wednesday, 29th March, the Oxford crew arrived at Putney, and took up their quarters at the Bells, where every attention was paid them.

Cambridge arrived on Saturday, 1st April, an ominous day, and were most comfortably entertained during their stay by Mrs Finch, Star and Garter. During the week following both crews rowed daily over the course, with the exception of Cambridge the last two days, who were evidently aware of their want of strength, and deemed it expedient to husband it somewhat more against the day of struggle. Oxford had brought such a reputation with them from *Alma Mater* for strength, weight, condition, and good rowing, while the misfortunes of Cambridge were not unknown, that the odds at the beginning of the week were about two to one on them; but after the beautiful rowing of Cambridge, their excellent manner of getting forward, and their apparently good condition had been seen, and the respective trials had been timed, these odds fell to evens, and those who had much money on Oxford drew long faces and were inclined to hedge. There was indeed a general opinion that Cambridge might pull through. However after Oxford had beaten the watermen, which Cambridge were unable to do, and a scratch crew from their own University had shown itself capable of 'holding' Cambridge for some distance, and 'outrowing' them at first, betting again assumed the odds of 5 and 6 to 4 on Oxford, freely offered and as shyly taken. It was now apparent that strength must have it. On the day before the race neither crew went out for more than a short breathing and a few starts. In the evening it was arranged that the start should take place as near 11 o'clock as possible, as it would then be about high water. Never did more genial or more brilliant morning attend upon a University Race, and at an early hour the stream of Hansom cabs, long and unbroken, which poured over Putney Bridge, was extraordinary. Ten steamboats crowded with the members of either University and their friends lay along the shore, and every nook and corner, house, roof, and window, from whence even a peep might be obtained, was filled with anxious spectators, while the towing-path was covered with hundreds afoot, and among the numerous horsemen many a fair equestrian.

Westminster attended in two eights, making a very good display of rowing. St John's College, Cambridge, and the Wandle Club, together with numerous four-oars, &c., were also on the water. Shortly after eleven, the umpire, C. J. Selwyn, Esq., formerly of Trinity College, Cambridge, and one of her most renowned oarsmen, who has so often officiated on similar occasions, took his seat in a cutter manned by eight picked watermen : and proceeded to the Bridge, when Mr E. Searle, time out of mind the able starter of these races, was started in a boat to do his office. In a few minutes the contending boats shot forth from the yard, and going down a short turn through the bridge returned by the centre arch, and took their stations amidst general cheering. The following are the names of the rowers :

OXFORD.

			st.	lbs.
1	W. F. SHORT	New Coll....	10	5
2	ALFRED HOOKE	Worcester...	11	0
3	W. PINCKNEY	Exon.........	11	2
4	T. H. BLUNDELL	Ch. Ch......	11	8
5	EDWARD HOOPER	Pemb.........	11	5
6	P. H. NIND [1]	Ch. Ch......	10	12
7	G. L. MELLISH	Exon.	11	2
str.	W. OLLIVER MEADE KING [1]	Pemb.........	11	8
cox.	T. H. MARSHALL	Exon.	10	3
	Average		11	1

CAMBRIDGE.

			st.	lbs.
1	R. C. GALTON	1st Trinity..	9	10
2	SPENCER NAIRNE	Emm.	10	2
3	J. COOPE DAVIS	3rd Trinity.	11	1
4	S. AGNEW	1st Trinity..	10	12
5	E. COURAGE	1st Trinity..	11	13
6	F. W. JOHNSON [1]	3rd Trinity.	10	13
7	H. BLAKE	Corpus	11	1
str.	J. WRIGHT	St John's....	10	2
cox.	C. T. SMITH	Caius.........	9	12
	Average		10	$9\frac{1}{4}$

Oxford having won the toss took the Middlesex side, and both boats being in readiness with the rowers stretching forward, all eyes were looking anxiously for the start, which was most admirably effected by Mr Searle, the oars of both boats dashing into the water simultaneously. Nothing

[1] Were in the crew of 1852.

could be more beautiful than this first burst of two such excellent crews, and though its duration as a strife for the mastery was not of long continuance, great was the admiration excited in the minds of all those oarsmen, spectators who had once borne their part too in many a similar struggle. After they had gone about a quarter of a mile the Oxonians began to show steadily ahead, and though opposite the Vice-Chancellor's (we cannot help retaining the name from old associations) Cambridge in a noble spurt regained nearly half a boat's length, before the Crab Tree was arrived at Oxford had cleared its length. On nearing Hammersmith Bridge a barge stood directly in the course, and gave both steerers an opportunity for a display of skill and judgment, of which the Cambridge coxswain availed himself promptly, going between the barge and the pier. Some complained that the Oxford boat was steered too suddenly wide of the barge, but it was making sure on the safe side, and there was not that 'pressure from without' which sometimes justifies great risk.

After the bridge Oxford was at least two boats' lengths ahead, rowing in splendid style, and though Cambridge rowed with the most unflinching pluck, and without deviating in the least from the goodness of their 'form,' it was quite evident that no change could be wrought, and eventually Oxford rowed past the flag-boat amidst the cheers of thousands, exactly 11 strokes in advance of their competitors; doing distance (they met the tide at

Chiswick) in 25 minutes 29 sec. Neither of the crews showed the least signs of distress at the finish; indeed their superb condition prevented the possibility of it. The style of their rowing was very similar, as indeed all good rowing must be, the chief difference being that Oxford was slightly higher on the feather. In Corney Reach, when the strokes of both boats happened to be in time together, they were rowing 39 in the minute.

Immediately on getting out of their 'ships' at Mortlake, both crews repaired to the 'Cedars,' the hospitable mansion of Mr Phillips, who entertained them at lunch, and in the evening they sat down to dinner with a numerous party of their friends at the Albion Tavern, in Aldersgate Street, where good fellowship and hilarity contributed to a most pleasant evening. After the usual toasts had been given and responded to, Mr Selwyn, who was greeted with loud and prolonged cheering, said that this was now the fifth generation of rowing men that he had had the honour of presiding over as umpire, and that he thought he was now no longer young and active enough to act in that capacity again. Besides there was one man among them so admirably fitted in every way for the post that he need hardly name him."

This is the account given in *Bell's Life*. From independent sources I learn that there was great consternation among old Cambridge men (who had not previously seen the Cambridge crew) when the two crews paddled to the starting posts.

Never up to that time had so indifferent a crew turned out from Cambridge, and the editor of *Bell's Life* was probably the only man who approved of their style of rowing.

Searle built both boats, which were 65 feet long. *Bell's Life* preferred the Oxford boat, though some thought it too heavy.

BIOGRAPHICAL NOTICES.

W. F. SHORT, Scholar, Fellow, Subwarden, and Tutor of New College. Junior Proctor, 1869.

A. HOOKE, M.A., graduated 1858; ordained 1859; perpetual curate of Wroxten 1863; vicar of Shotteswell, dio. of Worcester, 1864.

W. PINCKNEY, graduated 1857. Banker at Salisbury; J. P. for Wiltshire.

T. H. BLUNDELL, graduated 1857.

G. L. MELLISH[1].

T. H. MARSHALL, graduated 1856; President of O.U.B.C. 1855. If we except the case of Mr Egan in 1854, Mr Marshall is the only coxswain who has ever been captain of a University crew.

R. C. GALTON, graduated 1853 as Junior Optime.

S. NAIRNE, graduated 1856 as Senior Optime; ordained 1856 curate of Trinity, Weymouth; rector of Hemsdon, Ware, Herts.

J. C. DAVIS, educated at Eton and Trinity; in business in London; Lt.-Colonel of Volunteers.

S. AGNEW, graduated 1856.

E. COURAGE[1].

[1] Of these gentlemen I can find no trace.

H. BLAKE, graduated 1856.

J. WRIGHT, graduated 1857; ordained 1858; curate of Hucknall, Notts, 1858, of Plumtree, 1860; perpetual curate of Wem, Salop, 1865.

C. T. SMITH, graduated 1854 as double second; called to the Bar, 1857; practised as special pleader on the Norfolk circuit; Puisne judge at the Cape, 1869.

1855.

Henley Regatta.

At the end of 1854 the C.U.B.C. sent the usual challenge to row Oxford at Easter, 1855. No answer was however received till the end of February or beginning of March; and then it was to the effect that the affairs of the O.U.B.C. were in a very unsettled state, as their officers for the term had only been elected a few days before. The severity of the frost at Oxford had put a stop till then to all rowing, so that as far as the O.U.B.C. were concerned they would rather not row. They, however, would be very happy to meet the C.U.B.C. at Henley.

As the same sort of weather had been prevalent at Cambridge, the C.U.B.C. willingly consented to this arrangement in case Henley Regatta was fixed soon enough to enable them to get a crew. It was afterwards settled that the two clubs should meet at Henley, which they did. The two crews were:—

Cambridge.

			st.	lbs.
1	P. P. Pearson	Lady Marg.	11	0
2	E. C. Graham	1st Trin.	11	3
3	H. W. Schreiber	Trin. Hall	11	3
4	H. E. Fairrie	Trin. Hall	11	12
5	H. Williams	Lady Marg.	11	8
6	H. F. Johnson	3rd Trin.	11	6
7	H. Blake	Corpus	11	11
str.	H. R. M. Jones	3rd Trin.	10	2
cox.	W. Wingfield	1st Trin.	8	6
	Average		11	3⅞

Oxford.

			st.	lbs.
1	W. F. Short	New Coll.	10	7
2	T. S. Codrington	B.N.C.	10	7
3	C. H. Everett	Ball.	11	2
4	R. H. Denne	Univ.	12	6
5	T. H. Cruste	Univ.	12	6
6	P. H. Nind	Ch. Ch.	11	8
7	W. Pinckney	Exon.	11	2
str.	A. F. Hooke	Worc.	10	6
cox.	T. H. Marshall	Exon.	10	8
	Average		11	3¾

Of the Cambridge crew Johnson and Blake rowed the same oars in the University match at Putney in 1854. Of the Oxford crew Short was bow in that same match, Hooke rowed No. 2, Pinckney No. 3, Ninde No. 6, and Marshall steered. Jones and Graham rowed in 1854 for the Trin. Coll. boat at Henley.

Some little delay took place at starting in consequence of the wind, which was blowing half a gale from the Bucks shore; the Cambridge steerer had great difficulty in securing his bung, and we [*Bell's Life*] could not but admire the masterly and watermanlike manner in which Mr Marshall kept his boat's head to the wind and escaped all difficulty. At length an even start was effected and the great struggle commenced. The Oxford boat shot two or three feet in advance, but Cambridge in half a dozen strokes was even with them: a short race took place for a quarter of a mile, Oxford losing ground inch by inch, and before they had rowed half the distance Cambridge had cleared its length and taken its opponents' water. No change took place afterwards, and Cambridge were hailed the winners by about two lengths and a half. Both boats were steered as true as a die, but we are at loss to conceive why Oxford, having won the toss, should have given away a boat's length by choosing the wrong side. Each crew appeared in admirable condition, and rowed well. Messrs. Chitty and Meade King had given occasional assistance in coaching the Oxford, Mr Macnaghten the Cambridge crew.

"It is but fair," says Mr Marshall the President of the O.U.B.C., "to state that the defeat of Oxford this year for the Grand Challenge Cup was owing to no chance which might have altered the result of the race, but simply to the superiority of the Cambridge crew, who certainly rowed better together, and, I think, were in finer condition than our men, in fact they were as fine a University crew as could be turned out. We had many individually good men in our boat, some of whom had earned their reputation in former victorious crews, but there was a want of uniformity of style, and that even swing which must be present to constitute really good rowing. The wind (which rose after the sides were chosen) was certainly more disadvantageous to us than to our adversaries, who were under the lea of the bank for the first half mile of the course, but that could have made no real difference in the result of the race.

T. H. MARSHALL,
President O.U.B.C."

Lady Margaret (Cambridge) were beaten for the Stewards' Cup by the Royal Chester Rowing Club; but were victorious in the race for the Visitors', beating Balliol (Oxford), who had lost a man that morning through illness: the Johnians were however generally considered the better crew under all circumstances.

1856.

At one of the October term meetings of 1855 Mr Schreiber, the President of the C.U.B.C., proposed that a challenge be sent to Oxford.

He explained why it was the duty of Cambridge to send the challenge, even though they had won the Race at Henley in 1855: "That as the C.U.B.C. was almost always successful in matches on the London waters, only those matches were considered as the University races; besides that, at Henley other boats might enter against the Universities, and that therefore, though in every way a fair trial of strength, the contests at Henley Regatta could not strictly be called a University match."

This motion was received very favourably and carried. The challenge was accepted, and Mr Schreiber, who was in for classical honours, resigned the Presidency in favour of Mr Jones, of 3rd Trinity.

The books of neither the Cambridge nor the Oxford Boat Clubs contain any account of the training for this race. There is, however, a tradition that at Oxford no less than twenty-two men declined to row. Their crew, nevertheless, though much inferior in strength to the Cambridge, rowed in better style. The following narrative of the race itself is a comparison of the accounts given in *Bell's Life* and in the Cambridge book, assisted by oral tradition.

Owing to the state of the tide it was found necessary to row the race from Mortlake to Putney, instead of the contrary way as usual. At a quarter to eleven the rival crews made their appearance, both in old boats, built by Messrs Searle. The Cantabs having won the toss chose the Middlesex side, just below Barker's Rails, Mr Rich acting as umpire, and Mr E. Searle being starter, as usual.

The following are names of the crews :

CAMBRIDGE.

			st.	lbs.
1	J. P. SALTER	*Tr. Hall* ...	9	13
2	F. C. ALDERSON	*3rd Trin.* ...	11	3
3	R. L. LLOYD	*3rd Trin.* ...	11	12
4	H. E. FAIRRIE	*Trin. H.* ...	12	10
5	H. WILLIAMS	*Lady Marg.*	12	8
6	J. M'CORMICK	*Lady Marg.*	13	0
7	HERBERT SNOW	*Lady Marg.*	11	8
str.	H. R. M. JONES	*3rd Trin.* ...	10	7
cox.	W. WINGFIELD	*1st Trin.* ...	9	0
	Average ..		11	$9\frac{3}{8}$

OXFORD.

1	P. GURDON	*Univ.*	10	8
2	W. F. STOCKEN	*Exon.*	10	1
3	R. INGHAM SALMON	*Exon.*	10	10
4	A. B. ROCKE	*Ch. Ch.*	12	$8\frac{1}{2}$
5	RICHARD TOWNSEND	*Pemb.*	12	8
6	ARTHUR P. LONSDALE	*Balliol.*	11	4
7	G. BENNETT	*New Coll.* ..	10	10
str.	J. T. THORLEY	*Wadham* ...	9	12
cox.	F. W. ELERS	*Trinity*	9	2
	Average		11	$0\frac{5}{8}$

The start took place at exactly 30 secs. past 11 o'clock, and at the first dash of the oars the Oxford boat seemed to have already settled down to their work, while the Cambridge for some half-dozen strokes seemed hardly to be aware that they had started. This placed the Dark Blues some eight or ten feet in advance, which lead was considerably increased by an accident which happened to No. 6 in the Cambridge boat. A wave caught his oar, and so completely wrested it from his power that, reversed in the water, it became locked in the rowlock, and was not far from bringing the race to an untimely end by upsetting the boat. It grieves me to relate it, but Mr M'Cormick had caught such an immense shell-fish that its weight overpowered him, and he fell back into Mr Williams' lap, who with great politeness and presence of mind restored his oar to him, and him to his seat. This contretemps took place opposite the Ship at Mortlake, and fortunately both it and its remedy occupied less time in the action than the recital, or I fear me much the chances of the Light Blue of reaching Putney first would have been small. When the shock of this mistake was partially recovered, such a spurt as is seldom witnessed brought Cambridge on a level with their opponents, and gave them a trifling advantage. With about a yard and a half of their bow in front the Light Blue continued for about half a mile; and then they gradually increased their lead to half a length, and thus they continued, escaping the dangers of many sailing barges and other craft, by the most marvellous steering on the part of both, but more especially on that of Mr Wingfield, whose difficulties at this point were perhaps greater than those of his antagonist. He was called upon to decide whether he could get between the bank and a barge, which was going head on to it—those only who have been similarly circumstanced can judge of the nerve and prompt decision required—the man on board the lighter did all in his power to assist by throwing out a sweep ahead and stopping her way as much as possible, and the Cambridge boat just cleared through. Not much less in its degree was the promptitude required and displayed by Mr Elers who, now in the middle of the river, and going astern of the same lighter, had every prospect of being jammed into her by a sailing barge that was standing over to that shore. The nose of the Oxford boat was already sheered a bit over towards the Surrey side preparing to go astern, when suddenly the barge was put about, and no sooner did the quick eye of Mr Elers perceive a shake in her sails than he put his ship straight, and these dangers were thus cleverly surmounted. On arriving at Barnes Railway Bridge, which was reached in exactly 6 minutes—a time which speaks sufficiently of the pace at which the race was started—the Cambridge boat was at least half a length in front, an advantage which they soon improved so much as to draw themselves nearly clear. In Corney Reach a barge lying dead in the way of both boats drove Cambridge somewhat out of its course, and the boats again became level, Oxford putting on one of the most glorious spurts it has ever been our lot to witness. This famous bit of rowing on the part of the Oxonians caused the race here to commence as it were anew, and for some distance each boat alternately shot a foot or two in front, both boats rowing in beautiful form through that lumpy water and against a dead foul headwind, until they neared Chiswick Eyot, which was passed in 12 m. 50 sec. from the start.

From this point the succession of magnificent bursts on the part of each crew to obtain the mastery in this heroic strife has never been surpassed. Just below the Eyot Mr Elers again showed the greatest judgment and skill in passing a barge which lay in his course. He chose to go between it and the shore, and having done so wisely kept that course to which he had been driven, and made for the shore arch of Hammersmith bridge, which was reached in 16 min. 18 sec. This barge lost Oxford some ground, though having the smooth water on such a rough day made up for it to a certain extent. They however passed the Bridge half a length ahead, their opponents being well in the middle of the stream. The triumph of endurance was now to come, and the pluck and power with which each crew rowed exhibited the unflinching "game" that distinguished them. In shooting the water to the Crab Tree they remained as before, but there the Cambridge men laid out in such extraordinary style as to mend their position every stroke, and once more their stern peeped in front; both boats lying considerably over to the northward, and the Cantabs with a fine course before them nearer the shore. Nothing in the shape of rowing could surpass the gallant contest at that moment, both parties rowing with the most determined pluck; but superior strength of course triumphed, and off the Half Moon the Cantabs had nearly drawn themselves clear, but another spurt from Oxford reduced the distance off Searle's to half a length, in which position, with the advantage of a few more feet at the finish, Cambridge won.

The course was rowed in 25′ 45″.

The times given in *Bell's Life* differ somewhat from these. They are as follows: Barnes Bridge, 6 min. 0 sec., Chiswick Eyot, 12 min. 50 sec.; Hammersmith Bridge, 16 min. 50 sec., the winning post in 25 min. 50 sec.

BIOGRAPHICAL NOTICES.

J. P. SALTER, graduated 1858. In holy orders.

F. C. ALDERSON, educated at Eton and Trinity; graduated 1857; ordained 1861; curate of Ampthill, Beds. 61—63; Hursley, Hants. 1863—65; rector of Holdenby, diocese of Peterborough, 1865.

R. LEWIS LLOYD, educated at Eton, Trinity, and Magdalene; captain of boats at Eton, 1855; son of T. L. Lloyd, Nantgwilt; a barrister.

H. E. FAIRRIE, graduated, 1856; in business in London.

J. M'CORMICK, graduated 1857; ordained 1858. Played in the University eleven against Oxford. Late rector of Dunmore East, Waterford; perpetual curate of St Peter's, Deptford, 1867.

H. SNOW, graduated 1857, as fourth in First Class Classical Tripos; educated at Eton and St John's; Porson Scholar, Browne's Medallist for Latin Ode and Camden Medallist 1856; late fellow of St John's, assistant Master at Eton.

H. R. M. JONES[1].

W. WINGFIELD, graduated 1857.

P. GURDON, M.A. graduated 1858; ordained curate of St Andrew's, Halstead, Essex; Vicar of Assington, 1861—66; rector of Cramworth Reymerston, Norfolk.

W. F. STOCKEN, M.A., graduated 1856.

R. I. SALMON, M.A., graduated 1857; curate of St Michael's, Paddington.

A. B. ROCKE, student of Christ Church, graduated 1855.

R. TOWNSEND, graduated 1857.

A. P. LONSDALE, educated at Eton and Balliol; a barrister on the Northern circuit; Lieut. of Inns of Court Volunteers.

G. BENNETT, Scholar and Fellow of New Coll.

J. T. THORLEY, Private Secretary to Duke of Newcastle.

F. W. ELERS, graduated 1858, of Mount Ephraim House, Tunbridge Wells, Kent.

---

[1] Of this gentleman I can find no trace.

1857.

Oxford Books :—

"A short account of training and preparation for this race, which without doubt was about the most hollow beating ever given to Cambridge by Oxford.

"A challenge had been sent to Cambridge early in the October term and accepted readily by the authorities there. Accordingly two or three times a week in that term a crew was taken down, so that when the Lent term began we might know where to turn to get, at any rate, half-a-dozen of our crew. Consequently, at the beginning of the Lent term 1857, we were able to appear with at least six men already accustomed to the stroke and to row together. It was fortunate for us that Mr Thorley, our stroke oar in the close race with Cambridge in 1856, was still able to row. By these means and by constant practice we found ourselves on March 2, the day we commenced training, with a crew of good men, who could already row and swing well together; and I must not omit to say that never were a crew more willing to do their best, as they all took a great interest in rowing. Here I may mention by the way, that in choosing a crew it will be found better generally to get men who take an interest in the thing, though they be inferior oarsmen; in preference to good oarsmen, who do not care to implicitly obey the discipline necessary to training. The following was the crew we began business with five weeks before the match.

1 J. Arkell, 11 st. 3 lbs.; 2 P. Gurdon, 11 st. 3 lbs.; 3 W. H. Wood, 12 st. 6 lbs.; 4 R. Martin, 12 st. 4 lbs.; 5 E. Warre, 12 st. 7½ lbs.; 6 R. W. Risley, 11 st. 6½ lbs.; 7 A. P. Lonsdale, 12 st. 7 lbs.; 8 J. T. Thorley, 10 st. 3 lbs.

"For five weeks we trained steadily, and were most fortunate in not losing one member of the above crew either from illness or any other cause. Plenty of running both before breakfast and after rowing; a walk to Sandford, a spurt to Abingdon Lasher and a steady row up to Sandford, thence a run to Iffley and walk to Oxford, was our usual day's work, except when from weakness or other cause we were forced to do less. And certainly such a course of training we found to answer admirably. It will be seen that considerable changes in our weights were made before the race. Finally the great thing in getting together an University crew is to begin early; *in the October term take down a crew once or twice a week* and so get four or six men accustomed to row together; this is the secret of success in a Putney match, and as long as Oxford follows that plan, so long will she be successful.

"Our boat was built by Matthew Taylor of Newcastle-on-Tyne, and a beauty she was, 55 ft. long, 25 in. broad, in fact quite eclipsing in speed all boats turned out of late years by Searle or any southern builder. Taylor himself steered us during our training, *not to instruct Oxford in the art of rowing*[1], but to show us the proper way to send his boat along as quickly as possible[2]. For as the oars were all the same length (12 ft. 7 in.) and the rowlocks on a different level to the old-fashioned boats, the old style of high feathering and pulling out hard at the end was of no use. The Cambridge crew was heavier than the Oxford.

"A. P. LONSDALE."

We have thus seen how the Oxford men went to work. There is a full account also in the Cambridge Books of the training on the Cam: it bears so close a resemblance however to the accounts of the training of other years that it is hardly worth while to give it. The only point worthy of remark is that, either owing to the badness of the weather or the inferiority of the crew, the times recorded are a good deal longer than usual.

At this time and for some years afterwards there used to be races for the first division boats in the Lent term. This had the effect of preventing the 'Varsity crew from getting into regular practice before the second week in March; so that there was all the less time for attaining that uniformity of style which is the first thing which a crew must be taught if it is to do any good. Now at the Universities the different colleges have somehow or

---

[1] This appears to be a quotation from *Bell's Life*.
[2] One is inclined to ask, What is the difference between these things thus distinguished?

other managed to acquire different styles : and it is not perhaps surprising that this should be the case. For assuming as an axiom that there is one and only one true style of rowing, it is evident that any difference in style between two boats must be due to faults in one or both of them.

Thus, if at any time any fault be acquired or any wrong ideas instilled at a college, these particular errors are likely to be perpetuated in that college; the same will happen with regard to some different fault in another college. The consequence is that when the University crew is chosen, the different individuals have faults of very different kinds to get rid of. This *should* be done before the crew goes into really hard training, that there may be a month immediately before the race in which there is nothing to do but to get into the condition necessary for so severe a struggle as the race. Not the least advantage of this would be, that the individuals would be relieved from a good deal of anxiety dependent on the uncertainty which a new man naturally feels as to his proving worthy of his place. From personal experience, besides what has been told me by others, I know that this anxiety very materially affects the nervous system, and consequently interferes with the full development of muscle, and does not tend to improve the health. On the other hand, if the crew are not put together till within five weeks of the race, the two operations, of getting rid of faults and acquiring a uniform style on the one hand, and of fully developing the muscles and acquiring robustness of health (where that is necessary) on the other, have to go on together. It may perhaps be suggested, as is doubtless true, that the eradication of faults and the acquiring a particular style are the same with the formation of muscle to a certain degree, inasmuch as the difference between two styles consists solely in this, that in the one different muscles are used, or else the same muscles differently, from those in the other, so that in acquiring a particular style muscles formerly unused are brought into play, or else muscles that were used to a certain extent and in a certain line of action before, are used in a different line of action and to a different extent, greater or less, now. But that is not what I mean here by "fully developing the muscles." By that I mean the getting of muscles, already in use, into a fit condition to endure the strain that will be put upon them in the race.

Now the two operations above named are totally distinct from, and therefore are liable to interfere with, each other, if carried on at the same time. It is the obvious advantage which arises from separating the times of performing these operations, that has led to the practice of having trial eights in the October term.

Early in that term (I am speaking of Cambridge) the captains of the several college clubs send in to the President of the U.B.C. the names of such men as he thinks are likely material from which to form good oarsmen. All these men are in turn taken out in practising boats, and the best endeavours of the captain and his coadjutors are given to getting them all into an uniform style. Sixteen of the best are eventually formed into two crews, who race together at the end of the term. During this race they are all of course narrowly watched, so that a judgment may be formed of their "staying" powers as well as of their "form."

This has quite superseded an old race, which many old Cambridge men look back upon with feelings of regret, namely, the "Captains and University," in which the two crews were chosen, the one from the captains of the college boat clubs, the other from the University at large. It is a question that is being constantly asked by old men, "Why have you given up the Captains and University race? In my time, when Cambridge always used to win at Putney, we used to find out what men were worth having by means of this race. I think your giving it up must have something to do with your always getting beaten now."

Mr J. M. Ridley of Jesus, captain of the University in 1842, has given me the following reasons for preferring the old method.

"In former days the captain was almost universally the stroke oar of his boat, and it was doubtful how the different strokes would accommodate themselves to the stroke of another. This gave a greater amount of interest to the race.

"Moreover a spirit of rivalry was excited against those in authority (the captains)—and an opportunity was afforded of men being brought out who from pique might have been kept in the background.

"It also created a University as against a captain's opinion in rowing."

Both methods have been applied to the same end, namely, to pick out the best men for the University. The present method seems to have the advantage, in that through it more men are passed before the President's eye, and things are done more systematically; the only point in which, as it seems to me, it fails is that, as it lies nearly altogether in the hands of the college captains what men's names are sent in to the President, it not unfrequently happens that men are overlooked, who ought certainly to have been tried. The only remedy appears to be in extra vigilance on the part of the President, who ought to let his personal observation make up for the possible incapacity of a college captain, who is sometimes chosen rather for his personal and social qualities, than for his prowess as an oarsman or his discrimination in the art of rowing.

The following account of the race is given in the Cambridge book.

"On Saturday morning, April 4, at eleven o'clock, the two crews rowed to their stations at the 3rd and 4th piers of the Waterworks Bridge. Oxford having won the toss took the Middlesex shore. A very excellent start was effected, in which Oxford gained a slight advantage, and at about Searle's they were clear, and opposite the Vice-Chancellor's a good length ahead, which distance was kept till above the Crab Tree, when they increased their lead, and although Cambridge made several very plucky spurts, they did not gain any of their lost ground; but the Oxonians gained more and more till they ultimately came in winners by 32 seconds! time 22 min. 50 sec. Oxford rowed in a boat built by Matthew Taylor of Newcastle, and began their training a week before Cambridge, under the guidance of the wily Matthew, who was with them up to the day of the race; when their rowing showed that they had imbibed some of the North country style they had repudiated so much at Henley Regatta in the preceding summer. The boat was a beautiful specimen of work and finish, about 55 feet long, the bows being cut very short and the ribs, &c. very light and strong. Both crews rowed with round loom oars, for the first time. The tide was neap, and the boats, having started rather late, met the ebb at Chiswick Eyot.

"The Cambridge boat was built by Messrs Salter of Wandsworth.

OXFORD CREW.

			st.	lbs.
1	R. WELLS RISLEY	*Exon.*	11	3
2	P. GURDON[1]	*Univ*	11	0
3	J. ARKELL	*Pemb*	12	10
4	R. MARTIN	*Corp*	12	1

[1] In the crew of 1856.

			st.	lbs.
5	W. Hardy Wood	Univ.	11	13
6	E. Warre	Ball.	12	3
7	A. P. Lonsdale[1]	Ball.	12	0
str.	J. T. Thorley[1]	Wad.	10	1
cox.	F. W. Elers[1]	Trin.	9	2
		Average	11	9⅛

Cambridge Crew.

			st.	lbs.
1	A. P. Holme	2nd Trin.	11	8
2	A. Benn	Emm.	11	5
3	W. H. Holley	Tr. Hall.	11	8
4	A. Levin Smith	1st Trin.	11	2
5	J. Jordan Serjeantson	1st Trin.	12	4
6	R. L. Lloyd[1]	Magd.	11	11
7	P. Pennant Pearson	John's	11	4
str.	Herbert Snow[1]	John's	11	8
cox.	R. Wharton	Magd.	9	2
		Average	11	8

"After the race the crews rowed back to Putney, and then proceeded at once to the Cedars, Mortlake, the hospitable mansion of Mr Phillips, where they partook of a sumptuous repast. In the evening they were entertained at the 'Albion Tavern' by the Thames Subscription Club, who on this day gave their first anniversary dinner."

"We should render ourselves liable (says *Bell's Life*) to the accusation of injustice did we not mention the excellent behaviour of the captains of all the steamboats, who took especial care on this occasion to keep out of the way of the umpire's

[1] Were in the crew of 1856.

and each other's boats, which by forming a regular line across the river, and preserving it as much as circumstances would permit, not only afforded a good view of the race to all on board, but thus became themselves a magnificent spectacle when there was little else to interest."

BIOGRAPHICAL NOTICES. (OXFORD.)

R. W. RISLEY, graduated 1860; in holy orders; curate of St Mark's, Surbiton.

J. ARKELL, graduated 1859; in holy orders; rector of Portishead, dio. Bath and Wells, 1869.

R. MARTIN, M.A. graduated 1857; alive in 1869.

W. H. WOOD, graduated 1858; ordained 1859; late curate of St Peter's, Wolverhampton, and temporary head-master of the grammar-school; curate of St Luke's, Leeds, 1865; now of Theddlethorpe, Lincolnshire.

Rev. E. WARRE, educated at Eton and Balliol; Newcombe Scholar, 1854; graduated First Class Classics, 1856; fellow of All Souls; assistant master at Eton, 1860.

BIOGRAPHICAL NOTICES. (CAMBRIDGE.)

A. P. HOLME, graduated 1857; ordained 1859; minister of St Andrew's, Yarmouth.

A. BENN, graduated 1857; ordained 1860; curate of Atcham, Salop, 1860—63; rector of Woolfardisworthy, Crediton, 1866.

W. H. HOLLEY, B.A. eldest son of J. H. Holley, Esq. Oaklands, Devon.

ARCHIBALD L. SMITH, graduated 1858. Called to the Bar at Inner Temple, Nov. 1860; special pleader on the Home Circuit.

J. J. SERJEANTSON, graduated 1858 as Junior Optime; ordained 1859, curate of Stoke-upon-Trent.

P. P. PEARSON (Pennant), M.A., educated at Charterhouse and St John's; graduated 1857 as Senior Optime; of Bodfari, Flint; magistrate for that county, and High Sheriff 1859 and 1862.

Henley-on-Thames Royal Regatta.

Friday and Saturday, June 18 and 19.

Saturday.—The entry list had been nearly exhausted on Friday, and the only redeeming feature of this, the last day, was the eight-oar race between the Oxford University and the London Rowing Club. This produced a fuller attendance than on the previous day, although far inferior to what we have seen at Henley, notwithstanding the inviting character of the weather.

Grand Challenge Cup.

London Rowing Club 1
Oxford University Club 0

LONDON ROWING CLUB.

		st.	lbs.
1	J. IRELAND	9	7
2	F. POTTER	9	13
3	C. SCHLOTEL	10	11
4	J. NOTTIDGE	10	11

			st.	lbs.
5	J. Paine		11	10
6	Farrar		11	4
7	A. A. Casamajor		10	6
str.	H. Playford		9	11
cox.	H. Edie		9	0
	Average		10	7$\frac{3}{8}$

OXFORD UNIVERSITY BOAT CLUB.

			st.	lbs.
1	J. T. Thorley	*Wadham*	10	0
2	R. W. Risley	*Exon.*	11	3
3	R. Martin	*Corpus*	12	2
4	H. Wood	*Univ.*	11	13
5	E. Warre	*Balliol*	12	5
6	A. P. Lonsdale	*Balliol*	11	13
7	P. Gurdon	*Univ.*	11	2
str.	J. Arkell	*Pemb.*	10	11
cox.	F. W. Elers	*Trin.*	8	11
	Average		11	6$\frac{1}{8}$

The London Rowing Club had the Berks side. Mr Nind, formerly of Christ Church, Oxford, and one of the most accomplished oarsmen of his day, officiated as umpire in this race. From the very first stroke the London Rowing Club took the lead, and drew away, and after three hundred yards were their length clear. The Oxonians then began to pick up, pressing the Londoners with great severity, and fast decreasing for a time their advantage. Just below the Poplars the Londoners again drew away, increasing their advantage to a length and a quarter at the Grand Stand, where No. 4 in the

Oxford boat broke his oar; they however gallantly rowed on, and finished with about the same gap between them. Time 7 min. 55 sec.

The London Rowing Club likewise won both the Stewards' and Wyfold Cups for Four-oars and the Diamond Sculls, but were beaten for the Pairs by two of the Oxford University crew, Messrs Warre and Lonsdale.

1858.

The following is from the Cambridge Book :—

"Well is it that the records of this ever memorable crew have been preserved, for they will undoubtedly prove both beneficial and instructive to oarsmen in future times, when they consider of what sort and of what duration the training of this crew consisted, and *how the work was done.*

"Towards the end of the October term 1857, Mr R. L. Lloyd, who was then president of the C.U.B.C., took down an eight some five or six times, in which various men were tried, but nothing was fixed upon for certain till the beginning of the Lent term, 1858. Immediately this term began, the University eight also began to go down regularly; and after about 10 days' practising, in which many were tried and many rejected, Mr Lloyd called to his assistance a man not altogether unknown to fame; and this was none other but T. Selby Egan; he kindly promised to take in hand the crew of 1858, and right well did he fulfil his promise; for he might be seen four days out of every six steering his eight down the Cam in the most inclement weather that perhaps ever accompanied the training of any crew. After some few long rows to Bottisham lock and back, the following crew went into training on Wednesday the 24th of February; and wonderful to relate, the same crew, though in a somewhat different order, rowed in the winning race on the 27th of March 1858.

"1 W. J. Havart; 2 A. L. Smith; 3 H. H. Lubbock; 4 D. Darrock; 5 H. Williams; 6 R. L. Lloyd; 7 A. Fairbairn; str. J. Hall; cox. R. Wharton.

"The following is the log:

Wednesday, Feb. 24th. Rowed to Bottisham and back. Ran from Railway Bridge.

Thursday, Feb. 25th. To Clayhythe and back. Could not get further. Tornado from N.E. Ran from Railway Bridge.

Friday, Feb. 26th. McGregor, 2 Trin., rowed for H. Williams, who had a bad cold. To Clayhythe and back. Gale from N.E. Ran from Railway Bridge.

Saturday, Feb. 27th. McGregor rowed again for Williams. Egan steered; rowing very bad. Blown up accordingly. Men all weak.

Monday, March 1st. Men ran in the morning to the Observatory, which they continued to do till they left Cambridge, according as each man's condition allowed. Rowed nearly to Bottisham and back. Egan steered. Ran to Chesterton and back.

Tuesday, March 2nd. Rowed to Baitsbite. Wind too strong to go on, and Hall not well. McGregor rowed. Ran from Bridge to Searle's. Egan steered.

Wednesday, March 3rd. Rowed to Baitsbite Lock. McGregor rowed for Lubbock. Hall not well yet. Ran to Chesterton and back. Egan steered.

Thursday, March 4th. Rowed in a four. Havart, Darrock, Fairbairn, A. L. Smith or R. Lloyd. Rest of crew seedy.

Friday, March 5th. Rowed with our proper crew to Bottisham lock and back. Very good rowing most of the way.

Saturday, March 6th. Went down nearly to Clayhythe; got stopped by barges in Long Reach. Rowing at time A 1; "Bravo boys." Egan steered. Rowed over short Cambridge course at 30 strokes per minute in 9 min. Ran to Chesterton and back.

Monday, March 8th. Rowed to Clayhythe and back. Wind N.W. blowing a gale. Egan steered; rowing fair down; bad up. Ran up from Railway Bridge.

Tuesday, March 9th. Rowed to Upware and back. A gale from N.W. with snow. First day in Matt. Taylor's practising boat. Rowing against wind good. Egan steered. Got upset opposite Mrs Runkam's by barges on our way up.

Wednesday, March 10th. Rowed to Clayhythe. From steps to locks at Baitsbite 11' 55".

Calm day. Cambridge course 9′ 15″. Egan steered.

Thursday, March 11th. Rowed to Ely. P. Pearson steered. A calm day. 3h. 2m.

Friday, March 12th. Rowed back from Ely. Calm day. Rowing from Bottisham to Baitsbite excellent. Wharton steered; Fairbairn and Darrock both seedy. 3h. 15m.

Saturday, March 13th. Rowed to Plough and back in Magdalene Matt. Taylor. Egan steered; 7 and 4 both unwell.

Monday, March 15th. Rowed from locks to locks. Time 21′ 55″. River low. A breeze S.W. Stoppage of ½ minute by barges and by sculling boat. Egan up.

Tuesday, March 16. Locks to locks. Time 20′ 40″. A breeze from W. No water. No stream. Ran from Railway Bridge. Egan on bank.

Wednesday, March 17. Locks to locks, 21′ 8″. No water. Rather a side wind. Rowed about four lengths further than usual.

Thursday, March 18. Rowed in new Matt. Taylor racing boat. Went very steadily indeed. Time 20′ 46″. Stoppage ¼ of min. at Chesterton. Calm. Low water.

Friday, March 19. Locks to locks. Headwind. Time 21′ 7″.

Saturday, March 20. Locks to locks. Most perfect calm, very low water, and therefore no stream. Time 20′ 28″. The fastest on record.

[Oxford at Putney. 1st day of their rowing on Putney Course:
Putney—Hammersmith, 8′ 45″.
Hammersmith—Barnes, 9′.
Whole course from Waterworks to Ship, 21′ 7″.
Stark calm and good tide.]

Monday, March 22. The crew did not row: but went to Putney. Oxford time over the course 22′ 40″.

Tuesday, March 23. Mortlake to Putney. To Barnes Bridge 3′ 30″, and 22′ 24″ over course. Very slack ebb.

Wednesday, March 24. Mortlake to Putney. Raced watermen, gave them two clear lengths lead. Passed them at Chiswick Eyot, and won by the distance from Finch's in 21′ 22″ or 21′ 40″. Oxford, who rowed 10 minutes before, 22′ 10″ or 22′.

Thursday, March 25. Mortlake to Putney. Tremendous head sea in Corney reach. Boat half full of water. Time 22′ 40″. Oxford time with wind 22′ 2″.

Friday, March 26. From Waterworks to Hammersmith Bridge 8′ 15″.

Saturday, March 27th.

The Race.

Cambridge having won the toss chose the Middlesex side, and started from the third pier of the Waterworks.

The water was very lumpy up to the Crab Tree, owing to a wind against the stream, and the "boil" made by some 15 heavily laden steamers. The start was effected precisely at one o'clock, and both boats were immediately under weigh. Scarce was the word "off" given when Mr Thorley, the Oxford stroke, caught a very fine fish, which knocked him back into No. 7 and completely brought their eight to stand still. The Cantabs at this time had a slight lead, which they lost directly afterwards by fouling with their port-oars a barge which lay at anchor in their course.

Both crews were put completely out of rowing by these disasters, and for some time continued to row side by side in rather a wild manner. With the nose of the Oxford boat about level with the Cambridge cox. both crews continued to row up to the Crab Tree, when Cambridge began to draw rapidly ahead. The pace here increased, owing to wind not being so dead ahead, and Cambridge, who had now fallen into something like its usual style of rowing, passed under Hammersmith Bridge in 9′ 4″, about a length and a half ahead of their opponents.

The race was nothing now but a runaway one, as Cambridge improved its position every stroke, and passed the flag-boat off the Ship at Mortlake in 21′ 23″ from the time of starting, Oxford being some lengths, or more precisely speaking, "twenty-two seconds," behind.

It should be added to this, that such was the

pluck and determination with which the Oxford
men rowed up to the very end of the race, that
they only lost a second on the Cambridge crew
from Barnes Bridge to the finish. The time of the
winners was, from Putney to Hammersmith Bridge
9 m. 3 sec., Barnes Bridge 18 m. 3 sec., Mortlake
21 m. 23 sec. Thus the time of the Oxford men
from Barnes Bridge to the winning post was 3 m.
21 sec., which is not at all slow rowing, and speaks
to the courage and determination with which they
must have struggled on against the disadvantages
under which they laboured after the first few
strokes of the race.

The following remarks are from the *Field*, and
I give them because both sides of the case are
stated, together with the judgment of one who, I
should suppose, had no reason for partiality[1]. I
should not wish it to be supposed that I agree with
his remarks about the best weight for a crew.

Last year the Oxford crew were trained by Matthew
Taylor, of Ouseburn, near Newcastle, and rowed in a
boat built by him, which certainly seemed to suit them
exactly; and indeed, in our judgment, the crew altogether was by far the most perfect we have ever seen.
Nothing could be finer than Mr Thorley's stroke,
which was founded exactly upon the Clasper style,
with the addition of the elegant fall of the shoulders
and close management of the elbows which is only
seen to perfection among gentlemen amateurs. Again,
not only was the stroke good in itself, being long,
powerful, well pulled through, and clean-feathered, but

---

[1] Mr Cassamajor was at this time aquatic editor of *The
Field*.

it was exactly followed throughout the boat, so that the most critical eye would fail in detecting the slightest fault in time, the consequence of which was that Taylor's boat had full justice done her, and travelled to perfection. Why all this has been changed this year we are at a loss to know ; but certain it is that Taylor has not been the trainer, Mr Shadwell having kindly undertaken that office—that his boat has been replaced by one made by Searle—and that the stroke has been materially changed. Much has been written on the subject of waterman, as opposed to amateur, training for eight-oared races, and we are fully of opinion that, *cæteris paribus*, the amateur has the best of the argument ; but we confess that, in our opinion and as far as we know, Matthew Taylor has no equal among amateurs, and therefore we cannot believe that the change has been beneficial, even though we admit the claims of Mr Shadwell to be considered a firstrate oarsman ; and, from the experience he has had, he is doubtless equal to any one who could have been selected from among the graduates of his University. Still, as we have already remarked, we believe Taylor to be *sui generis*, combining the practical skill of the waterman with the mental intelligence of the amateur ; and after his wonderful success last year, we cannot help wondering at the O.U.B.C. venturing on a change. With regard to the boat used on this occasion, we believe her to be good enough for the crew, and that Mr Searle deserves no part of the blame for the failure which was experienced, especially as, from an accident at the start, the thowl of the stroke rowlock was broken, and, as a natural consequence, the boat could not have full justice done her—though, from a close inspection of the rowing throughout the race, we are scarcely inclined to believe that the loss is entirely attributable to that cause, for reasons which we shall give after describing the contest. On this subject, however, we have received a communication from a gentleman on behalf of the Oxford crew, which is to the effect that in their belief, and after inspecting the injury done to the boat in company with the captain and trainer of the Cambridge crew, the race was lost entirely through the mishap. The following is the account sent us by him of the accident, which, we have no doubt, occurred exactly as described :—

"At the fourth stroke from the start, a wave in the troubled water, coming from a steamer floating near at hand, struck the stroke oar with such force as to twist the wrought iron outrigger and the iron case of the thowls out of their places; so that the former was bent out of shape downwards, and the thowl, upon which the whole pressure of the oar comes, started outwards to the extent of one-third of its whole perpendicular height. Thus there was no longer anything left to row against; and the crew was at once deprived of their stroke, upon which of course they entirely depended for time. The rowing, which the day before had been as uniform and precise as any ever witnessed, became consequently a mere scramble—the captain being unable to retain his oar in the water, and the rest following hap-hazard his vain endeavours to row a reasonable stroke. Never was any crew brought to the post in more perfect order and condition; but this great mishap threw them all out, and in an instant two months' careful preparation was totally marred. Cambridge, in fact, had nothing to row against."

We will therefore assume that the injury done was a bending outward of the thowl, so as to make the fulcrum for the oar somewhat unstable, while the opening between the thowl and stopper was made wider than before, and the cord connecting them together was broken. But it must be remembered that there was no swell on the river; that the water, though slightly rippled by the breeze, was not at all lumpy; and that there was no steamer near the Oxford side at the place of starting. Hence it is clear that, whatever the nature of the accident, it was solely attributable to a miss in catching the water by Mr Thorley, which occasioned what is commonly called a "crab"—however improbable such an event may appear in a finished oarsman, who had twice before rowed stroke in a similar match. We hazard below an opinion on the precise cause of this remarkable mistake, upon which we leave our readers to form their own opinion. The total weight of the rowing crews was as follows:—In 1857 the Oxford men, independently of the coxswain, weighed 87 st. 13½ lb [1], being within a fraction an average of 11 st.; while in 1858 the total weight was 94 st. 1 lb., or an average of 11 st. 10⅝ lb., the increase being partly accounted for by the growth in weight of the old members and the relative greater weight of the new. This change is of some importance, as it bears upon the interesting question relating to the most advantageous weight for a boat's crew in the present day, which, we believe, should not average much above 11 stone, beyond which few men pull their weight in an outrigger boat. In the old-fashioned build it was of less importance; but even then a crew averaging more than 11 st. 7 lb. each was seldom first-rate. So much for the defeated, and for the possible causes of their defeat; and now let us see, by contrast, how we may account for the success of their antagonists. *Imprimis*, it was not from being *much* lighter men, for their total weight was 92 st. 7 lb., giving an average of 11 st. 8 lb. nearly; but certainly this difference can scarcely be supposed to account for their superiority—more especially when we find that last year the total weight of the Cambridge rowing crew was 92 st. 5 lb., or only 2 lb. less than on the present occasion. All the crew were new men, except Nos. 2 and 6, together with Mr Wharton, who again officiated as coxswain. Mr Hall rowed an excellent stroke, not nearly so high on the feather as Mr Snow's of last year, but still partaking slightly of the "soaring" style. It was, however, extremely well pulled through, and finished very clean; while the time was good, and the stroke was backed up throughout the race. Indeed, it appeared to us that the last year's defeat, as it usually does, had made the Cantabs as careful in their practice as the wonderful success of their opponents had acted prejudicially on them. The light-blues are, however, much indebted to the

---

[1] This does not agree with the weights I have given above and which I have every reason to believe correct. The total weight was 93 st. 3 lbs. The whole passage contains what is now considered an exploded idea, but it is interesting to see the change in opinion that has taken place in so few years.

training of Mr Egan, the well-known old and experienced coxswain and trainer of that University; and to his unremitting attention and skill we believe they are indebted for their success. The following are the names and weights of the respective crews:—

CAMBRIDGE.

			st.	lbs.
1	H. H. LUBBOCK	Caius	11	4
2	A. L. SMITH[1]	1st Trinity	11	4
3	W. J. HAVART	Lady Marg.	11	4
4	D. DARROCH	1st Trinity	12	1
5	H. WILLIAMS	Lady Marg.	12	4
6	R. L. LOYD[1]	Magdalen	11	13
7	A. H. FAIRBAIRN	2nd Trinity	11	12
str.	J. HALL	Magdalen	10	7
cox.	R. WHARTON[1]	Magdalen	9	2
		Average	11	7$\frac{7}{8}$

OXFORD.

1	R. W. RISLEY[1]	Exon	11	8
2	J. ARKELL[1]	Pembroke	11	3
3	C. G. LANE	Christ Church	11	10
4	H. AUSTEN	Magdalen	12	7
5	E. LANE	Balliol	11	10
6	W. H. WOOD[1]	University	12	0
7	E. WARRE[1]	Balliol	13	2
str.	J. T. THORLEY[1]	Wadham	10	3
cox.	H. S. WALPOLE	Balliol	9	5
		Average	11	8$\frac{7}{8}$

The boat in which the winners rowed was quite new, being built for them by Matthew Taylor, and appeared to carry them well, having a very full floor, especially amidships, but falling away rather rapidly to a sharp entrance and run. She seemed remarkably stiff, and certainly nothing could be more beautiful

---

[1] Were in the crew of 1857.

than the smooth even way in which she travelled when her crew settled down to their work above the cricket-ground. The Oxford boat was built by Messrs Searle, last year, for Brazenose College, and has always been considered a capital specimen of their well-known skill as boat-builders. She is, perhaps, not quite so full in her waist as the Cambridge boat, but, being fuller at stroke and bow than the Newcastle model, she is quite as floaty, and carried her crew well enough, but seemed to shiver a little, either from weakness in herself, or from deficiency in the rowing together of her crew, which latter we believe was really the case, probably in consequence of the accident. Whether or not the accident which occurred to Mr Thorley's rowlock militated to any great degree against the success of his crew, it must be remembered that it was entirely the fault of that gentleman, which is the more extraordinary in so old and practised an oarsman; but still so it was, and therefore Cambridge is fairly entitled to the credit to which she may lay claim. According to the description inserted above, the thowl was damaged exactly as it always is when "a crab" is caught; and, if the "crab-catcher" had been a young oar, he would undoubtedly have been blamed—*first*, for catching that unfortunate animal; *secondly*, for not releasing his oar at once after he had caught it—which, however, he was prevented doing by the cord passed from thowl to stopper; and, *thirdly*, he would have been soundly rated for not being able to row under the difficulties in which his own awkwardness had placed him. Such we believe to be the plain unvarnished tale relating to this unfortunate accident, which we would gladly tell in a different manner, thereby sparing the feelings of Mr Thorley and his friends, if we could do so consistently with the facts of the case as far as we are ourselves cognisant of them. Fortunately, this gentleman may fall back upon his previous well-earned fame, and there is less reason to be tender of him than there would be in the case of a younger aspirant to aquatic honours. He has had his share of glory, and he may now be content to take the rough as well as the smooth. Were we to give an opinion as to the immediate cause of the "crab," we should, to a certain extent, relieve him from the blame, as, from what we saw of the rowing of No. 6, we believe that he was out of time at the moment, and threw his water upon the stroke's oar, which was thus struck out of place. But, as we were not near enough to see the precise nature of what took place, we can only throw it out as, in our opinion, a more probable cause than that which is assigned by our correspondent. Our chief anxiety is that the facts should be carefully weighed, as proving, in our opinion, that the success of last year occasioned an over-confidence on the part of the one crew, resulting in carelessness, which was still further promoted by the extra vigilance and regular training of the other. This is, however, the old tale, which will, we suppose, be told again and again to the end of time. Thus ended this last act in the drama, which is always a comedy to one party and a tragedy to the other; but as, in spite of this necessary result, the two are always merged in broad farce as soon as the legs are under, instead of over, the mahogany—so on this occasion the losers pledged the winners, and the winners pledged the losers, as University men only are capable of doing. Indeed, instead of being a ground and cause of jealousy, as might be expected, this annual trial of skill, pluck, and strength seems to cement the bonds of good-fellowship which exist so strongly between all those who have matriculated at either seat of learning.

Mr Warre, President of the O.U.B.C., says as follows:

"The training that the crew went through was perhaps the most perfect in system that has ever been acted upon. The consequence was that not one of the crew ever suffered from the usual weakness from boils which in most crews torment men in training..........The dinners were at the Cross, and the diet was the usual beef and mutton, varied occasionally with fish and poultry, *and there was always a plain pudding* of rice, sago, or tapioca afterwards. To this system must be attributed the good health of the crew. A certain amount of claret or port was allowed each man after dinner... The boat, though it might have been better had it been new, was a good one, and the loss of the race is undoubtedly attributable to the accident above-mentioned..........The only thing that critics remarked was wanting in the crew was that precise and sharp catch hold of the water at the beginning of the stroke; that it was caught together every one agreed, but perhaps the above criticism had a truth involved in it which is worth the notice of future captains, which is that it is the *beginning* of the stroke that makes the boat go, and whether or not a cause of failure this time is still in all cases to be equally remembered.

E. WARRE,
(<i>President Easter Term</i> '58.)"</div>

BIOGRAPHICAL NOTICES.

H. H. LUBBOCK, graduated 1858; Curate of Stow-cum-Quy, 1859—60; Rector of Gunton, Norwich, 1866.

W. J. HAVART.

D. DARROCK, B.A., graduated 1859; Lt. of Camb. Univ. Volunteers; Lord of the Barony of Gourock, Renfrewshire.

H. WILLIAMS, educated at Marlborough and St John's, LL.B. 1860; ordained 1862; Curate of

Bedwell, Stafford., 1862—67; eldest son of Rev. Hugh Williams, Vicar of Bassaley, Newport.

A. H. FAIRBAIRN, graduated 1859; ordained 1860 to the curacy of Wargrave; Curate of Wilton, 1863; Perpetual Curate of Knowl Hill, dio. Oxon., 1864.

J. HALL, graduated 1862; died 1868, aged 33; eldest son of James Hall, Esq. of Scarborough Hall, Yorkshire, the Master of the Holderness hounds.

C. G. LANE, graduated 1860; ordained 1862; Curate of Little Gaddesden, 1866; chaplain and librarian to Earl Brownlow.

H. AUSTEN.[1]

E. LANE, graduated 1860; Fellow of All Souls; ordained 1862.

H. S. WALPOLE.[1]

Henley Regatta.

This took place on Monday and Tuesday, July 21 and 22.

The London Rowing Club were the holders of the Grand Challenge Cup. The only challengers were the C.U.B.C. and the Leander.

It had been hoped that the O.U.B.C. would have entered, and they had indeed begun to practise. Several disasters however occurred, and it was altogether found impossible to send a crew which would represent the University in a fitting manner. In the trial heat the Cambridge were victorious. The Leander crew consisted of mem-

[1] Of these gentlemen I can find no trace.

bers of the two Universities, and to Mr Egan was assigned the difficult task of reconciling their different styles. The final heat was rowed the second day. The following is from the *Field*:

In spite of the change in the London crew[1] the betting at starting was in their favour, the odds varying from 5 to 4 to 2 to 1. Nothing could be finer than the style of the Londoners as they rowed down, but want of condition will tell even in a healthy man; and with one notoriously out of health in the crew, the *cognoscenti* were too well aware of the defect to back the side which would otherwise have been almost considered certain winners. The Cambridge had won the toss, and of course took the Berkshire side, which piece of luck just gave them the cup; but the loss of the Londoners was the gain of the spectators, as it produced such an exciting and evenly-contested race as is seldom seen in this kind of sport. From the start the London Club showed in front, their only chance being to get the lead to the Poplars, but the Cambridge crew stuck to their work (after the first few strokes, which were rather wild) in the most steady and determined style, and prevented their antagonists from accomplishing their object, of taking the Berkshire water. The Londoners rowed fully forty-six strokes per minute during the whole of this long struggle, while the Cambridge crew reached forty-two in the early part of the race, and even forty-four, according to one gentleman who counted them; in going round the point, when putting on their grand spurt, they actually accomplished forty-eight strokes per minute. Nothing could exceed the smartness and precision of Mr H. Playford's stroke, except the backing up of No. 7; and indeed the whole crew are to be equally admired in their several places, the only defect being the want of stamina and condition of No. 4. If the palm for elegance is to be conceded to London,

---

[1] No. 4 was a substitute; Mr Catty, who had been rowing No. 3, was taken ill on the Sunday and was unable to row; Mr Schlotel went to No. 3, and Mr Ditton, who was quite out of condition, took his place at No. 4.

efficiency, strength, and pluck may be claimed for the Cambridge gentlemen, who certainly deserve great credit for their determination to "do or die" throughout the race; and the farther they went the more their long, dragging stroke told in their favour. At the Poplars the Cambridge boat slightly overlapped the London boat, and their coxswain keeping a capital course, and not giving way a single yard to his opponent, though strongly pressed, the sons of the Thames were obliged to abandon their hope of taking the Berkshire water from the fear of a foul, and were therefore compelled to row outside the Cantabs, which Master Weston (though only a youth of 14) succeeded in doing in most beautiful style, not leaving much more than a yard between the blades of the oars. Here the stroke of the Cambridge boat called upon his crew in the most brilliant style, and on their well backing him up, they rapidly gained upon the London Club, and on entering the final piece of straight water, the C.U.B.C. was more than half a boat's length ahead; but the Londoners here being on even terms, again put on a final spurt and diminished the distance slightly, so as to be about a third of a boat's length behind at the winning post. The excitement was, of course, extreme, such a race having seldom been witnessed by the oldest patron of the sport present. The time was variously taken at 7 min. 32 sec. to 7 min. 38 sec. We ourselves made it 7 min. 34 sec., being the fastest race on record, we believe, by nearly half a minute.

The three crews were as follows:—

THE CAMBRIDGE CREW.

		st.	lbs.
1	G. A. PALEY	11	3
2	A. L. SMITH	11	2
3	T. HAVART	11	2
4	D. DARROCH	12	2
5	A. FAIRBAIRN	11	12
6	R. L. LLOYD	11	13
7	N. ROYDS	10	0
str.	T. HALL	10	3
cox.	J. T. MORLAND	8	4

THE LONDON CREW.

		st.	lbs.
1	L. Paine	10	3
2	F. Potter	10	0
3	C. Schlotel	10	11
4	E. G. Ditton	10	10
5	W. Farrar	12	2
6	J. Paine	12	5
7	A. Cassamajor	11	0
str.	H. Playford	10	4
cox.	H. H. Weston	6	0

THE LEANDER CREW.

		st.	lbs.
1	J. Wright	11	2
2	P. Pearson	11	8
3	T. Craster	12	8
4	H. Fairlie	12	10
5	E. Courage	12	4
6	A. B. Rocke	13	0
7	A. O. Boyd	10	10
str.	A. Lovesdale	12	7
cox.	E. Adams	8	5

1859.

In the Michaelmas term of 1858, according to a suggestion of Mr Warre, late President of the O.U.B.C., Mr Arkell his successor instituted a new system of choosing men for the University boat. This was the trial eights. The nature of this system I have already[1] explained. Mr Arkell in

---

[1] See pp. 230—1.

his remarks on the race says, "It will not do to trust too much to the judgment of the College captains, for a constant watch ought to be kept on the river for likely men, who may now with advantage be brought into shape." After the race between the two trial eights the custom at Oxford[1] has always been to pick the eight best men out of the two boats to row up to Oxford, and "although there are necessarily numberless faults in such a crew, yet they may be said to form a foundation on which to build the crew that is to represent" the University at Putney the next year. Speaking of the race of 1858, he says:

"The system of trial races instituted in last October term was a great assistance to us, and enabled us to begin work with the crew settled soon after the beginning of the Lent term, exactly eight weeks before the race."

Throughout the training Mr Arkell was assisted by Mr Lonsdale, who coached the men separately in pairs in the mornings, a practice which did them all much good.

The following is the log of the Oxford crew.

The crew was first considered formed on Friday, Feb. 18th, after we had been up just 3 weeks. It was 1 Baxter, 2 Risley, 3 E. Lane, 4 Clarke, 5 Morrison, 6 Lawless, 7 C. G. Lane, 8 Arkell, cox. Robarts. This crew practised regularly for

[1] This practice was introduced at Cambridge in 1868 by Mr G. Morrison.

the next three weeks, 6 and 8 being occasionally changed, but eventually Arkell kept the after oar. Active training began on

Monday, March 14th. Rowed over long course, *wind* strong ahead, about 34 per min. Time 24' 10". *Boat*, John the Balliol.

Tuesday, March 15th. C. G. Lane's father up. Warre rowed for him. Twice to Iffley.

Wednesday, March 16th. To Abingdon Lasher. Strong stream, but wind very strong against us. Slow stroke. Time 23' 15".

Thursday, March 17th. Too rough to row till evening. Run to Sandford. Once to Iffley in new boat.

Friday, March 18th. In new boat again. Once to Iffley before torpids. Second time scratch crew waited for us at the Gut and licked us up. Condemn new boat, and telegraph to Mat. Taylor to bring his new one directly.

Saturday, March 19th. Again in John the Balliol. To the Lasher at Abingdon. No wind. Stream very strong. Time 22' 10".

Sunday, March 20th. Walk to Islip to lunch.

Monday, March 21st. Below locks again. Lonsdale on the bank to Iffley. No stream or wind. Time 22' 20".

Tuesday, March 22nd. To the Lasher. Time 22' 45". Stroke too quick. Warre and Lonsdale on bank.

Wednesday, March 23rd. Twice to Iffley, and run round the meadows.

Thursday, March 24th. E. Lane bad with boils. Warre rowed for him: did not go below locks.

Friday, March 25th. Rowed in Pembroke boat to-day. A scratch crew waited for us in the Newnham Reach: took two lengths start. We gained on them and just passed them at the corner above the Poplars. Time 22′ 10″.

Saturday, March 26th. Rowing not so good. Warre and Lonsdale on the bank. Wind against us from the island. Time 22′ 50″.

Sunday, March 27th. Walk round by river to Evesham: lunch and back by road.

Monday, March 28th. E. Lane obliged to withdraw for boils. Take in Thomas and alter the crew as follows:

1 Baxter, 2 Clarke, 3 C. G. Lane, 4 Lawless, 5 Morrison, 6 Arkell, 7 Risley, 8 Thomas. Wind strong against us. Did not go well.

Tuesday, March 29th. Same order. Wind high. Time 23′ 26″. Risley cannot row bow side.

Wednesday, March 30th. Snowing all day. Twice to Iffley. Arkell 8, Thomas 7, Risley 6. Rest as before.

Thursday, March 31st. Frosty and cold, but fine for rowing. Lonsdale, Pinckney and Marshall on the bank. No wind. Time 21′ 55″.

Friday, April 1st. Wind blowing a hurricane against us. Time 25′ 45″.

Saturday, April 2nd. Another very windy day. Time 24′ 5″. Average weight, 11st. 13 lbs.

Sunday, April 3rd. Walk round by Newnham. Lunch at Harcourt Arms.

Monday, April 4th. Wind still very high. Time 23' 55".

Tuesday, April 5th. Hot, with head wind. Time 22' 55".

Wednesday, April 6th. *Very hot.* Slight wind against us. Stroke too quick. Time 23 min. Send boat on to Putney. Average weight, 11 st. 8 lbs.

Thursday, April 7th. Go to Putney by express. Very hot indeed. Rowed about 4.30. Rather too late for the tide. Calm but hot. Time 21' 45".

Friday, April 8th. Much cooler. Paddle in the morning, and try starts. Row about 5 o'clock. Very rough above Hammersmith. Raining slightly. Time 23 min.

Saturday, April 9th. Paddle and try starts in morning. Row about 6.30. Wind very high indeed and water very rough. Time 24' 20". Run back across common. Cantabs arrive but do not row.

Sunday, April 10th. Walk, some to Windsor, some to Richmond.

Monday, April 11th. Both crews row with the ebb in the morning. The Cantabs from the Ship to Putney Bridge, 22' 23". We start at Barker's Rails and reach Searle's in 23' 30", but from Ship to Searle's in 20' 30". Paddle and try starts in evening.

Tuesday, April 12th. Both crews row same distance as yesterday. Cantabs 22 min. Oxford 20′ 25″.

Wednesday, April 13th. We row with the flood: wind very high against tide. Time 23′ 30″. Cantabs row with ebb against the watermen. Wind strong with them. Time 21′ 10″.

Thursday, April 14th. Calm day, with slight breeze from North. Try starts to Hammersmith Bridge in morning. Go to be photographed in afternoon.

Friday, April 15th. Row the race and win it easily. Wind blowing hurricanes. Cf. newspapers.

There is a pretty full account given of the training at Cambridge, but there is nothing worthy of remark in it except that the time to Ely and back was a good deal better than last year; being 2 h. 45 m. going down and 2 h. 55 m. coming back, against 3 h. 2 m. and 3 h. 15 m. of last year respectively.

In the account given of the race I find the following comments by the Secretary :—

" Friday the day of the race was ushered in with heavy clouds and half a gale of wind, which made the water so rough that anything like rowing was out of the question, and although Cambridge continued favourites at about 3 to 1, good judges felt sure that their boat could never live through the surf which was rolling, especially since they had lost the toss and had to row on the outside.....

"This year we gave in to Oxford, and agreed to

row the race on Friday; chiefly to get rid of an old claim of Oxford against us[1]. As we have now satisfied that claim, our successors will, we hope, consider how they agree to row on Friday again, as on this occasion every sort of person complained bitterly of the alteration to the newspapers and privately to the President of the U.B.C., who received several letters about it.........

"The late President of the U.B.C. wishes to add his recommendation that no challenge should be sent to Oxford or accepted from them which does not leave it to the discretion of the Umpire, or some person appointed, whether the day is fit for rowing, so that the race may in future be a matter of rowing instead of a wretched scramble, and that the lives of the crews may not be endangered as they undoubtedly were in 1859."

The following graphic report of the race is taken from the *Times* newspaper. It and all other accounts seem to show that the loss of the race was due to the superior watermanship of the Oxford men, which showed itself in their choosing a boat able to carry them through the rough water :—

It is not, perhaps, too much, even though we are speaking of London weather and Thames squalls, when we say that it would not have been easy to pitch on a more unfavourable day for an eight-oared race than yesterday proved. The wind blew violently in raw gusty squalls from the north-west, and raised an

---

[1] I confess I am unable to see wherein any concession lay, or how Oxford gained any advantage except quite accidentally from having the race on Friday.

amount of broken water when it met the tide that boded very ill indeed for the safety of the light racing cutters. The day, too, was intensely cold, and almost every half hour was varied by a heavy storm of hail and snow. The aspect of a muddy river under such circumstances is endurable only in one of Vanderveldt's pictures. The reality is as unpicturesque as it is unpleasant; yet, notwithstanding these drawbacks, which must have exercised a considerable influence on the attendance, we seldom remember a race which was better attended, or which, on the whole, appeared to excite more interest. The interest shown, however, was more to witness the race than to speculate as to its result. It in fact appeared to be taken as a matter of course that Cambridge must win, and even heavy odds in their favour found but few takers; as the saying is, "very little was done for Oxford," so the Oxonians had to do everything for themselves, and they did it in splendid style. Both banks of the river at Putney were crowded with spectators as the hour for starting drew near, and the towing-path was covered with horsemen, nearly all of whom showed the Cambridge colours, which were certainly the popular tint of the day. The river swarmed with craft of all kinds, from outriggers, which were scarcely safe, to overcrowded steamers, which were very unsafe indeed. The Oxford crew showed soon after 12, and were regarded much in the light of men going on a forlorn hope, or who at best were about to make a very gallant but a very hopeless struggle. Their boat was severely criticised, " it was too short," " it was too broad," " it was too heavy," it was everything but what was right. The crew, too, having the odds against them, were immediately discovered to be wonderfully deficient as they rowed down against the tide to the starting-place at Putney Bridge. Certainly their rowing during this short course gave no evidence of the exquisite skill and vigour with which they afterwards pulled the race, neither did it justify the vaunts of Cambridge and the over-confident assertions that there would actually be no race after all. The Cantabs were afloat about the same time as their opponents, and their rowing was all that could be wished—regular as if the whole crew were one piece of machinery, though the stroke was manifestly slower than that of Oxford. Both the competing boats were made by the same builder at Newcastle, but before Cambridge had got twelve yards from shore it was apparent that their boat was too light for the rough water they had to encounter, besides which she appeared to have no stiffness, so that it was hoped they would change it even at the last moment. Oxford won the choice of station, and took the Middlesex side, which gave them a considerable advantage in point of wind and smoother water. Soon after 1 o'clock the word was given, the oars flashed in the sun like polished steel, and with a bound that seemed to lift them from the water both boats were off at a tremendous pace. For a short distance, until the "way" was well on them, they kept together, straining every nerve to the utmost ; but after the first 200 or 300 yards Oxford drew steadily ahead, and gained so much while their opponents were forcing by main strength their boat through the broken water, which almost swept over it, that at the end of the first mile Oxford was two or three lengths ahead. As the boats flew past, the fleet of steamers which lined the banks, and were laden almost to the water's edge with eager spectators, fell in their wake, and the race with all its fierce excitement commenced in earnest. The steamers rolling heavily from side to side as if they must capsize, and almost threatening to overwhelm the rival cutters, hemmed them in closely, and, with deafening cries and cheers, stimulated the losers to greater efforts. Their boat gains evidently, but there are still two long weary lengths between them and their opponents. The steamers, boats, and everything in dangerous confusion, fly pell-mell under the Suspension Bridge, the steamers fouling one another, and almost unmanageable in their overcrowded state, the rival cutters just able to keep ahead of their high-pressure pursuers, which almost jeopardise the lives of the rowing crews. At Hammersmith the wind is violent, and dead in the teeth of the competitors, with an ugly stretch of broken water for the Cambridge boat. As they labour through this it is seen at once that some of their crew are sorely distressed with this last spurt, and that the boat itself is ankle deep in water. For the latter evil there is no remedy, and it gets worse each minute. The Oxford boat was not too dry, but the first and second oars in the Cambridge boat were almost hidden by the water, which broke completely over them, and made the boat heavier with every stroke. While their antagonists were thus impeded, the Oxfords improved their distance, and at last got considerably ahead, and even the steamers, in spite of the shouts and signals from the umpire's boat, in spite of all the rules of fair play, began to pass a little ahead of the poor Cantabs, leaving them to contend as they best could with their trail of broken water. Past Barnes Railway Bridge the water was very rough; Oxford, now far ahead, went through it gallantly, but not so Cambridge, whose boat was almost waterlogged. Wave after wave broke into it—the track of steamers passing ahead made matters worse. Yet still, though their sinking condition was seen, the gallant crew pulled to the last, and were in the act of rowing desperately when the boat sank under them. In another minute, and amid a lot of straw hats, oars, and flannel shirts, they were all seen striking out just as manfully to gain the shore. Some were instantly picked up by boats, others swam to land, and all escaped without any worse mishap than a ducking on a very cold day. The accident, as we have said, in no way influenced the result of the race. At Hammersmith the chance of Cambridge was hopeless. After the accident, Oxford rowed the couple of hundred yards which yet remained to be accomplished very quietly, and came in winners amid tremendous cheering.

There is no doubt but that much of the blame for this mishap, such as it was, rests on the steamers, and unless some precautions are taken to prevent a large number of these overcrowded and unmanageable vessels from pressing on the boats while rowing, it is not impossible but that sooner or later some dreadful accident must happen. Throughout the race Cambridge did its very best to win, but with scarcely a chance from the first. The rowing of the Oxford crew astonished even their warmest supporters. The last year's defeat of Oxford is thus wiped off in the most triumphant manner.

The following were the crews:—

OXFORD.

			st.	lb	s.
1	H. F. BAXTER	Brazenose	10	12	
2	R. F. CLARKE	St John's	11	13	
3	C. G. LANE[1]	Ch. Ch.	11	9	
4	V. LAWLESS	Balliol	12	3	
5	G. MORRISON	Balliol	13	1	
6	R. W. RISLEY[1]	Exeter	11	2	
7	G. THOMAS	Balliol	11	4	
str.	J. ARKELL[1]	Pembroke	10	12	
cox.	A. J. ROBARTS	Ch. Ch.	9	1	
	Average of crew		11	8¾	

CAMBRIDGE.

			st.	lb	s.
1	N. ROYDS	1st Trinity	10	6	
2	H. J. CHAYTOR	Jesus	10	13	
3	A. L. SMITH[1]	1st Trin.	11	11	
4	D. DARROCH[1]	1st Trin.	12	4	
5	H. WILLIAMS[1]	Lady Margt.	12	6	
6	R. L. LLOYD[1]	Magdalene	11	9	
7	G. A. PALEY	Lady Margt.	11	7	
str.	J. HALL[1]	Magdalene	10	2	
cox.	J. T. MORLAND	1st Trin.	9	0	
	Average of crew		11	5½	

I may state on excellent authority that the Cambridge boat took in a great deal of water going down to her place and started in much the roughest water and kept too far out. She was nearly full at Hammersmith Bridge. The steamers kept too near but were never ahead and never gave the boats any

[1] Were in the crew of 1858.

swell; they were all astern or abreast. The account from the *Times* was clearly written by some one who knew nothing about rowing. It is evident bosh to say that the "accident in no way influenced the result of the race."

The accident, if such it may be called, commenced to take place as soon as the crew pushed from shore, and may I think be considered as the sole cause of the result. For a finer crew I believe never left Cambridge, and their pluck and power were amply shown by the glorious struggle they made when in such hopeless circumstances.

All the papers unite in condemning the conduct of the steamers. The *Field* says:

> We cannot but express our unqualified disgust at the conduct of those who commanded the steamboats, in keeping their craft so close upon the Cambridge gentlemen. We are confident that this must have not only intimidated the rowers, but also greatly impeded their progress. The only exceptions were in the Venus, Jupiter, River Queen, Waverley, and two other boats, the names of which we did not notice; but the management of all the others, not excepting even that of the umpire, was greatly to be condemned, and if again persisted in will perhaps drive away all University matches from the London water.

BIOGRAPHICAL NOTICES.

H. F. BAXTER, graduated 1860; ordained 1861; curate of St Thomas', Scarborough, 1861—63. curate of Bushbury.

R. F. CLARKE, graduated, 1860. Scholar and Fellow of St John's College. Joined the Roman communion and, having been obliged to leave his own college, has migrated to Trinity.

Hon. V. F. LAWLESS. Now Baron Cloncurry, educated at Eton and Balliol. Captain in Kildare Militia, 1860.

G. MORRISON, 2nd Class Lit. Hum. 1862; J. P. for Wiltshire. Has proved himself one of the most, if not the most, successful of trainers of eight-oared crews, having had the training of most of the last nine victorious Oxford crews. Is now engaged in training the Cambridge crew.

G. THOMAS (now Treherne), graduated 1861. A solicitor in London.

A. J. ROBARTS, graduated 1859.

N. ROYDS, graduated 1859; ordained 1861. Curate of Woodford, Notts. 1861; P.C. of Moggerhanger, Beds., 1863-64. Rector of Little Barford, St Neots, Beds., 1864.

H. J. CHAYTOR, graduated 1861.

G. A. PALEY, graduated as Senior Optime 1860.

J. T. MORLAND, graduated 1861.

Henley Regatta.

The following is from the Oxford Book:

"When it appeared that the Cambridge eight would enter for the G. C. Cup, *hoping* to meet the Oxford eight, it was immediately determined by the O.U.B.C. to send a crew and show the world that the result of the match in April at Putney was not entirely owing to the weather. Unfortunately the two Universities did not meet, for the prize was gallantly carried from the grasp of both by the London Rowing Club: yet it was sufficiently shown that had the light blue been matched with the dark, the honour of Oxford might have been safely entrusted to the crew that represented her at Henley in 1859."

The Steward's Cup was won by III. Trinity, who beat the London Rowing Club. The winning crew were: 1. R. Beaumont, 2. Collins, 3. Ingham, str. Holland, cox. T. Gaskell.

This is the last occasion on which a University crew has contended at Henley, and many University oars, I believe, think and hope that it will long remain so. It is thought that the Universities are at a considerable disadvantage; because weight, which is necessary over the long course, is rather an encumbrance at Henley. Over the former, "a good big man is better than a good little man," but it seems that this is not the case at Henley. I cannot but think however that part of the deterioration of University Rowing, which has, so say our seniors, set in of late years, is due to the unwillingness of the University Boat Clubs to measure their strength with outsiders. Surely the same causes which operated to raise them to the highest rank amongst amateur crews would also do much to keep them there. We have seen what a large share the Leander matches had in helping Cambridge to rise to the splendour of the unrivalled glory she had in 1839, 1840, 1841, when it was no vain-glorious boast in her to strike the medal with the motto: "Granta Victrix."[1]

Just as it is allowed that if the University Boat Race were discontinued, rowing at the Universities would wane, so it appears to me that by confining our rivalry to ourselves we are throwing away one means of preserving our excellence in it as an art.

Healthy emulation is the *sine quâ non* of maintaining excellence in any art. How futile would be the annual Exhibition at Burlington House, how inane the Royal Academy, had we not "breathing on the deathless canvass records of the years of old"! How hopeless again would be the task of the professor in guiding his pupil to excellence, if he could only point to these untold glories, and could not pit one student against another! How would the Student despair of imitating the living flesh of Rubens' goddesses or the bloom of "Murillo's soft boy-faces," and how would his hand fail when he contemplated the "poet's loveliest fancies starting into shape and substance at the touch of Raphael"! But emulation stirs up the innate powers, and little by little educates one and another, until perhaps one may perchance arise who will even rival these bygone worthies. So we have the traditions of former days; and as we have not got the living example to imitate, we need all the more to use to the utmost the means we have.

[1] p. 69.

1860.

There was a good deal of difficulty in arranging the preliminaries of this race. In the October term Mr J. Hall of Magdalene, who was President of the C.U.B.C., sent the usual challenge to Mr G. Morrison, the President of the O.U.B.C., to row some time in the "week before Passion week." This was of course accepted, and the race was fixed for Friday, March 30. Soon after the commencement of the Lent term, however, Mr Morrison called Mr Hall's attention to the fact that the tide was very inconvenient on Friday, and proposed Saturday. The Cambridge men also found that an examination, which had been lately instituted at Trinity College, and which was a necessary stepping-stone to the degree, was fixed for Wednesday and Thursday, the 28th and 29th of March. Mr Hall consequently suggested that as an alteration was to be made, it would be better to have the race fixed for Easter Monday. "Now this," said Mr Morrison, "would entail upon us the necessity of being at Putney more than a fortnight, and besides would have kept us in training through Passion week, which would have set the Dons against us. Consequently I refused to consent to Easter Monday." Mr Hall next endeavoured, in order to make the situation more nearly equal for both sides, to have a stipulation made that neither crew should practise at Putney before the race. Mr Morrison replied "that the challenge came from Cambridge, and was accepted by Oxford to row at such a time and such a place; by such conditions only were they bound; that Cambridge might withdraw the challenge if they thought fit, but in doing so they alone would have to bear the blame." *Bell's Life* says:

"Mr Morrison as President was bound to the interests of his University, and it was not for him to throw a chance away, however he may have regretted such seeming want of generosity. Cambridge had made a false move in the game, and the consequences rested with her. Mr Hall, however, was not the man to withdraw a challenge once given, how careless soever he might have been in its wording. So like a brave but desperate chief he replied that on the day appointed he and his crew would be there—practice or no practice he would be there to give all points that Oxford were contented to accept. But the Gordian knot was to be severed by an unexpected stroke. Whether the immersion at the last race had suddenly raised rowing to take rank among the *in-duck-tive* sciences we know not; but certain it is that the Master of Trinity stepped down from his high place to take it kindly by the hand, and by suspending the standing orders at once smoothed away all difficulty, and left the Trinity men free to leave Cambridge with the rest. This exceptional recognition [of rowing]...... shows that the long list of distinguished oarsmen who have obtained University honours, together with the general beneficial results to the community conferred by Christian muscularity, have not passed unheeded. We have said 'exceptional' because it cannot be expected, nor would it be fitting, that such cases should be set up as precedents to be acted upon hereafter, but rather as a warning to future *officials* to take well their vantage ground before they enter on a treaty."

"Let us now turn to the active proceedings on the water."

The crew selected from the two trial eights at Oxford was as follows: 1 McQueen, 2 Raikes,

3 Somerset, 4 Young, 5 G. Morrison, 6 Baxter, 7 Strong, str. Norsworthy. In the Lent term other men were tried but found unworthy in various respects, and as will be seen some of these were changed. It was thought that Norsworthy was not suited to the important place of stroke, so Risley who rowed in that place the year before at Henley Regatta was asked to do so again; and, after some difficulty arising from his father's objections, actually took his seat as stroke of the Oxford crew of 1860 when the boat went into training on Feb. 23. Halsey took Somerset's place, and after that no more changes were made in the crew up to the day of the race.

At Cambridge the formation of a crew, and consequently its practice, was delayed somewhat later than usual. The serious business of selection was not entered upon until Saturday, Feb. 25th, when two eights were manned for that purpose. The crew was considered fixed on Feb. 28th, when they commenced training with the same crew as that which rowed in the race, with the exception of Heathcote, who succeeded to Wailes on the latter's showing signs of indisposition. They kept rowing to Bottisham with occasional visits to Ely until March 17th, when they got into a new boat built for them by Searle, and then they kept rowing over the so-called four mile course from Jesus sluice to Baitsbite. The stream was, as at Oxford, somewhat stronger than usual, but even allowing for this, their "times" over the distance were so extraordinary that it was no wonder they left Cambridge full of confidence themselves and prime favourites with their University. The last three days they rowed the course in 20 min. 10 sec. These may be compared with those of the crew of 1852, which once only on a "very calm and favourable day" did the distance in 20 min. 50 sec.

Oxford were the favourites from various causes till the crews arrived at Putney, when Cambridge so impressed people with a favourable idea of their speed that the betting dropped nearly to even. The Oxford men arrived at Putney on Saturday, March 24th, Cambridge on Monday the 26th. That day both boats went over the course, Cambridge on a strong ebb and with a fair wind, in 21 m. 20 s.; Oxford on good flood tide but against a light wind, in 21 m. 52 s.

There was a general anticipation of a very close race; and such it really turned out to be. The crowds that attended the race were immense. Saturday, March 31st, the day of the race, was drizzly and windy, but did not cause much rough water.

"We anticipated a good race," says the *Field*, "nor were we disappointed: we do indeed really pity the true rowing man of the past or present day who was absent from the match, and whose feelings of excitement, caused by the description of such a contest, must be mingled with those of regret that he was not a witness thereof.

"Almost simultaneously, at a quarter-past eight, both the eight-oared boats destined to be so closely tested were launched into the Thames—that of the

Cantabs from Simmons's (late Searle and Son's) yard, and that of the Oxonians from the boat-house of the London Rowing Club. The former is a new boat, 57½ feet in length, built expressly for the occasion by Edward Searle, of Stangate, Lambeth; the other boat, built last year by Matthew Taylor, of Newcastle-on-Tyne, is some 3½ feet shorter than Searle's, and is the same ship which so safely carried Oxford to victory last year. Cambridge was first to push off and paddle down to their station, the outer one from the Middlesex side, at the Putney Aqueduct; Oxford in about one minute after followed and took their position by choice (they having won the toss) on the Middlesex side, to leeward of their determined adversaries. This choice of station under ordinary circumstances would have been correct, but was on this occasion a mistake, because the tide had made its mark, and therefore was either still or making down stream; besides, the wind was blowing hard on the Middlesex shore, and thus caused a nasty popple to rebound from the bank. The stern of each boat was held level by men in two boats moored respectively to the third and fourth piers of the aqueduct, from the Middlesex shore—we say the sterns were level, because the Cambridge, being a longer boat, her stem was a few feet in advance. Mr Edward Searle was the starter.

"For the first time in a University Race, there was a false start, for no sooner was the word given than an ugly old wherry came creeping across the bows of the boats, and had not Mr Searle with the greatest presence of mind instantly by voice and gesture re-called them, most unpleasant consequences might have been the result. A few moments sufficed for them to get back to their places, and at exactly 28 minutes past eight the word 'Off' was finally given. Neither started so well as the first time, and Cambridge got a slight lead; but Oxford soon settled down to their rowing in good form, at a very quick stroke, getting that great pace on which was noticed in their practice. Before arriving off the Star and Garter the quick rowing of Oxford had brought them up level, and they continued so till off the Club boat-house. To get that far Oxford was compelled to be taken close in the

Middlesex shore, under the sterns of two barges, very improperly left moored right in, and swung by the wind right across, the course. On coming out above these craft, being about a quarter of a mile from the start, Cambridge were taken rather too much over to the south, while Oxford very properly came nearer the centre of the river, gradually going in advance, being at the half-mile post a quarter of their length ahead, and rounding Craven Cottage point first by nearly half a length. This advantage they kept gradually increasing (their rowing now being most excellent, in perfect time, and with beautiful uniformity); Cambridge, though rowing most pluckily, with great vigour and length of stroke, did not catch the water so well at the first grip, nor in very good time, so that it looked as though the Oxonians were winning; and many bets were accordingly offered upon the latter with but few takers. Just below the Crab Tree, the Dark Blue was almost clear of its antagonist, and it appeared as though the Oxford coxswain, thinking to be quite clear in a few more strokes, steered out towards his opponents, ready to take their water on the first opportunity; but the experienced eye of Mr Morland at once detected his rival's object: he called upon his stroke and crew for a spurt, and Mr Hall did spurt most admirably, as he in many a race had done before, and, being nobly followed by his crew, it was observed by all that the quickened rowing of the Light Blue oars was fast drawing their boat up alongside that of Oxford, who likewise spurted in their turn. After passing the Crab Tree both boats steered badly, getting too near the Surrey shore, so that Oxford, who was in dangerous proximity to her opponents, had to turn her nose outwards in order to give Cambridge room to pass the pier at Hammersmith Bridge, under the centre arch of which both had agreed to steer. A fine race now took place to get first through Hammersmith Bridge. So even was the race that at the Soapworks the oars rowed respectively by Messrs Risley and Fairbairn came into contact, and the same thing again occurred before reaching Hammersmith Bridge, Mr Risley's oar being on one occasion knocked for the moment out of his grasp. Time, 9 min. 28 sec. from the start.

"Here Cambridge drew on their antagonists and, notwithstanding a most splendid spurt on the part of Mr Risley, passed Hammersmith Bridge 3 ft. in advance.

"The lead which Cambridge had now obtained was not, however, to be wrested from them by the admirable and plucky rowing of their antagonists; and, although it was but a lead of a few feet, that was a considerable advantage, for they were on the side of the river whence blew the wind, and on which were the points to be rounded before entering into the two next reaches, namely, Chiswick and Corney. In rounding into the first-named reach Cambridge increased the lead to half a length, but Oxford appeared on rowing past Chiswick Ferry to have crept up a little; however, on rounding the second point and getting into Corney Reach, Cambridge went still further in advance, and in rowing up to Barnes continued to gain gradually, they both steering under the Middlesex arch of the railway-bridge, the Light Blue oars first by a boat's length and a half. Immediately after, Oxford made a splendid spurt and slightly drew up, but being met with a corresponding one from Cambridge, they again dropped back, not, however, resigning this grand struggle till the very goal, the remainder of the distance being accomplished by a succession of the most plucky spurts on the part of both that were ever made at the conclusion of a race of such bitter and long-continued punishment. The great power of the Cambridge men kept them in advance, and they passed the Ship Tavern at Mortlake the brave winners by a length and a half only, having rowed the distance—one-half with little better than no tide, and the other half against the young ebb, making it equal to about five miles and a half with an ordinary tide—in 26 min. 5 sec. The number of strokes rowed per minute averaged by Cambridge 38 to 41, by Oxford 42 to 44. Some say that Oxford at times rowed as many as 46, but this is open to doubt.

"Immediately after the race the Oxford crew landed at Mortlake, and returned by land to Putney. Cambridge, after lying on their oars for some five or ten minutes, paddled back through the crowd of steamers and other boats amidst loud and repeated cheering.

"Later in the morning both crews as usual repaired to the domicile of the hospitable Mr Phillips, The Cedars, Mortlake, where they were entertained at breakfast; and in the evening they again met at dinner, in accordance with their usual custom, at the Albion Tavern, in Aldersgate-street, City.

"The Thames Subscription Club held their dinner on the following Tuesday. None of the Cambridge crew could be there, but the Oxford men were, and the toast of the 'University Boat Clubs' was responded to by Mr Baxter, Sec. of the O.U.B.C."

The crews were:

CAMBRIDGE CREW.

			st.	lbs.
1	S. HEATHCOTE	1st Trinity	10	3
2	H. J. CHAYTOR[1]	Jesus	11	4
3	D. INGLES	1st Trinity	10	13
4	J. S. BLAKE	Corpus	12	9
5	M. COVENTRY	Trin. Hall	12	8
6	B. N. CHERRY	Clare Hall	12	1
7	A. H. FAIRBAIRN[1]	2nd Trinity	11	10
str.	J. HALL[1] (captain)	Magdalene	10	4
cox.	J. T. MORLAND[1]	Trinity	9	0
	Average of crew		11	7¾

OXFORD CREW.

			st.	lbs.
1	J. N. MACQUEEN	University	11	7
2	G. NORSWORTHY	Magdalene	11	0
3	T. F. HALSEY	Ch. Ch.	11	11
4	J. F. YOUNG	Corpus	12	8
5	G. MORRISON[1] (captain)	Balliol	12	13
6	H. F. BAXTER[1]	Brasenose	11	7
7	C. I. STRONG	University	11	2
str.	R. W. RISLEY[1]	Exeter	11	8
cox.	A. J. ROBARTS[1]	Ch. Ch.	9	9
	Average of crew		11	10½

[1] Were in the crew of 1859.

The Oxford President says; "Our course of training was the same as last year, and a better one could not be wished for. As to the cause of our defeat, all I can say is they were a stronger crew than we were. For on the day of the race we were in as good condition and as perfect as at any time in our practice, though one or two of us were not so good as might be wished; and before concluding I must record our best thanks to J. Arkell, without whose assistance we should have been much worse than we were.

G. MORRISON,
President."

BIOGRAPHICAL NOTICES.

S. HEATHCOTE, graduated 1861.

D. INGLES, B.A., graduated 1861; late curate of Stoke-upon-Trent, now of Cookham Dean, Maidenhead.

J. S. BLAKE, B.A., graduated 1861; ordained 1862. Curate of Felixstowe, Suffolk, '62—'64; Heigham, Norfolk, '65—'66; St Jude's, Portsea, 1866.

M. COVENTRY, graduated 1862, as Senior Optime.

B. N. CHERRY, graduated as Junior Optime, 1862. Ordained 1863. Curate of Grimley with Hallow, dioc. of Worcester.

J. N. MAC QUEEN, graduated 1861. Emigrated to India as an indigo planter.

G. NORSWORTHY, M.A., graduated 1861. Lives near Maidenhead.

T. F. HALSEY, educated at Eton and Christ Church; graduated 1861. Magistrate for Herts. and the liberty of St Albans. Captain of Herts. Yeomanry. Of Gaddesden Park, Herts.

J. F. YOUNG, graduated 1860. Died of typhus fever in London.

C. ISHAM STRONG, graduated 1860. Went into the army.

Henley Regatta.

No Oxford boats put in an appearance at the Regatta this year, but though the Cambridge men had been gone down more than a fortnight First Trinity were there to dispute the possession of the Grand Challenge with London, who it will be remembered beat both the Universities the year before. First Trinity won the race after a most plucky struggle on the part of London. First Trinity[1] also won the Stewards' Cup; beating the Londoners, who gave in as soon as they were "collared."

The President of the O.U.B.C., after giving in detail the reasons why Oxford did not send in a crew, goes on to say, "No praise is too great for the First Trinity. They were perfect, better than most University crews; but they had only attained this perfection by the most constant practice together, and hard work. Oh! that some of our

---

[1] This four-oar was a treat to see as it rowed down to its post. No crew that has gone from Cambridge since 1860 has been so "lively" in getting forward as this 1st Trinity crew.

colleges would follow their example, and shew a little more spirit in them than they do at present.

G. MORRISON,
President."

The Trinity crew were:

		st.	lbs.
1	G. H. RICHARDS[1]	10	2
2	G. COX	10	12
3	H. S. WRIGHT	11	2
4	D. INGLES[1]	10	12
5	J. LYLE	11	12
6	T. E. BEAUMONT	11	12
7	S. HEATHCOTE[1]	10	1
str.	N. ROYDS[1]	10	10
cox.	J. T. MORLAND[1]	9	2
	Average of crew	10	$13\frac{1}{8}$

Royds, Ingles, Cox and Heathcote rowed respectively as stroke, three, two, and bow in the four.

1861.

Neither crew appeared on Putney water till the Monday before the race, which was fixed for Saturday, March 16. On Tuesday Cambridge raced the London twelve over the course, but did not pass them till just before Barnes Bridge. Time over the course, the weather being very stormy, 24 m. 10 s.

Oxford also rowed up over the course about half an hour after this race, their time being 23 min. 38 sec.

On Wednesday morning Cambridge had another hard race, this time against the following picked eight of watermen: 1, H. Phelps; 2, G. Driver; 3, F.

---

[1] These gentlemen were members of a University crew either before or after this time.

Kelley; 4, T. Mackinney; 5, J. Mackinney; 6, T. Pocock; 7, G. Hammerton; 8, H. Kelley; J. Phelps, cox. The watermen received two good lengths' start. The race was rowed from the Ship at Mortlake down to Putney, with a strong wind and tide. The watermen at once increased their lead to four or five lengths, and though on nearing the Soapworks, Cambridge on the side of the turn, and having a good tide under them, began to draw up, and continued gradually to do so to the finish, the watermen beat them by nearly a length and a half. Time, 21 min. 12 sec. Oxford also rowed the course down from Mortlake; time, 22½ min.

On Thursday morning Cambridge were the first out, and practised starting several times in coming down. Soon after them, the same crew of watermen that beat them on Wednesday raced the Oxford men down stream. The watermen received about two lengths' start, besides having the better station (Middlesex), and at first they drew still further in advance. The Oxford men overhauled them at Chiswick, and were five lengths ahead at Hammersmith; and won by a ¼ mile; time, 20 min. 35 sec. There was a strong wind blowing favourably in nearly every reach.

Friday morning both were out at the same time; Cambridge rowed hard down from Hammersmith to Putney, their rowing being very good, and their swing and time much more uniform than on any other occasion that we have seen. They were just under 8 minutes doing the distance, and rowed forty-two strokes per minute. Oxford merely rowed up to just below the Crab Tree, and practised starting. They seldom rowed more than thirty-eight strokes to the minute.

Every time the two eights were seen out rowing the Oxonians became stronger favourites, and certainly such was fully warranted by their appearance as a crew, as all rowed in admirable form and with beautiful uniformity. The Cantabs, however, were remarked as rowing with considerable power, and thereby retained many staunch supporters.

In consequence of the prevailing south-westerly strong winds, and quantity of land-water coming down the river, it was decided that the race should be rowed before eleven o'clock on Saturday, nearly an hour earlier than anticipated.

Twelve or thirteen steamboats, many of them private, and some largely patronised by ladies, were chartered to accompany the race as usual; numbers of boats were also afloat on the course between Putney and Mortlake.

About a quarter to eleven both the boats, which had been built expressly for the occasion, that of Cambridge by Searle, and that of Oxford by Salter, were launched respectively from Simmons's and the London Club boat-houses. Without the least delay the crews took their stations, Oxford in the centre of the river; Cambridge, having won the toss, some thirty yards on the Middlesex side of them; Mr Searle, the starter, being in a boat between the two, ready to give the signal to start.

As near as could be, they took the first stroke together, and then Cambridge, being quicker in their rowing than Oxford, appeared to get to their full speed directly, but for several strokes neither obtained any advance in position of the other. Just before reaching the Star and Garter, Cambridge showed a slight lead, and their stroke then quickened into a tremendous spurt, the effect of which placed about half of their boat in advance. Oxford had now got into their best rowing, and were working in that admirable regularity of action which proclaims the perfection of a crew. Off the Duke's Head tavern the bursting pace of the Cantabs had drawn their boat still more ahead, but in a few more strokes that advantage was lost by the error of their coxswain, who instead of keeping straight up the river suddenly sheered off to starboard, going from outside of a small yacht to inside another one riding in a direct line not fifty yards above the first. This sudden double use of the rudder—first to go in and then to get straight again—of course checked the speed of the boat most materially, so that when the two eights came off the Club boat-house clear of the craft moored above Putney, Oxford had a lead of a few feet. The long rowing of the latter now showed its superiority over the quick distressing stroke of its opponent, and gradually did Oxford creep further ahead till just below Craven Cottage, where a steamboat (Citizen D), lying in the course right ahead of them, shamefully put her paddle-wheels in motion, and caused a most awkward rolling swell. Into this the Oxford coxswain could not avoid taking his boat without fouling the oars of the Cambridge crew, of whom his boat was then not quite clear. As the swell rolled over the canvass of the bows of the Oxford boat it of course threw the crew out very much. During this interruption Cambridge had drawn up slightly, but in less than half a dozen strokes afterwards the rowing of the Oxford crew was as regular as ever, and Cambridge again steering badly by hugging the shore so close on rounding Craven Cottage point as to get into slack water, the former drew their boat clear in advance, and continued steadily increasing their lead up the remainder of the course. At the Crab Tree Oxford led by nearly three lengths, and at Hammersmith Bridge by six lengths, which they reached in 8 minutes 50 seconds from the start. Cambridge here was 25 seconds behind Oxford. On nearing Chiswick a sailing barge was standing straight up the reach, for which the Cambridge boat appeared to be steered as if intending to bump her, until almost near enough to effect the bump, when Mr Gaskell suddenly sheered clear of her, but on the wrong side, going to leeward, instead of to windward on the side of the point. During this Oxford of course had improved their lead, and they passed Chiswick about 10 lengths ahead. In Corney Reach, Oxford was slightly put out by a barge, their coxswain in his turn going on the wrong side of it. Barnes Railway Bridge was reached by the leading boat twelve or fourteen lengths ahead, and in 19 minutes 45 seconds after the start. This lead they slightly increased to the Ship tavern at Mortlake, and passed the flag boat easy winners by 14 or 16 lengths, and 47 seconds ahead of their opponents: their time in doing the entire distance being 23 minutes 30 seconds, with a very bad tide and a head wind in the latter part of the course. As they rowed by the steamers to return both boats were loudly cheered, though not with that enthusiasm which the crews of last year received after their gallant struggle.

Below are the names and weights:
OXFORD CREW.

			st.	lbs.
1	W. CHAMPNEYS	*Brasenose*	10	11
2	E. B. MERRIMAN	*Exeter*	10	1
3	H. E. MEDLICOTT	*Wadham*	12	4
4	W. ROBERTSON	*Wadham*	11	3
5	G. MORRISON[1]	*Balliol*	12	8
6	A. R. POOLE	*Trinity*	12	3
7	H. G. HOPKINS	*Corpus*	10	8
str.	W. M. HOARE	*Exeter*	10	10
cox.	S. O. B. RISDALE	*Wadham*	9	0
	Average of crew		11	4¼

CAMBRIDGE CREW.

			st.	lbs.
1	G. H. RICHARDS	*Trinity*	10	4
2	H. J. CHAYTOR[1]	*Jesus*	11	3
3	W. H. TARLETON	*St John's*	11	0
4	J. S. BLAKE[1]	*Corpus*	12	10
5	M. COVENTRY[1]	*Trin. Hall*	13	3
6	H. H. COLLINGS	*Trinity*	10	11
7	R. U. P. FITZGERALD	*Trin. Hall*	11	2
str.	J. HALL[1]	*Magdalen*	10	6
cox.	T. K. GASKELL	*3rd Trinity*	8	3
	Average of crew		11	4⅛

In the Cambridge crew Mr Coventry was the captain, and in the Oxford Mr Morrison.

REMARKS.

As the winners, let us speak first of the Oxonians. The more praise is due to these gentlemen for being young oarsmen, and not only for having obtained a great victory, but also for the formation of a crew which was one of the most perfect eights that ever rowed. It is somewhat strange that such admirable style and uniformity should have been obtained by these gentlemen, because no one individual undertook

---

[1] These gentlemen were in the crew of 1860.

the task of "coaching" them in their training. They were, however, occasionally looked after by Mr Baxter, of last year's crew, and Mr Lane of the 1859 and '58 crews. When watching the crew at work they strongly reminded us of that splendid eight sent to Putney by the O.U.B.C. as their representatives in 1857, and which attained a similarly easy victory. If any deserve more praise than another in this year's crew, we would award it to Messrs. Hoare, Morrison, and Champneys. When this crew first began to prepare themselves for this match, they did so under some disadvantages, being all inexperienced, with the exception of their captain, and having the discouraging fact of knowing that their opponents would muster several of the victorious crew of last year. Their University, therefore, has every cause to be highly proud of possessing such a crew of accomplished oarsmen.

As regards the Cantabs, we are of opinion that they formed a crew quite up to the average, their glaring fault being want of uniformity, which we believe to have been greatly caused by their rowing in a boat the work[1] of which was not suited to their style of rowing. Messrs. Richards, Chaytor, and Fitzgerald, were decidedly the best oarsmen in the crew; while, though the rowing of Messrs. Hall and Coventry was good, we do not consider it equal to last year's.

The Oxford Book, having three printed accounts of the race from the newspapers, goes on to say:

"The accounts given in the papers on the foregoing pages are tolerably correct. That of the *Field* is the best, except that it tries to make out that there was a race up to Hammersmith, whereas the race was over at Craven Point. But before saying anything more of the race itself, let

---

[1] The word "work" here means the arrangement of the rowlocks where the "force" is applied. Thus a person is said to be seated "too near *his work*," when he is sitting too near *the point of application of his work*.

us see what had been done before the glorious 23rd of March. Early in the October term it was decided at a captains' meeting to send a challenge to Cambridge, though many persons thought that it was folly to do so, so bad did our prospects look: of the eight of '60 only Mr Halsey and myself remained, and the eights of the previous summer had been so excessively bad that no new oars had been found. However the challenge was sent and accepted, and measures were taken to supply the lack of men by placing the Fours earlier than usual, so as to give about four weeks for the practice of the Trial Eights. In these no old oars were allowed to row, and out of the men sent by each college the strongest men were selected, for good rowing was not to be got, but luckily there was plenty of good raw material. At the beginning of the Lent term a crew was formed of the following men: Carr, Robertson (Wadh.), Poole, Merriman, French, Medlicott, Hoare, and Champneys. These were selected from the Trial Eights, neither Mr Halsey nor myself rowing at first, but being employed in coaching. After about a fortnight Mr Carr refused to row, and Mr Hopkins was taken out of the Corpus Torpid to supply his place, and soon afterwards Poole and Robertson were removed to make way for Halsey and myself, and we began training on *Wednesday, February* 13."

[Here follows the log of the crew, in which the chief point worthy of remark is the shortness of the times in which the long course was done. They were 23 m. 30 s.; 20 m. 30 s.; 21 m. 30 s.; 23 m. 30 s.; 21 m. 30 s.; 21 m.; 20 m. 35 s.; 21 m. 3 s. Average 21 m. 38½ s. At Putney they were 23 m. 30 s.; 24 m. 30 s.; 21 m. 45 s.; 20 m. 35 s.; 23 m. 30 s.; including the race. Average 22 m. 46 s.]

"Our training differed in many respects from any before described in these books, so a longer account than usual may be pardoned. In the morning the old system of a mile run before chapel was dropped, and a walk of ½ a mile substituted, which was found a great improvement. Breakfast of chops and steaks, bread-and-butter and tea. Lunch ½ a pint of beer and bread-and-butter or a sandwich, or glass of sherry and biscuits, which suited some men better. At half-past two started for our row; after which we always had a run for 1 mile or ½ a mile, in the earlier part of training usually 1 mile. A clean jersey for rowing in every day was insisted upon. For dinner we had four days a week beef and mutton, on the others fowls, fish (on Sundays), and once or twice a light pudding. We were always careful to have the same beer; 1 pint every day. After dinner two glasses of port, never allowed large glasses, but occasionally after hard work an extra glass. For supper a bason of gruel, or a cup of chocolate; and to bed at 10.30 sharp. We rowed twice to Wallingford, about 20 miles down stream, which had a decidedly good effect. Also during the week at Putney we used to run for two or three bursts of 100 yards each in our morning walk, which also we found beneficial. So much for our training, which brought the crew to the post in as good a condition as any crew ever was. During our practice Mr Finch of Wadh. sometimes rode down, but (not being a University oar) could hardly do much for us, and once or twice Mr Baxter and Lane (but the turning point in the formation of the crew was Mr Warre's visit on March 21st). So that we laboured under the disadvantages of hardly any coaching from the bank and of having only one old oar in the boat, so that our winning must be attributed to the willing patience of the crew and to the great strength and size of its members, for it was one of the biggest crews ever sent from Oxford.

G. MORRISON,
President."

1862.

In the October term of 1861 Cambridge for the first time adopted the plan of having trial eights. They were rowed as a time race over the usual racing course from Little Bridge to the Railway Bridge.

Immediately on the commencement of the Lent term of 1862 two trial crews were sent down the river under the superintendence of Mr Richards the President and Mr Collings the Secretary of the U.B.C., and at length the following crew went into training on March 10th. 1, J. G. Buchanan; 2, J. G. Chambers; 3, E. Sanderson; 4, H. H.

Collings; 5, B. P. Gregson; 6, R. U. P. Fitzgerald; 7, R. B. Ransford; 8, G. H. Richards; cox. F. H. Archer.

The log of the crew presents little more than a series of changes which must have had a bad effect on the members thereof. The times which they took to go over the Cambridge course were good: on one occasion they rowed from lock to lock in 19 m. 9 s., which was the shortest time in which it had ever been done.

At Oxford Mr Morrison the President had serious difficulties to deal with. At the beginning of the term it was thought that there would be four old men in the boat, but eventually only one of them was able to take his place. The men from the trial eights were in a very rough condition. " Hence men began to despair of our winning the race; and we were usually advised to write to Cambridge and say that we could not get up a crew. Let no future captain ever despair, for if matters do not look well few will encourage him, while most will abuse him, but let him make up his mind to depend entirely on himself, and never to be influenced in the least by what is said of him or what he hears. * * * * It will be hardly necessary to give an account of the various changes in the places of different men, for they were made for reasons purely connected with trying to get some form into the boat, by trying to counterbalance one man's faults against another's; for instance, if one man rowed it out too much at the end, to put a man behind him who did not finish his stroke." The following hints are given "to any one who may find himself expected to lick Cambridge with little experience and with no one to assist him." " In the first place never mind what is said about you : next recollect that the man who appears the best oar in October is often not the man to choose. Take a good big man as early as you can and lick him into shape. Above all fix on three or four men (never mind how they row) early in November at least, and stick to them, and don't bother yourself because not more than one or two old oars can row; old oars often do more harm than good. Again, the best oar is not always the best man to have in a crew, especially if he is likely to make a row in a crew. Cambridge lost last year very much owing to this. Again, if you want really good form, you must work the College crews in the summer term and make the committee do the same. ... Next, as to training; lay down certain rules and never let a man break them in the very least thing. Large wine-glasses and such things will lose you a race sooner than anything else. Be very sure that you know your men. Experience has taught the writer of this that *all men cannot be trusted* ...

G. MORRISON,
President."

The *Field*, after giving an account of the practice on the Thames, says :

The time of the rival crews both up and down was taken over and over again, the result showing that there were but a few seconds' difference in the two boats. The seats of the coxswains in both eights were during the week preceding the race shifted further aft upon the canvas, as the boats were too much by the head; that is to say, the steerers were not sufficiently heavy to keep the sterns depressed to their proper draught of water.

The following account is from *Bell's Life*:

The morning of Saturday, the 12th of April, the day of the race, was fine, but excessively cold, the wind blowing a smart breeze from the N.N.E., although the sun shone brilliantly.

J. W. Chitty, esq., of Exeter College, Oxford, acted as umpire, while the duties of starter were undertaken by Mr Edward Searle, of Stangate.

The two eight-oared cutters were in the water at the same time, a few minutes before 12, and the following crews took their places in them, namely :—

OXFORD.

			st.	lbs.
1	W. B. WOODGATE	*Brasenose*	11	6
2	O. S. WYNNE	*Chr. Ch.*	11	3
3	W. B. R. JACOBSON	*Chr. Ch.*	12	4
4	R. E. L. BURTON	*Chr. Ch.*	12	5
5	A. MORRISON	*Balliol*	12	8½
6	A. R. POOLE[1]	*Trinity*	12	5
7	C. R. CARR	*Wadham*	11	2½
str.	W. M. HOARE[1]	*Exeter*	11	1
cox.	F. HOPWOOD	*Chr. Ch.*	7	3
	Average of crew		11	11⅜

CAMBRIDGE.

1	P. F. GORST	*(Lady Marg.)*	10	4
2	J. G. CHAMBERS	*3rd Trinity*	11	8
3	E. SANDERSON	*Corpus*	10	10
4	W. C. SMYLY	*1st Trinity*	11	5

[1] Rowed in 1861.

			st.	lbs.
5	R. U. P. FITZGERALD[1] *Trin. Hall*		11	3
6	H. H. COLLINGS[1] ... ...*3rd Trinity*		11	2
7	J. G. BUCHANAN ....*1st Trinity*		10	12
str.	G. H. RICHARDS[1] ...... *1st Trinity*		10	5
cox.	F. H. ARCHER............*Corpus*		5	2
	Average of crew		10	13⅛

The Oxonians, who had won the choice of stations, took the Middlesex side, an advantage, as the wind lay. Very little time was wasted at the start, the rival eights being at the post barely 10 minutes altogether. They were soon alongside, and at 8 m. past 12 Mr Searle gave the order "to go."

Cambridge, catching the water first, obtained a momentary lead. Immediately afterwards the Oxonians, pulling a steadier stroke, were up with them, and they rowed a fine race dead level opposite the Star and Garter; when foot by foot the Oxford boat went in front till they led by half their length. The Cantabs held them well till the Point, but in their great anxiety for rapidity the rowing was rather wild; and the Oxonians gradually increased their lead, till they went clear of their opponents at Craven. The Cantabs here settled down to their work, but failed to near the Oxonians, who still increased their lead. Off the Soapworks Mr Richards put on a fine spurt, but it was rendered unavailing, for by this time they were so far astern that the steamboats began to surround them, and when this misfortune happens to the sternmost boat in a match it is well known that all chance of even making a decent race by any recovery of lost ground is completely gone. The greatest offender was "Citizen J," who at one time was actually ahead of Cambridge. Under Hammersmith Bridge, reached at 10 m. 30 s. from the start, the Oxonians led by three lengths; and this lead they continued throughout, although the Cantabs rowed with great pluck. Off Chiswick they put on another very fine spurt, but it

---

[1] Rowed in 1861.

was too late, as the Oxonians, whose last mile was a splendid specimen of rowing, and their very best since their coming to London, had added two more in lengths to their lead : and at Barnes Bridge, reached in 21 m. 15 s., they led by more than a hundred yards ; and ultimately won by 20 strokes, or 30 seconds; having rowed the distance in 24 min. 40 sec. There was no tide, with a dead-noser through Barnes Elms Reach. The steering in both boats was good, as the difficulties were not few.

Of these two crews it is scarcely necessary to say more than that if they did not reach the consummate excellence of some which we have been accustomed to look back upon as the highest standard of form and beauty, they were yet a good average specimen of University rowing ; and while Oxford lacked somewhat the quick recovery and forward reach, Cambridge would have done well to have rowed a little deeper. The four after-oars of Oxford, especially Messrs. Poole and Hoare, were very good ; and in the Cambridge boat judges seem to have singled out Messrs. Gorst, Fitzgerald, and Buchanan, for especial praise.

Such is the account of the race in *Bell's Life*. The one in the *Field* is so different that I give it separately, for I could not combine the two so as to give a single account which should be consistent and still give the leading features of both reports.

On the word being given the oars of both crews took the water nearly at the same moment, but, one of the after oars in the Cambridge boat missing a stroke, the Oxford eight showed her bow slightly in front. Opposite the Star and Garter this advantage was increased to a third of a length, the leading crew rowing powerful strokes ; and off the London Rowing Club boat-house they were about three-quarters of a length in advance. Here the Cambridge boat was steered somewhat out of her course, being brought outside one of the craft that usually lie almost in every one's way, but this in no degree affected the result of the race, as it was patent to every one who was in the slightest degree acquainted with matters aquatic, that the Oxford must win, if they did not come to grief by the way. On going by Craven Cottage the Oxford boat was more than clear, and the Cambridge, coming in behind them, forced them, as it were, to take their water. Up to this point the Cantabs had rowed tolerably well, though short, but upon approaching the lumpy water they became somewhat unsteady. Crossing over just above Craven Cottage by a long shoot, the Oxford crew, who were very well steered throughout, passed under the Surrey arch of Hammersmith Bridge, upwards of four lengths ahead. The Cambridge crew were, as last year, taken through the centre arch of the bridge, considerably out of their true course, and it could not be urged in excuse that what they lost in distance they gained in strength of tide, for there was but little of that. Moreover the eddy of the westernmost pier is not the least on the river. From Hammersmith the Oxonians increased their lead, and won a very easy race by 35 seconds, or 25 strokes, doing the distance in 23 min. 30 sec. The time was quick, considering the bad tide and the foul wind in Barnes Elms Reach.

The winning crew rowed quite as well as in the latter part of their practice. They pulled their oars well through the water, though one or two of the forward men were, to our thinking, now and then a trifle shorter in the stroke than Mr Hoare. They rowed from thirty-nine to forty strokes a minute, which was much faster than on their first arrival at Putney, but yet not too quick to be effective. The oarsmen most deserving of mention are Messrs Hoare (who pulled very pluckily considering the state of his arm, and nearly all the way above Chiswick with one hand), Carr, Poole, Morrison, and Woodgate; and the coxswain is deserving of very great praise for the manner in which he handled the lines. We believe he has, previously to this race, piloted a winning Eton crew against their brethren of Westminster, between Putney and Chiswick Eyot. Mr Champneys would have taken an oar as last year, but his medical adviser would not allow it.

With respect to the Cambridge crew, we are compelled to say that their rowing in the race did not realise the expectations that were previously raised, and it fell far short of the form exhibited by them during their practice. It is true that a losing crew never appears to row as well as a winning boat, but still the stroke was too short and jerky, though there is no doubt they were somewhat incommoded by the rough water. One thing is certain, and that is, they were most shamefully used by the steamers, and especially by Citizen J. Most of the boats lay off Craven Cottage and the London boat-house, and many of them put their paddles in motion before the crews had passed, rendering the water very lumpy. Several of them kept too close upon the Cambridge boat up the Crab Tree Reach, and the captain of Citizen J is deserving of especial censure for his most disgraceful behaviour. It would be a thousand pities for the race to be driven away to other waters, but such is far from being improbable, if other measures fail to put a stop to this greatest of nuisances.

The steering of Mr Archer was very bad, independently of the mistake in taking the middle arch at Hammersmith, in relation to which we can only express our surprise that the president of the Cambridge University Boat Club should have consented again to follow the advice which was so loudly and so justly condemned last year. The oarsmen most deserving of mention are Messrs. Richards, Collings, and Fitzgerald.

Both boats were built by J. and S. Salter, of Oxford. The difference in the total weight of the two crews was nine stone, from which, deducting say two stone for the difference in the steersmen, there was seven stone more rowing weight in the Oxford crew than in the losing boat; a decided advantage, more especially in rough water. Good big men are, as a rule, better than good little men. The Oxonians have now won nine out of the nineteen matches that have been rowed. The majority of the races in which Oxford has been victorious have been won with ease; whereas the closest and most exciting matches have resulted in favour of Cambridge.

1863.

Mr Smyly was elected president of the C.U.B.C., Mr Hoare of the O.U.B.C., after the race of 1862.

There was nothing particular in the trial eights at either Oxford or Cambridge. The Oxford Book makes no mention whatever of the training or practice of the crew of 1863, nor does it even give a report of the race. The Cambridge Book only gives extracts from the *Field*. This course, too, I shall pursue.

The race was fixed for Saturday, March 28.

The rival crews arrived at Putney on the evening of Saturday, the 21st of March, both taking up their customary quarters. On Monday, about four o'clock in the afternoon, the Cambridge crew pulled gently down to the Aqueduct, and rowed the course hard with the flood, doing from thirty-seven to thirty-eight strokes a minute; time, 21 min. 44 sec. The Oxford crew about half an hour after rowed the course, doing thirty-five strokes a minute, and performing the distance from the Aqueduct to the Ship in 20 min. 57 sec. The men rowed well and with a better swing than their opponents, though there appeared hardly life enough in the boat; the time kept might also have been better.

On Tuesday morning both crews rowed up towards Hammersmith and returned; the Cambridge on this occasion made the questionable experiment of shifting a crew into a strange boat only four days before the race. They made use of this boat, which was built by Searle, in the afternoon, Mr T. S. Egan handling the lines in lieu of the regular coxswain. They pulled down a trifle below Putney Bridge, and then rowed over the course in 21 min. 31 sec., with a very good tide under them. The number of strokes varied considerably, ranging from thirty-five to thirty-nine over different parts of the course, and they certainly did not appear to go so well as on the previous day.

The Oxonians went out about half an hour previously, and rowed the course in much better form than the day before, pulling thirty-six strokes to the minute, and increasing the pace as they progressed up the river. The distance was compassed in 20 min. 37 sec.

On Wednesday morning the Oxonians raced a picked crew of watermen from the Ship at Mortlake to Putney Aqueduct. The latter received two lengths' start, and won by the same distance; time, 21 min. 16 sec. In the evening the Cambridge men rowed against a London Twelve-oar from Putney to Hammersmith, and beat them by two or three lengths; time, 8 min. 40 sec.

The following is a table of the time of the two boats during their practice, each having taken their own:

OXFORD.

	m.	s.
Monday.—Putney Aqueduct to Ship, Mortlake..	20	50
Tuesday.— Ditto ditto ..	20	35
Wednesday.—Ship to Putney	21	15
Thursday.—Barker's Rails to Putney	24	35

CAMBRIDGE.

	m.	s.
Monday.—Putney Aqueduct to Ship	—	—
Tuesday.— Ditto	21	17
Wednesday.—Ditto to Hammersmith Bridge...	8	37
Thursday.—Ditto to Ship	22	10

Owing to the state of the tides it was found necessary to row the race down from Mortlake to Putney. The account of the race given below is compiled from three accounts, one of which describes the race as seen from the towing-path, the other two from the steamboats.

The time for starting, which had been announced to the select few on Friday night for nine o'clock, was afterwards still further postponed to 9.30, the captains fearing that the tide would not turn till then. But in accordance with the experience of the last few days, it was running down at "the Rails" pretty strong soon after 8.30, and the race might very well have been rowed at that hour. In spite of the early period of the day, the attendance was never greater than on this occasion, vehicles of all descriptions streaming along the Putney and Hammersmith roads in one uninterrupted file, with horsemen innumerable intermixed. The block at Hammersmith Bridge was at one time so great that it was feared it could scarcely be kept clear, but by the exertions of the police their arrangements were good enough to keep all going. On nearing Barnes Railway Bridge we found their efforts were of no avail, as nearly 300 horsemen were penned in there by the carriages, and unable to reach the starting-place; and the towing-path at the Point, just below which the start took place, was in consequence only occupied by a dozen horsemen and two or three hundred pedestrians. The boats for both crews were taken up there by their watermen, whilst the crews themselves went by road to the starting-point. About fourteen steamers had arrived at Mortlake when the Cambridge men got into their boat. The Oxford men, who had won the toss and chosen the Middlesex shore, soon followed them to the buoys which had been moored just above the high bridge on the towpath off the Kew Meadows. The Middlesex station is of great advantage in rounding the first corner, and besides this the set of the ebb there makes it still more favourable.

The crews were :—

	OXFORD.		st.	lbs.
1	R. SHEPHERD	Brasenose	11	0½
2	F. H. KELLY	University	11	5½
3	W. B. R. JACOBSON[1]	Ch. Ch.	12	4
4	W. B. WOODGATE[1]	Brasenose	11	11
5	A. MORRISON[1]	Balliol	12	4
6	W. AWDRY	Balliol	11	4
7	C. R. CARR[1]	Wadham	11	3½
str.	W. M. HOARE[1]	Exeter	11	7½
cox.	F. HOPWOOD[1]	Ch. Ch.	8	4½
	Average of crew		11	8 9/16

[1] Were in the crew of 1862.

	CAMBRIDGE.		st.	lbs.
1	J. C. HAWKSHAW	*Trinity*	11	0
2	W. C. SMYLY[1]	*Trinity*	11	4
3	R. H. MORGAN	*Emmanuel*	11	3
4	J. WILSON	*Pembroke*	11	10
5	C. LA MOTHE	*St John's*	12	3
6	R. A. KINGLAKE	*Trinity*	12	0
7	J. G. CHAMBERS[1]	*Trinity*	11	6
str.	J. STANNING	*Trinity*	10	6
cox.	F. H. ARCHER[1]	*Corpus*	5	9½
	Average of crew		11	5¾

A long delay of more than half an hour occurred, owing to the obstinacy of three or four of the captains of the steamers, who would not comply with the orders of the umpire (backed by the river police) to keep behind the boat of the former gentleman. At a quarter to ten they had all come back just behind him, and we anticipated a start at that time, but from some cause it was delayed a few minutes, during which the foremost boats, like two-year-old racehorses, broke away, and would not be persuaded to return to their stations for some time. At length this difficult feat was accomplished, and at twenty-five minutes after ten we were treated with the start. Both crews dropped their oars into the water at the same moment, the Cambridge having perhaps a trifle the best of it in point of time, but the Oxford gaining a foot in the first two strokes. Gradually their long powerful stroke told against the Cantabs, who lost ground foot by foot, and in the first 300 yards the Oxford coxswain was opposite No. 5 of the Cambridge, both rowing steadily, and without any of that flurry which is so often seen at the start for this exciting event. At the Ship at Mortlake the Oxford were leading a clear length and a half round the point, the Cambridge dropping into their wake. It was evident here that the race was over, barring accidents. The race from this point was, in fact, a repetition of the last two University

---

[1] Were in the crew of 1862.

matches, for Oxford, having once got a good lead, increased it all the way down, passing under Barnes Bridge three lengths ahead; and having still further added to the distance between the boats at Hammersmith, they reached the winning flag off the Star and Garter, Putney, easy winners by at least twenty lengths, the time being about 45 secs., having completed the distance in 23 min. 6 sec., with a strong ebb and a very favourable breeze.

In consequence of the rapid pace at which the tide was making down, the eights completely distanced the steamboats, who saw little or nothing of the race beyond the start.

The *Field* says that the form of the Oxford crew was so decidedly superior that it looked almost any odds on them, and odds varying from 6 to 4 to 5 to 2 were offered against Cambridge at the start. Had they been fortunate enough to have obtained the Middlesex shore they might have made a race for a short distance, but without any ultimate prospect of success.

Among the men who rowed best in the Oxford boat we may mention Shepherd, Woodgate, Morrison, and Hoare; and in the unsuccessful crew, Hawkshaw, Smyly, Kinglake, Chambers, and Stanning.

After the race the crews breakfasted with Mr Phillipps, of the Cedars, Mortlake, and in the evening the dinner went off as usual.

1864.

The Matches between the Universities had now been won an equal number of times by each. Cambridge had won in 1836, 1839, 1840, 1841, 1845, 1846, Easter 1849, 1856, 1858, 1860. Oxford in 1829, 1842, December 1849, 1852, 1854, 1857, 1859, 1861, 1862, 1863. This was the first time since 1836 that they had been equal, and both sides consequently made the most strenuous exertions, Cambridge to regain the superiority she had lost, Oxford to get the lead, which she had never yet had since the races were brought to the London water.

At Oxford Mr Carr of Wadham succeeded to Mr Hoare, and at Cambridge Mr Hawkshaw of Third Trinity to Mr Smyly.

In the trial eights Mr Pocklington for the second time rowed stroke to the winning boat, Mr Senhouse of Ch. Ch. being the stroke oar of the losing.

The rowing gave good promise for Putney in 1864. The style was the same as in the last few years, long, even and swinging, the greatest pains being taken to teach the men to finish the stroke clean with a square blade, as well as to catch the water at the beginning.

The crew which rowed up from Sandford after the race was Roberts, Fenwick, Beachcroft, Warman, Parson, Senhouse, Parker, Pocklington.

At Cambridge a novel method was pursued. A crew was picked so as to represent the University boat as nearly as possible, and the other men who were thought worthy were divided into two trial eights. The place of the race was shifted down from the old course to Sandy's Cut below Ely (see map No. V.), which is a beautiful piece of water for a race between two boats. There is only a very slight bend in the middle of this course, just opposite the Engine-house; it is not perceptible to you when rowing, but after you are well past it you can see that you have come round a corner.

The races lasted three days: on the first two the University boat gave the other two boats two lengths' start over the course, which was two miles long. It beat them both easily. On the third day the two defeated boats had a race, which resulted in one gaining a very easy victory.

Of the training and practising of the Cambridge boat there is no mention in the U.B.C. books; but of the Oxford there is a very full account.

The race was fixed for Saturday, March 19; and from the beginning of term, Jan. 16th to Feb. 10th, Mr Carr tried various crews, with the men in various places in the boat. On Wednesday, Feb. 10, the crew which rowed in the race rowed over the long course, and on Thursday, 11th, began the regular training, on the same system as had been followed in the three previous years. As this is the case I think it will be unnecessary to give the log of the crew.

They had very rough weather during training; on Wednesday, 10th Feb., they met floating ice which cut the bows of the boat as they were going up stream, and they had to get out opposite Nuneham and walk up.

On Friday, 19th, they went to Wallingford; and this was the only occasion on which they did go.

On Monday, March 7th, they raced with a scratch crew in which were the two Morrisons with

Carr for stroke. The river was in a high flood, and such a gale of wind was blowing that both boats filled. The University crew all got drenched to the skin, but thanks to the waterproof bags had dry coats to run up to the island in. These waterproof bags were, I believe, introduced by Mr G. Morrison, and seem to have been of the greatest use; each man has one in which he puts his coat while he is rowing, keeping them under the thwart.

The crew left for Putney on Wednesday, March 9th, but as the Warden of Wadham refused to grant Mr Carr an exeat before Saturday, he had to stay at Oxford, "congratulating himself in this, that he was able to put the crew in such good hands as those of Mr George Morrison, who had kindly gone to Putney with them."

The *Field* says:

The Oxford crew took their first long row over the course about 4 p.m. (Friday). In consequence of the late heavy rains and spring tide, the river had for some days been very full of water; and with a whole gale of wind blowing down the Putney Reach on the flood, there was a nice little sea opposite the Star and Garter, and at the Aqueduct. The start was thus a matter of some difficulty, but getting off pretty well, they rowed strongly through the wash, although at the half mile the wind and waves once all but brought them to a standstill. They kept on, doing their best under these disadvantages, and finished opposite the bottom of the Kew Meadows, some little distance above the Ship. The time to the Ship was 24 min. 28 sec., to where they stopped 26 min. 28 sec.

During the same week changes were made in the Cambridge crew, and evidently for the better; although their rows have been taken generally under the most adverse circumstances. They had their first pull over the Ely course (starting from Adelaide Bridge) on Monday, rowing for the first time also in their new ship, built by Mat Taylor; under these conditions much progress was not to be expected, and, to make matters worse, a strong head wind was blowing up the reach, causing a heavy surf. Shortly after starting, the button came off one of their oars, when they went ashore and waited until another was brought from Ely, rowing home well pleased with their craft. On Tuesday they went over the course without let or hindrance, doing the three miles and a half in twenty-one minutes. On Wednesday they were supplied with a new set of oars, and started in the middle of a heavy and blinding snow storm. As a heavy swell striking and locking Selwyn's oar, caused it to break, again they had to take to the shore and wait until another was procured. There was on this day, we are glad to say, a marked improvement in their rowing, attributable either to the previous day's hard row, or to the new oars above-mentioned, there being a more square and better hold of the water, with more freedom of the men's bodies. On Thursday, the weather being much finer and the wind less, they went over the course in good style, still showing an improvement. They took their last pull at Ely on Friday, and left on Saturday evening for Putney.

On Saturday, 12th, the Oxford men again went over the course from Putney to Mortlake, but the time was not accurately taken. The Cantabs arrived at Putney that evening.

On Monday both crews rowed over the course; Cambridge had the best tide, but a stronger wind against them. The times were: Oxford 24 min. 8 sec.; Cambridge 25 min. 5 sec.

On Tuesday both crews again rowed over the course, this time from Mortlake; the Cambridge men had the stronger tide and the better wind. Time, Oxford 20 min. 26 sec.; Cambridge 20 min. 32 sec.

On Wednesday Cambridge beat the watermen over the course, having given them three lengths' start. Time from Mortlake to Putney 21 min. 35 sec.

In order to get the steamers to behave as well as possible, the following notice was published :—

Caution to Steamers.

The boats will start from two barges moored off the Star and Garter.

We have agreed that the race shall not start with a single steamer in front of the boats.

If the captains of steamers do not abide by these orders the race shall be rowed with the ebb.

J. C. HAWKSHAW, Capt. C.U.B.C.
C. R. CARR, Capt. O.U.B.C.

The force of the threat to have the race rowed with the ebb lies in this, that in case the steamers are refractory, you have only to wait long enough and they will be nearly all aground. As however rowing with the ebb does not give so fair a race, the best endeavours are always made to get the steamboats to be reasonable on this occasion.

In order to prevent them lying up ahead—the starting-place was altered from Putney Aqueduct to two barges moored off the upper end of the Star and Garter, or more correctly, opposite the Duke's Head, at Putney. This left plenty of room for captains to keep well behind, but it is almost unnecessary to say that very few were actually astern when the word was given. Four or five lay up ahead under the Fulham shore, and several others gradually drove up on the Putney side as high as Simmons's yard, and even higher, before the men were off, thus obscuring the otherwise fine view of the start that many of the shore folks would have had.

The Prince of Wales for the first time honoured the match with his presence, and the start was put some time earlier than had been intended, to enable him to be present at a drawing-room which had been fixed for two o'clock that day.

The morning of Saturday, the day of the race, was

glorious, and in every respect suitable for the great event then about to be decided. The sun shone brightly, and the atmosphere was almost as genial as in the middle of spring, although the wind blew from the east; still it was by no means cold, and the breeze, though slight, materially assisted the flood, and caused a gentle ripple on the surface.

Betting had ranged during the week from 6 to 4 to 5 to 4, and again up to 7 to 4 on Oxford. Just before half-past 11 the following crews were ready for the contest :—

OXFORD CREW.

			st.	lbs.
1	C. ROBERTS	*Trinity*	10	9
2	W. AWDRY[1]	*Balliol*	11	4½
3	F. H. KELLY[1]	*University*	11	9
4	J. PARSONS	*Trinity*	12	9
5	W. B. R. JACOBSON[1]	*Chr. Ch.*	12	3½
6	A. E. SEYMOUR	*University*	11	3
7	M. BROWN	*Trinity*	11	3
str.	D. POCKLINGTON	*Brasenose*	11	5
cox.	C. R. W. TOTTENHAM	*Chr. Ch.*	7	3
	Average		11	7½

CAMBRIDGE CREW.

			st.	lbs.
1	J. C. HAWKSHAW[1]	*Trinity*	11	3
2	E. V. PIGOTT	*Corpus*	11	9
3	H. WATSON	*Pembroke*	12	4
4	W. HAWKINS	*St John's*	12	0
5	R. A. KINGLAKE[1]	*Trinity*	12	4
6	G. BORTHWICK	*Trinity*	12	1
7	D. F. STEAVENSON	*Trinity H.*	12	1
str.	J. R. SELWYN	*Trinity*	11	0
cox.	F. H. ARCHER[1]	*Corpus*	6	6
	Average		11	11½

[1] Were in the crew of 1863.

The Oxonians, having once more won the toss, chose the Fulham station. The stern of each eight was held by a person in a small boat, made fast to each barge, and Mr E. Searle, of Lambeth, gave the word from another small boat between the lighters.

The word being given, the oars of both crews took the water together, but there was more strength applied to the first few strokes by the Cambridge crew than by the favourites; in addition to this an important oar among the latter bungled his start, consequently the Cambridge boat went away with a lead, though it soon proved to be of a very transitory nature. Amid the greatest excitement and the loudest cheering the bow of the Cambridge boat shot in front, gaining gradually, until off the end of the Bishop of London's garden she was a third of a length in front. This was the greatest lead the Cambridge crew ever obtained, although to persons looking from astern and askew it appeared as if they were nearly, if not quite, a length ahead. The steady rowing of Oxford, who were very close to the Fulham bank, now began to tell, and inch by inch they reduced their opponents' lead, until opposite the centre of Finch's field the two boats were as level as when they started. Now comes the most peculiar feature in the race, for when once level the Oxford boat began to leave its adversary in the most rapid and extraordinary manner; so much so, that we have heard doubts expressed whether the representatives of the Cam were really in condition. At the site of the half-mile post Oxford led by half a length, which at Craven Cottage they had increased to one length, and as they rounded the bend they took the Cambridge water, and opposite the second creek on the tow-path shore were two lengths ahead, the coxswain of the latter crew steering his boat anything but well. From this point to the finish the race was devoid of interest for it was evident that, short of falling out of their boat, or being run down, nothing could prevent the success of the Oxford men. The crews now began to cross the water for the Soapworks point, and off the Crab Tree a gap of three lengths at least separated them. This was increased to four or five lengths at Hammersmith Bridge, reached, according to our timing, in 7 m. 50 s. The Oxford boat continued to increase its lead through Corney Reach, being forty strokes ahead off the bathing place, both being steered rather wide in the reach above Chiswick Church. Barnes Bridge was passed by the first boat in 17 m. 10 s., too many lengths ahead to be accurately counted. They stopped rowing off the Ship, fancying they had arrived at the post; but, discovering their error at once, they rowed on to the winning-boat, which was placed as far above the Ship as the starting-barges were above Putney Aqueduct. The time of the winners was 21 m. 40 s., and that of the losers 23 m.

The account of the race in the Cambridge Book makes the difference in the times only 27 secs. The Oxford Book says it was won by 20 lengths. The winners rowed in the same boat as last year, which was built by J. and S. Salter. The Cambridge men rowed in a new boat built by Mat. Taylor of Newcastle.

The crews paddled back to Putney, and on their way down fell in with the George Peabody, with the Prince on board, when first one and then the other gave him a hearty cheer, which was duly responded to by himself and the passengers on the steamer.

Concerning the style of the rowing in the two boats, the *Field* says:

The form of the winning boat was very good, taken altogether, though we have seen better crews. The great points of fine rowing were, however, not wanting. There was the long forward reach, the simultaneous catch, and firm hold of the water at the very beginning of the stroke, the long drag through the water, the perfect swing of the bodies so essential in a crew, and the clean feather. The men were tall and powerful, and although one or two looked a little delicate, they did not appear by any means over-trained. Not one but rowed straight fore and aft, there being no rolling in or out of the boat, and no jerking. Their start was certainly rather scrambling, but before a couple of hundred yards were covered, the crew had fallen into the long, powerful swing, which found such favour during their practice on the Thames.

As regards the losing boat, we regret that we have nothing favourable to say. Their start was good, but the rowing was too hurried for such a long and trying course as the Metropolitan. The feather was not clean enough nor high enough, which was evidenced by the splashing at Hammersmith. There was none of that uniformity or simultaneous swing which characterized the Oxford boat, and every man seemed more or less to do his work in his own peculiar fashion.

The crews lunched at the hospitable mansion of Mr Phillipps, " The Cedars," Mortlake, and in the evening dined as usual as guests of the Thames Subscription Club.

Thus, alas! Oxford won the conquering match, and took the lead which Cambridge had lost the year before.

1865.

At Cambridge Mr Hawkshaw was succeeded by Mr J. G. Chambers: at Oxford Mr Carr held the office of President until the end of 1864, and so had the management of the Trial Eights at the end of that year.

The two strokes were Lambert of C.C.C. and Forster of University College, but neither of them rowed in the crew of 1865. Mr Lambert won.

At Cambridge the strokes were Guerney of

Emmanuel and C. B. Lawes of 3rd Trinity. Mr Guerney had the heavier crew, and won by nearly a boat's length over a course 2½ miles long.

Mr Carr was succeeded by Mr A. Morrison of Balliol, brother of Mr G. Morrison. Between him and Mr Chambers there was some considerable correspondence on a subject which came into greater prominence the following year. The Cambridge men wished to have a limit made as to the "standing" of the men in the University crews; they proposed "that no one should be allowed to row in a University after the termination of his fourth year from his first day of residence." Mr Carr brought the matter before the meeting of the O.U.B.C., but as the proposal met with no seconder the matter dropped for the time.

The race was fixed for Saturday, April 8th.

The term being a very long one, there was plenty of time for practising and getting rid of faults before the crews went into training.

The Cambridge Secretary says, "At the time of commencing training we were fairly together, and had got rid of that abominable dig now so frequent in Cambridge rowing, and caught the beginning sharply; the great apparent requirement being length forward."

The Oxford Captain says, "As regards the training and the race this year, I think that the Oxford crew was not up to the average of former years; this I consider to be due principally to the fact that we carried out too far a practice which had in former years been a decided success; I mean the selecting men entirely on account of mere strength, without regard to their form or neatness of rowing. The result was that, owing to the total want of watermanship which some of the crew showed in our spurts with the watermen on the Wednesday before the race, the Oxford University eight presented one of the most deplorable spectacles which the rowing world has lately seen....

" There was very little choice of oars from whom it was possible to select the crew, but in this, as indeed in almost every matter throughout the whole course of training, I was guided by the assistance of my brother, Mr George Morrison."

The following is taken from the *Field*, and describes the appearance of the two crews as they were three weeks before the race, that is on Monday and Tuesday, March 20 and 21.

On the first-mentioned day the Oxford men rowed over the short course between Oxford and Iffley Lock for the first time in their new eight, built by the Salters; she appears to be a very nice boat, and carries them well. The first point that attracted our attention was the apparent size of the men, who gave us the impression of being a very powerful, heavy set of oarsmen; but this idea was to a certain extent dispelled on seeing them out of their boat between the two rows; for some of those who appeared the biggest men in the boat were actually the least in stature when on *terra firma*. This is attributable to their broad shoulders, thick, long bodies, and, comparatively speaking, short legs. There appeared to be plenty of strength in the crew, a fair catch of the water, and, above all things, length and swing, although as a crew they are still very rough and unpolished.

On Tuesday the Cambridge crew rowed down to Clayhithe and back in the old out-rigger which they have been lately using. The men are a powerful crew, but, unlike the Oxford eight, they appear bigger out of their boat than in it; they are tall—averaging, perhaps, 6 feet—the stroke being the shortest man in the boat, and he measures 5 ft. 10 in., or rather more. They are better together than their rivals at Oxford, but we question whether they will improve so rapidly or so much during the last fortnight of training. Their rowing is very lively, the only question being whether at this distance of time from the race it is not a little too quick, thirty-four and thirty-five strokes being done in the minute. The catch at the first part of the dip has been diligently engrafted, but several of the men in the centre of the boat have a tendency to clip the beginning of each stroke. There is, however, plenty of dash, and the time is far better than that of the opposing crew; but yet we looked in vain for that long drag and lengthy swing which is so desirable a qualification for a long distance. Lawes' rowing has much improved since the trial eights in the Michaelmas term, and, taken altogether, the crew were much better than we expected. There was still the same absence of finish we have previously noticed, but we cannot help thinking that by the time the men arrive on the Thames they will meet with general approbation.

There is a very full account of the practising at Putney in the *Field*, from which it appears that the Cambridge crew were very fast for a short distance, but generally fell to pieces after three miles or so had been traversed.

Saturday, the long-looked for 8th of April, at last arrived, and a more glorious day for the annual encounter between the Universities of Oxford and Cambridge could not have been wished for. The morning broke with a thick fog, but as noon approached the vapour gradually dispersed, and the sun shone down upon the Thames with all the brilliancy and power of midsummer.

About half-past twelve the crews walked down to their respective boat-houses from their head-quarters—the Cambridge men to Simmons's yard; and the Oxonians to the London Rowing Club shed. The former were first afloat, but they were speedily followed by their opponents, and both paddled down to the starting-point. The same plan was pursued as last year, two barges having been anchored off the upper end of the Star and Garter, and the sterns of the two eights were held by men in small boats made fast to the lighters in question. This left plenty of room for all the steamers to lie astern of the crews, but, as usual, nothing could be worse than the behaviour of the captains of these craft.

Oxford, for the fourth time in succession, won the toss, and took the Fulham station, the Cambridge boat being, of course, outside. Whilst the crews were preparing for the start, several of the steamers behaved most disgracefully, notwithstanding the efforts of the umpire, Mr Chitty. The two crews therefore returned to the boat-houses, and this had the effect of restoring the steamers to order, though some of them after all had gone in advance before the start took place.

Betting varied; even money, 5 to 4, and 6 to 4, being in their turn laid upon Oxford, as far as we could learn: but during the race all sorts of odds, from 2 to 1 to 10 to 1, were betted on Cambridge.

The course lay from the lighters off the Star and Garter to a flagboat moored the same distance above the Ship as that which intervened between the Aqueduct and the two barges. In this flagboat John Phelps, of Fulham, was stationed as judge, in case the finish was close; and Mr Edward Searle of Lambeth started the eights from a skiff between the two lighters. The crews were made up as follows—the undermentioned weights having been obtained by us from head-quarters the evening before the race:

OXFORD.

				st.	lbs.
1	R. T. RAIKES	*Merton*		11	0
2	H. P. SENHOUSE	*Ch. Ch.*		11	1
3	E. F. HENLEY	*Oriel*		12	13
4	G. C. COVENTRY	*Pembroke*		11	12
5	A. MORRISON[1]	*Balliol*		12	6
6	T. WOOD	*Pembroke*		12	2
7	H. SCHNEIDER	*Trinity*		11	10
str.	M. BROWN[2]	*Trinity*		11	4
cox.	C. R. W. TOTTENHAM[2]	*Ch. Ch.*		7	13
	Average			11	11¼

CAMBRIDGE.

				st.	lbs.
1	H. WATNEY	*Lady Marg.*		11	1
2	M. H. L. BEEBEE	*Lady Marg.*		10	12
3	E. V. PIGOTT[2]	*Corpus*		11	12
4	R. A. KINGLAKE[2]	*3rd Trinity*		12	8
5	D. F. STEAVENSON[2]	*Trin. Hall*		12	4
6	G. BORTHWICK[2]	*1st Trinity*		11	13
7	W. R. GRIFFITHS	*3rd Trinity*		11	8½
str.	C. B. LAWES	*3rd Trinity*		11	7
cox.	F. H. ARCHER[2]	*Corpus*		7	3
	Average			11	10

At three minutes past one o'clock Mr Searle dismissed the crews on their way. The oars of the Cambridge men were the first to take the water, but neither boat made a very brilliant start, although after a couple of strokes had been rowed the Cambridge crew went to the front at a tremendous pace. So fast, indeed, did they get away, that they led by half a length at Simmons's and one length off the Bishop's Creek. By this time the leading boat had been taken out about mid stream by its coxswain, so as to get well away from the crowd of steamers pressing on in the rear. The Oxford coxswain, on the other hand,

---

[1] Was in the crew of 1863.
[2] Were in the crew of 1864.

had fetched too close in towards the Fulham bank out of the strength of the tide, and he unfortunately got within the draught of one or two of the steamboats that lay up under the Middlesex shore, his progress being thereby considerably impeded—in fact, it really looked as if the Oxford crew were "settled." At Craven Cottage, where Mr Tottenham was obliged to steer out so as to clear a whole fleet of rowboats congregated at the Point, Cambridge led by two lengths, rowing forty-three strokes to Oxford's thirty-nine, and were still increasing their lead, which at the Crab Tree amounted to three lengths, Mr Archer throwing the whole of his back wash on to the Oxford boat.

Along the tow-path rushed frantic pedestrians, followed by a crowd of galloping horsemen, raising a cloud of dust, the shouts of "Cambridge!" "Cambridge!" rising strong and distinct above every other sound. On rounding the Soapworks corner both the boats kept the centre of the river, probably to avoid the crowd of small boats lying under the shore arch of Hammersmith Bridge. Here the long, steady, telling rowing of Oxford on the outside began to look very formidable, albeit the Cambridge crew appeared to hold on with unabated speed. By the time the eights reached Hammersmith Bridge the lead of Cambridge had begun to decrease, and as the boats emerged from the shadow of that structure there was a space of three-quarters of a length between the Cambridge stern and the bow of the Oxford boat—in a word, the former led by one length and three-quarters. The sight was without question one of the finest we ever witnessed. On the bridge, on the tow-path, and on the raised bank above the tow-path, was a countless sea of faces; in the foreground the two eights racing as it were for very life, the Oxford boat holding its ground, but neither gaining nor losing one inch: thus the race passed Biffen's. Steadily Oxford reduced the gap off the Lead Works, until at the bend of the river opposite the Doves a bare half length separated the two boats, each crew striving its utmost, one to gain, and the other to retain the lead. Opposite the Oil Mills Oxford had gained a few feet more, one-third of a length being the intervening space. No further alteration occurred for another hundred and fifty yards, when the nose of the Oxford boat once more gained, but by inches only, until it just overlapped the rudder of the Cambridge boat. Half a dozen strokes and Cambridge were again clear for another hundred yards; and we must say that never before did we watch so intently the stern of one boat and the bow of another. A little way up Chiswick Eyot, for the second time did the Oxford boat overlap its opponent's stern, and again was the leading boat drawn clear: a third attempt ended similarly. Rather more than half-way up the Eyot, the Oxford boat once more, and for the fourth time, gained, on this occasion overlapping as far as Mr Archer's seat; but a brilliant spurt from Mr Lawes, in which he was tolerably well backed up by his crew, again took him clear, and a space of several feet once more divided the boats. For the moment we thought Oxford could not effect their object, for the same relative positions were maintained until off the roadway below the Waterworks mound, opposite the upper end of Chiswick Eyot, where for the fifth and last time the Oxford eight went up and again overlapped. It was painfully exciting to witness, from a position immediately abeam of the two boats, these repeated endeavours to get up; but all doubt was now speedily removed, as slowly but surely the bow of the Dark Blue boat reached the coxswain—a spurt from Cambridge, but of no avail—then stroke, then 7, 6, 5, 4, 3, 2, bow, and they were level—as level as when they were held at the start. This was immediately off Chiswick Church. No sooner were the boats alongside than Oxford, in the better tide, rapidly commenced to leave their adversaries, who were kept too close to the tow-path shore, and in the bight, where the eddy causes the mud bank, so conspicuous at low water, to collect, the difference in the rowing of the two crews was beyond measure striking —Oxford rowing that long swinging stroke which has again and again stood them in such good stead, whilst Cambridge became shorter and less effective, the crew falling to pieces when collared, exactly as in their practice. The race was now over, and the Oxford crew drew themselves clear off the White Cottage above Chiswick Church, where both eights made a long leg for the Middlesex side of Barnes Bridge. At the bathing place Oxford led by barely two lengths, at Barnes Bridge by nearly three, and finally won easily by three lengths and three-quarters, to be particular, or in round numbers, four lengths. Time, 21 min. 24 sec. from the start. The losers appeared much distressed, and several of the men rowed the last mile and a half terribly out of shape. Whilst swinging across the tide, a tug came up with the flood and stove in the Cambridge boat, so that the crew were unable to row her down again to Putney. The Oxford men, on the other hand, after a short rest paddled back to their boat-house.

The *Field* makes the following remarks on the rowing in the two boats :—

First, as to the Oxford crew. They were, to our thinking, scarcely up to the average of the last three or four years, and Nos. 4 and 6 had much to learn in the art of rowing, although, physically speaking, strong men. At the same time, we think Mr Henley, who weighed 12st. 13lbs., too heavy for such a forward place as No. 3. The one essential qualification for success was not wanting: we refer to long, clean, steady fore-and-aft rowing, accompanied by good body swing. The men's arms were stretched out to their full limits; they caught hold of the water at once, and they rowed their strokes right through, finishing with the handles up to their chests. No part of the stroke was missed, and the rowing, although strong, was pre-eminently light.

Concerning the rowing of the losers during last Saturday's race, we must now say a few words. The number of strokes at which they started was far too great ever to continue over the whole distance; and although it may be a very easy thing for a steam-engine to make forty-three and forty-four strokes a minute, and to keep them up, yet such a task could never with reason be expected of any human being. The pace commenced to tell its tale upon more than one man in the Cambridge boat before passing under

Hammersmith Bridge, and upon yet another and another as Chiswick Eyot was gained. When caught and left astern by Oxford, the majority of the crew fell out of shape, and the short, laboured rowing of the losers thence to Mortlake contrasted most unfavourably with the easy and commanding pulling of the winners. Lawes' rowing was strong and plucky, but it had many faults, including that of burying the oar too deep; and however good he may be behind another, yet he is not the man for the stroke thwart of a 'Varsity boat. Moreover he had the blade of his oar pared down and reduced in width[1]. He, Griffiths, and Steavenson, did more work, from first to last, than any other three oars in the eight, and it was a thousand pities that men composed of such sterling stuff should, to a certain extent, be thrown away for want of good coaching and the exercise of a little common sense and judgment.

These words, though strong, are those of one who, not being a University man, would not, I should say, have any bias to one side or another. I have given them here, because I think they were probably the only criticism from the pen of any amateur of considerable authority who was neither a Cambridge man nor an Oxford man.

The boats rowed in were two new eights built for the occasion by Messrs J. and S. Salter, of Oxford, of the following dimensions:—Oxford

---

[1] This extraordinary statement, though neither quite true nor quite false, was never contradicted, although Mr F. M. Arnold wrote to *Bell's Life* making the accusation. I believe the exact truth was, that Mr Lawes rowed in practice till within a day or two of the race with an oar which was reduced in width. This oar having been accidentally broken Mr Lawes declined to have the one pared down which was substituted for it. I have therefore the greater pleasure in being able to give the exact truth, as the statement in the text would imply that Mr Lawes very cheaply got the credit of rowing pluckily when he would really have been doing less work than the rest.

boat: Length, 56 ft. 5 in.; breadth, 2 ft. 1 in.; depth at stem, 8 in.; at stern, 7¼ in.; amidships, 13½ in. Cambridge boat: Length, 56 ft. 5 in.; breadth, 2 ft. 1½ in.; depth at stem, 8 in.; at stern, 7¼ in.; amidships, 13½ in. Both eights were built of cedar—the wood being fellow planks, the fittings inside partly of pine for lightness of appearance—both of similar mould, the Cambridge boat having rather more floor and being a little wider, as she was made for a crew averaging 12 st., or 3 lbs. more per man than Oxford, and they were built sufficiently large to carry the crews through rough water.

The Oxford President says: "Cambridge took the lead and kept it so far that by far the largest majority of the spectators, even those on the umpire's boat, had made up their minds that Oxford was beaten. And I must admit that my own feelings were somewhat of the same nature. This however was not the case with Mr Brown, who had before arranged to start with a slow stroke, so as to prevent a repetition of the scene which we had exhibited with the watermen, and who never lost heart. Indeed I do not think it too much to say that the credit of the Oxford victory was almost entirely due to his admirable coolness and rowing, in refusing to spurt before he felt sure that our men had cooled down to their work.

"ALLAN MORRISON,
"*President.*"

1866.

Mr Kinglake succeeded to Mr Chambers in the office of President, Mr Brown to Mr A. Morrison.

In 1865 the Cambridge trial eights were again rowed over the Ely course.

The strokes of the two Cambridge boats were Jerwood of Trin. Hall and Bonsey of St John's. Neither of them rowed in the University boat either before or afterwards. Jerwood won after a splendid race.

At Oxford it is curious to notice that the same two men handled the after oars who did so in 1863, viz. Mr Pocklington of B.N.C. and Mr Senhouse of Ch. Ch., and the same result ensued, Mr Pocklington having now for the third time won the race.

Towards the end of 1865 the question about the seniority of men rowing in the crews was reopened. Mr Kinglake wrote to say that, unless the Oxford men would agree to some limitation, he did not feel sure that the C.U.B.C. would send a challenge to row. This was doubtless the proper course to take, for the experience of 1860 shewed that unless the arrangements were made before the challenge was sent, there was no chance of gaining any concession afterwards. I remember however that at the time Mr Kinglake was blamed in the newspapers for breathing such a suggestion; the idea being that it would be a disgrace to the University to decline sending a challenge. This, however, appears to me to be a very false notion on the matter. Surely if a challenge is to be sent at all, the challengers have the right to put it in what terms they like, it being at the option of the challenged party to accept it or not. In the same way, it was clearly a most reasonable thing on the part of Mr Kinglake to try to find out whether or no the challenge he wished to send would be accepted at Oxford. In consequence of Mr Kinglake's letter a deputation of Oxford men came over to Cambridge to try to adjust matters: the result of their consultation was the framing of the following rules. "That no pass or Πολλ. man may row after one year has elapsed from the date of his having passed his final examination. That no honour man may row after the end of his fourth year from the date of his commencing residence." These regulations were agreed to by the officers subject to the approval of their respective clubs.

This was in the October term; and the matter having got abroad, a protest signed by 56 old Oxford "Blues" was sent to the officers of the O.U.B.C. The result of this was that the O.U.B.C. rejected the proposed limitation.

Now looking at this from a Cambridge point of view only, I think we have great cause to congratulate ourselves on this termination of the negociation.

The reason why a change was desired from our point of view was this. Honour men at Cambridge must take their degree (or rather pass the examination which entitles them to their degree) in the eleventh term at the latest after their first term of residence. Thus if a man enter in October 1870, the latest examination he can go in for, in order to take his degree with honours is the Classical Tripos of 1874. Men usually go down within a term of having taken their degree, and thus at Cambridge a man who entered in October 1870 would not be likely to stay up longer than to be able to row in the race of 1874.

At Oxford, if a man matriculated in October 1870, he might defer the time of his examination for honours till the October term 1874, and thus he would not improbably stay up another term for the race of 1875. This is I believe the only advantage which the Oxford men possess over us in this point. We are on exactly even terms with regard to Πολλ. men. So that the only object of the rule was to exclude those few honour men, who might take four years and a term in taking their degree, from rowing in the University boat. It is not in my power to give the exact number of men who would probably have been affected by this rule, but I think it would have been exceedingly small; for Mr Allan Morrison says that in the three crews in which he had rowed, "*none* of them were of more than four years' standing." If then the O.U.B.C. had consented to the rule, they would have been making an almost valueless concession, which still would have been a concession.

and for which they might at some time have claimed something which it would have been inconvenient to agree to, but still impossible to refuse.

I ought to mention that Mr Kinglake wrote a letter to the *Times* denying that he had accompanied his proposals by a menace that he would not send a challenge unless they were acceded to. I think it unnecessary to give his letter, because I consider he was perfectly justified in making such a menace if he had chosen. To my mind it is perfectly optional for the losing side to challenge or not, and no one has any claim to be consulted as to when, or in what terms, the challenge is sent. The challenged party has the right of accepting or rejecting it; the public generally of going to the race when it does come off, or of staying away.

After this dispute was closed, the challenge was sent in the usual form and duly accepted. When the challenge was sent it was hoped that the President would have the cooperation of every individual member of the Club whose services might be required; but unfortunately two men of the greatest reputation in the University as oarsmen declined to row when they were solicited to do so. The justification which they had for pursuing so questionable a course is best known to themselves, but I believe that I am right when I state that no reasons were *given* which would have any weight with a man who allowed any other ground for his actions than his own personal convenience, and who acknowledged that the University Boat *Club* had any claim on his gratitude as a rowing man. It is unnecessary here to record their names, or recount the retribution which followed "non pede claudo" upon the error they made. Their reputation remains in the University as a warning, unneeded I hope, to others not to follow in their steps.

After this untoward defection, the President Mr Kinglake, with the greatest pluck and determination, set to work to form a crew worthy to represent the University on the Thames. In this he was ably assisted by Mr Steavenson the Secretary, and for the last four weeks of training Mr Chambers, the President of the year before, made his appearance to coach the crew. They went up to Putney about ten days before the race, and "though by no means free from faults" when they left Cambridge, yet "having some time at Putney before the race, they set to work with a determination to do their best, and they improved so rapidly during their stay at Putney as to satisfy the most ardent wishes of their friends.

"The night before the 24th of March there was a tremendous gale, and it was feared that there would be a very heavy sea on the next day. The morning however broke very fairly, and at 7.50 A.M. the two crews were at their stations.

"Oxford took a slight lead at the start, but Cambridge soon came up, and both crews rowed level though wide apart to the Dung Wharf: here Cambridge drew ahead a little and passed under Hammersmith Bridge half a length ahead; they kept their lead, rowing in good form and time to the end of Chiswick Eyot: here on entering Corney Reach both crews encountered the rough water; they however kept their respective distances, Cambridge slightly in advance on the outside and Oxford sheltered under the Middlesex shore; about the middle of Corney Reach Cambridge were impeded by a barge, and had to put the rudder on hard twice to prevent a foul; when they again got straight Oxford were half a length ahead, and had moreover got the corner by Barnes Bridge: thus there was no struggle for the lead. Cambridge spurted and drew up to Oxford, but could never get on even terms with them, and Oxford finally won by two lengths, after a very exciting and even race." (Cambridge Book.)

Mr Willan, who kept a private log for his own amusement, says:

"We had the usual sort of weather while at Oxford, such as snow and sleet while rowing the long course, and floods to walk through on the way back.

"We had very bad weather at Putney, returning nearly every day with the boat nearly full of water.

"We trained for five weeks and one day; during that time, allowing for Sundays, we had fourteen days in the gig-boat and seventeen in the racing-boat.

"We had eight days' practice at Putney.

"We rowed the long course at Oxford ten times; six in the heavy, four in the light boat. Beside the long course we rowed once to Wallingford,

23 miles. We rowed the whole course at Putney four times.

	st.	lbs.
Average weight at beginning of training	12	1½
Do. „ end „	11	12½."

The Cambridge crew arrived at Putney on Wednesday, March 14, and rowed over the course on the ebb the same day, the weather being fine but the ebb not strong.

The Oxford crew did not arrive till Thursday afternoon.

Their times over the course are as follows:

	Cambridge.	Oxford.
Wednesday, March 14.	21' 15"	—
Thursday, „ 15.	23' 25", weather bad.	—
Friday, „ 16.	Short distance rowing.	21' 26"
Saturday, „ 17.	21' 39"	—
Monday, „ 19.	22' 23"	20' 35"
Wednesday, „ 21.	21' 59"	Not taken.

On Saturday, the 17th, one of the Oxford men, who had been obliged to go to the University, returned too late for the crew to row over the course. On Thursday the Oxford men had some spurts with the watermen and with a Kingston eight, Cambridge with a London Rowing Club eight.

Friday was given to rest, with the exception of a little paddling.

The following account of the race is taken from the *Field*.

The start was fixed for an early hour on Saturday, March 24, viz. half-past 7, on account of the neap-tide, which could scarcely be expected to hold out against a westerly wind after 8 o'clock. As the time for starting drew near, the customary fleet of paddle-steamers, private yachts, and tugs attended; but in order to prevent the great nuisance, not to say danger, which results from their driving up almost on to the racing boats when at their stations, and half drowning the crews with the surf from their paddle-wheels, arrangements had been made by the Thames Conservancy Board, which most effectually put a stopper on their tactics, and for once enabled the crews to have an unmolested and satisfactory start. It was managed in this way. Across the river, off the Star and Garter, a number of barges were moored in line, in order that the steamers might make fast to them, and so spare the crews the broken water to which they have hitherto been regularly treated. As each steamer dropped up through Putney Bridge she was hailed by an officer in authority, and directed to make fast to the craft at anchor; this order was promptly obeyed. Some little distance in front of the line of steamers—viz. just off the Duke's Head—two lighters were moored, nearly in mid-stream, and to them were made fast two watermen's skiffs, with an occupant in each, for the purpose of holding the stern of each eight. There was thus a clear and considerable interval between the crews and the steamers, and when the word was given by Mr Searle the two competing boats were off, and well ahead, out of danger, before the paddles of the latter had made half-a-dozen revolutions.

The crews embarked about a quarter before 8 o'clock, and put off to their stations; Oxford, who won the toss for choice, taking the Fulham, and Cambridge the outer or midstream station. The Fulham station is usually considered an advantage, but such was not the case in the present instance, because the breeze, which rose with the flood, blew across the river from the Putney shore, and the Surrey station was consequently to windward and in smoother water, there being more rough water under the Fulham shore than elsewhere, besides which the tide had almost ceased to flow, and just drained up in the centre. This was the fifth consecutive occasion on which Oxford won the toss, and it is a remarkable coincidence that each time she has gained the choice of station she has also won the race. Mr J. W. Chitty, of Exeter College, Oxford, acted as umpire.

In consequence of the start taking place some distance above Putney Bridge, viz. just below the Duke's Head, the winning-post was shifted as far above the Ship at Mortlake as the starting-barges lay above the Aqueduct. John Phelps, of Fulham, was in the flag-boat to act as judge, if necessary.

The following was supplied to the *Field* by a well-known oarsman of the London Rowing Club, who accompanied the race on horseback.

At 12 m. to 8 o'clock Mr E. Searle gave the signal to go ; and, for a wonder, the Oxford crew were the first to get way on their boat, and lifting her off before the Cantabs had fairly got hold of the water, immediately led by several feet. This advantage, however, was not of long duration, for directly the Cambridge men settled down to their work they drew up to Oxford, and then began one of the most exciting and best-contested eight-oared races ever rowed between Putney and Mortlake. From the London Club boat-house to Craven Cottage there was nothing to choose between the two crews, which raced for the Point alongside one another, although very wide apart, owing to the Cambridge coxswain keeping out in the centre of the river, where he was not only well to windward, but had the benefit of the last drain of the neap flood-tide, the Oxford crew being very close in under the Fulham or lee shore. At Craven Cottage the two boats were still perfectly level; but, after passing the Point, Cambridge forged a trifle ahead, and opposite the Grass Wharf led by about four yards. No alteration occurred during the long leg which both crews made across the water for the Soap Factory, until after passing the Crab Tree, when the Oxford crew, rowing very powerfully, again came up, and at the Point immediately below the Soap Works Wharf the two eights were once more level. Thence to Hammersmith Suspension

Bridge the Cambridge crew had the best of the course, and the best of the water, and edging Oxford out somewhat, put on a spurt and went ahead, passing under the centre span of the bridge with a lead of three-quarters of a length. Immediately after shooting the bridge Oxford again overhauled the leading crew, and—for the third time subsequently to the start—became level with their antagonists as the boats passed Biffen's Yard. From Biffen's to the Doves Oxford held her own, but Cambridge, having the inside of the horse-shoe bend on the towpath side, yet again showed a few feet in front at the corner opposite the Upper Mall, between the Doves and the Oil Mills. Entering Corney Reach, where, owing to the foul westerly wind, the water was very lumpy, and when opening out the straight stretch for the White Cottage, the strength of Oxford again told a tale, and at the bottom of Chiswick Eyot they were once more alongside Cambridge, neither having any perceptible advantage. This state of things did not long continue, for by the time the two boats were abreast of the middle of Chiswick Eyot Oxford was two yards ahead. At the upper end of the island Cambridge put on a spurt, and although taken too close in to the Surrey shore, and over the mud-bank opposite Chiswick Ferry and Church, they actually led by a quarter of a length as they turned the corner and entered the long reach for Barnes Bridge.

The distance from the White Cottage to Barnes Railway Bridge would in all probability have been the scene of the most interesting part of the whole race, had not the evenly-balanced chances of the boats been brought to a sudden and abrupt termination, which happened after this manner: a little below the bathing-place in the Chiswick meadows a sailing-barge, which had just gone about, was standing across the course of the rival eights, and the Cambridge coxswain, instead of holding on his course, pulled his right-hand yoke-line hard, and suddenly fetched in towards the Middlesex shore, so as to pass ahead of the obstacle in question, and yet outside the Oxford boat, which was making up along the Chiswick bank, and so lost considerable way. When both boats had passed clear of the barge they found themselves level, the Cambridge crew having by this unfortunate manœuvre lost what little advantage they possessed. Had Mr Forbes kept on his course, or even used his weather-line ever so little, he would have crossed the wake of the barge, which, by the time he came up, would have stood off clear. No sooner were the Oxford crew level than they rapidly commenced to go in front, and simply rowed away from Cambridge, notwithstanding all the efforts of the latter. It was merely a question of time when Oxford would pass her antagonist, but the affair of the barge brought the result about some few hundred yards before it would actually have happened. From the bathing-place to the winning flag-boat off the Kew Meadows, Oxford increased her lead, passing under Barnes Bridge about a length and a-half ahead, notwithstanding a most determined spurt from Mr Griffiths just above the Bull's Head, and winning by three lengths in 25 m. 35 s. Slow time, but the tide had commenced to ebb before the crew reached the Ship. On their return both crews were loudly cheered, but there appeared to be more enthusiasm displayed towards the Cambridge crew than towards their conquerors.

The crews were,

OXFORD.

			st.	lbs.
1	R. T. RAIKES[1]	Merton	11	0
2	F. CROWDER	Brasenose	11	11
3	W. FREEMAN	Merton	12	7
4	F. WILLAN	Exeter	12	2
5	E. F. HENLEY[1]	Oriel	13	0
6	W. W. WOOD	University	12	4
7	H. P. SENHOUSE[1]	Chr. Ch.	11	3
str.	M. BROWN[1]	Trinity	11	5
cox.	C. R. W. TOTTENHAM[1]	Chr. Ch.	7	13
	Average of crew		11	12¾

[1] Were in the crew of 1865.

CAMBRIDGE.

			st.	lb.
1	J. STILL............................	*Caius*	11	6
2	J. R. SELWYN[1]............	*3rd Trinity*...	11	6
3	J. U. BOURKE	*1st Trinity* ...	12	3
4	J. FORTESCUE	*Magdalen* ...	12	2½
5	D. F. STEAVENSON[2]...	*Trinity Hall*	12	5
6	R. A. KINGLAKE[2]......	*3rd Trinity*...	12	9
7	H. WATNEY[2]	*St John's* ...	10	11
str.	W. R. GRIFFITHS[2]	...*3rd Trinity*...	11	9
cox.	A. FORBES................	*St John's* ...	8	0
	Average of crew		11	11⅝

The crews afterwards enjoyed the hospitality of Mr Phillipps, of Mortlake, and of the Thames Subscription Club in the evening. Mr Denman, as usual, presided.

In commenting on the crews the *Field* says that if Mr G. Morrison had trained the crew throughout, Oxford would with its unusually good raw material have turned out one of the most slashing eights that have ever been seen.

There was no lack of a good reach forward, of a firm and early catch of the water, or of a long and fairly rowed out stroke, but the form of the crew was decidedly not up to the average.

The Cambridge crew were a great improvement on their predecessors, and came to the post a really good crew, lacking however that all important quality—strength. The chief improvement on the crew of 1865 was in the stroke oar, Mr Griffiths having taken Mr Lawes' place; he rowed in the most brilliant manner during the race, his

---

[1] Rowed in 1864.   [2] Were in the crew of 1865.

steady sweeping stroke being the subject of universal admiration from first to last.

1867.

The Trial Eights at Oxford had to be put off from the day they were originally fixed to the next, owing to the high winds: and at Cambridge they had to row the race with the stream and wind instead of up stream as usual.

The strokes of the winning and losing crews at Oxford were T. Crump of Wadham, and L. A. Kershaw of Pembroke: at Cambridge, J. W. Pinckney of 1 Trinity and A. J. Leavens of Queens'.

There is no account whatever of the race or training in the Cambridge Books.

At Oxford "the great difficulty in the formation of the crew this year was the retirement of Brown from the stroke oar, and having therefore to select a fresh stroke." Crump of Wadham, J. Hall of University, and Fish of Worcester, were in their turn tried and found wanting. Eventually Marsden of Merton (who, by the way, was formerly at St John's College, Cambridge), was put in that place. The coaching was generally done by Woodgate of B.N.C., and sometimes G. Morrison and others came up for a day or two.

"We had on the whole very bad weather[1], and

[1] The weather during the period of training this year

towards the end of training the floods had risen to a greater height than ever was known before, and every day it snowed and blowed so hard that we could not by any means get below Sandford, and of course no coaching could be had from the bank. It at last got so bad that we were fairly driven away, and started for Putney on March 29th, where we took up our quarters as usual at the White Lion."

The weather at Cambridge was also very bad, and for one whole fortnight the crew never came in without getting a drenching. They were coached during the greater part of training by Rev. W. Maule, 1st Trin., whose cheery manner was of the greatest assistance in keeping up the spirits of the crew, and by Mr D. F. Steavenson of Trinity Hall during the latter part of their time at Cambridge, and during the whole of the time they were in London.

The crews arrived at Putney, Oxford on Friday, March 29, Cambridge on Saturday, March 30.

The *Field* says that the Cambridge men were on their arrival as nearly fit to row the race as possible, and during the early part of their first week in town their rowing was really a pleasure to behold.

They seem however to have been overtrained

reminded one of the Yankee's description of the English climate:

> "Fust it rained and then it blew,
> And then it friz and then it snew,
> And then it hailed and then it thew,
> And friz again, Oh, horrible!"

some time before the day of the race, and consequently got stale.

The times of the two boats over the course were as follows:

			Oxford.	Weather.	Cambridge.
Monday,	April	1st.	——	——	20' 45⅛"
Tuesday,	,,	2nd.	24' 45⅛"	Light headwind.	——
Wednesday,	,,	3rd.	20' 19⅖"	O. rowed on a strong ebb with a fair wind. C. rowed on a good tide with a bad wind at the start.	23' 48⅖"
Friday,	,,	5th.	20' 7"	Good ebb and fair wind.	——
Saturday,	,,	6th.	19' 5"	To Barnes Bridge on strong flood.	——
Monday,	,,	8th.	——	Heavy gale of wind.	——
Tuesday,	,,	9th.	21' 6"	Wind fair but squally.	21" 25"

On Wednesday Oxford rowed from the Ship, and at Hammersmith were picked up by an amateur crew, who led them till beyond Craven Cottage, when the Oxford men overhauled them and got the lead just above Bishop's Creek, where both stopped. Cambridge had a spin with the London twelve-oar, in which they overhauled the Londoners before Craven Cottage.

On Thursday Cambridge had some spins with Leander, and Oxford with a watermen's crew. Friday was devoted as usual to a few starts, but Mr Willan was unable to row on account of a very severe boil.

After giving the log of the crew while at Putney, the Oxford Book speaks thus of the day of the race.

"April 13. It turned out a filthy morning, raining and blowing like anything: there were nevertheless quite as many steamers and spectators as usual. We were delayed some time at the start owing to the bad behaviour of some of the steamers; we were however at last got off at 9 o'clock, and after a fearful race won by ¾ths of a length."

After giving a list of the crew it goes on:

"As I write Tottenham's name, I cannot help contributing my mite to the universal praise of his splendid steering, and also of his great assistance in coaching and encouraging the crew when in practice; this being also the fourth time of his steering Oxford to victory.

" F. WILLAN,
"*President*, 1867."

Bell's Life, in giving an account of the race, makes the following admirable remarks:

We have read in really respectable newspapers that false weights of the Cambridge crew were put about and published "for the purpose of influencing the betting!" Now, of course, the notion that the weight of a yet unformed crew—the men themselves not even yet decided on—could influence betting, is nothing else than unmitigated nonsense, but to the uninformed and innocent it might also be dangerous nonsense, and suggestive of evil. It is however another of those descending steps by which the dignity of this race is year after year suffering, and before it is reached it should be borne in mind that there is a last round of every ladder. When rowing first came into vogue at the Universities, and for years after, the reward of merit was honour, and honour alone. Now-a-days no one, who takes up athletic sports as a pastime, is content unless his labours are continually rewarded in the shape of gold, or silver, or pewter; the uttermost mediocrity, indeed, considering itself ill used if it failed to attain the latter. Would it not be well for our modern athletes to call to mind what was the reward of the victor in the Olympic Games, in which the most skilful competitors could not hope to attain a prize without a preparation as severe as any of our own day? At the present time, when there is a great outcry against the expenses of a University education, it might be advisable for members to reason seriously with themselves whether in healthy recreation and amusement such luxurious prizes are necessary, for undoubtedly they form a serious item in the annual bills of many an undergraduate whose parents can ill afford such, nay more, who probably pinch themselves in many ways to give him the benefits held out by Alma Mater. We are not singular in our ideas upon this topic, for our contemporary, the *London Review*, no mean authority in University matters, in speaking of the amusements at the Universities, says:—'College athletic sports are still the order of the day, although some are found to cry out bitterly against the waste of time and the general habit of betting to which they lead. Probably the most objectionable feature in them (which not a few of the athletes individually acknowledge) is the obligation which fashion seems to lay upon all Colleges to provide a very handsome and very expensive Strangers' Prize. There is neither rhyme nor reason in enforcing a subscription for a cup of £15 or £20 to be won by somebody who gives his whole mind (!) to the trade of running; however, it is hopeless arguing against the tyranny of public opinion.' 'Public opinion!' but of what public? surely not that of the wise, honest, upright, reasoning public! No! but of that by whom, and for whom we have endeavoured to show, attempts have been made to lower the University Boat Race from its pinnacle of honour, integrity, and fame, and debase it among those events capable of being affected by the fluctuations of the odds. Such attempts have, of course, failed, as, when guarded against, they must always do; but that is no reason they should not be again repeated, and holding the high honour of our Universities, their members, and their sports at heart, we have considered it our duty to point out that such attempts have been made, and are likely to be tried again, and we have therefore tendered our solemn warning and protest against them.

It is now time to turn our attention to the Boat Race of 1867, and to introduce it with a short remembrancer of 1866. For the first three miles nearly of that year's celebrated race the hopes of Cambridge were greatly and most justly raised. They had a good lead, were rowing in better form than their opponents, and victory seemed secure, when a sailing barge standing over ahead of them towards the Middlesex shore caused an error in judgment on the part of their steerer, who took upon himself the dangerous risk of endeavouring to head it. Nothing but the superhuman endeavours of his already wearied crew, endeavours too which had to be made with the rudder hard on, saved them from being run down, and the consequence was the immediately forging ahead of the Oxford boat, and practically the termination of the race. Much was said at the time and has since been said as to what the probable result would have been had no such occurrence taken place, and of course the matter is open to doubt. But we cannot help thinking that the notion that Oxford, although certainly slightly gaining at the time, would ultimately have passed the Light Blues, was a good deal founded on the recollections of the year before, and the habit which they had acquired of winning. But it should be remembered that only four or five minutes remained to effect this great change; it should be borne in mind that the depression of spirits in a crew who all at once lose sight of an enemy they had been rowing ahead of, is even more than equalled by the refreshed hopes of those who have been rowing a weary stern chase, and again catch sight of the foe. Nor is it a certainty that Oxford would have pulled themselves together again into the good form which had once been entirely beaten out of them, unless all this had happened. Be that as it may, it is one of those practical and bitter lessons which may be useful to those who come after. If a vessel, beating to windward, is standing across ahead of you in your road, the invariable rule is to approach her, holding on your straight course as if about to run under her, but in your own mind determined to go astern. What at a distance appears an immoveable log upon the waters you will find on a near approach to possess a most fatal swiftness, and should you in error attempt to head her she will drive you irresistibly to despair and certain ruin. If taken properly she may prove of priceless worth, for you coax your adversary, if he is alongside of you, or nearly so, up to her very side; with a gentle turn of the wrist, almost imperceptible but to yourself, you just escape her rudder, and your adversary must ease his oars or rush full tilt upon the destructive wall.

The following account of the race is from the *Times*. It is evidently from the pen of a man who either is peculiarly ignorant of rowing or has a happy knack of concealing his knowledge. I have consequently thought it advisable to append a few notes, which are chiefly criticisms of Mr Vincent.

In the hypercriticism which has been so liberally showered on the Cambridge crew during their training, a mass of nonsense has been talked and written about their not "catching" the water, "clipping" their stroke, not rowing from their legs, and so on *ad nauseam*. The plain truth is that Cambridge in her best days, when she won year after year four times in succession, never launched a better crew upon the Thames than that which rowed the race on Saturday. The beauty of their style, the quickness of their start, the uniform precision of their feathering[1], and the speed of their "spurts" when Mr Griffiths choose to put them on, have never been seen on the river before. The odds which were offered against them were due more to the traditional prestige which Oxford has now acquired than to any real difference in the crews. No one who saw the boats at exercise over their ground

---

[1] This is hardly the point to which an oarsman would have looked first; rather he would have looked for "uniform precision" in the stroke.

could feel confident of the result of the race for either side. Oxford, with their deep[1] stroke and very high style of feathering, seemed certainly likely to win in heavy and lumpy water; and heavy and lumpy water they had on Saturday. Had there been a better tide, with light wind and a smooth surface, it is possible that Cambridge would have gone in a winner. As it was, however, the Oxford men rowed best under the conditions in which both started. Their crew, too, were decidedly the stronger, and never, unless in dangerous emergencies, put on those "spurts" in which Cambridge excelled, but which take it out of the crew so much as to be fatal to their endurance in so long a race.

Oxford had been out as usual for a little paddling in the morning; the Cambridge crew did not take the water till the start. It was nearly 9 o'clock before they passed down to their boats, and sixteen finer or better trained young men it would have been difficult to find in England.

The following is a list of the crews:—

OXFORD CREW.

			st.	lbs.
1	W. P. BOWMAN	*University*	10	11
2	J. H. FISH	*University*	12	1
3	E. S. CARTER	*Worcester*	11	12
4	W. W. WOOD[2]	*University*	12	6
5	J. C. TINNÉ	*University*	13	4
6	F. CROWDER[2]	*Brasenose*	11	11
7	F. WILLAN[2]	*Exeter*	12	3
str.	R. G. MARSDEN	*Merton*	11	11
cox.	C. R. W. TOTTENHAM[2]	*Ch. Ch.*	8	8

[1] The writer probably means that the Oxford crew covered the blades of their oars; but so does every crew which is worth anything.

[2] Were in the crew of 1866.

CAMBRIDGE CREW.

			st.	lbs.
1	W. H. ANDERSON	............*1st Trinity*...	11	0
2	J. M. COLLARD	............*St John's* ...	11	4
3	J. U. BOURKE[1]	............*1st Trinity*...	12	9
4	Hon. J. H. GORDON	.........*1st Trinity*...	12	3
5	F. E. CUNNINGHAM	.........*King's*	12	12
6	J. STILL[1]	............*Caius*	11	12
7	H. WATNEY[1]	............*St John's* ...	11	0
str.	W. R. GRIFFITHS[1]	............*3rd Trinity* ..	12	0
cox.	A. FORBES[1]	............*St John's* ...	8	2

They took the water a little before 9, and, going easily to the starting-point, turned up the river and waited with poised oars till the word was given. It must be remembered, as we have already said, that Oxford, with her usual luck, won the choice for place, and of course took the best—the Middlesex side. At two minutes to 9 the word was given, and, like a flash, both boats were off. It could hardly be said which was the first to catch the water, and it is almost unnecessary[2] to say that both crews were to a certain extent flurried, and did not settle to their practised form for the first 300 yards or more. Then Cambridge began to draw their boat a little ahead, but never for more than a few feet, when the Oxonians quickened their deep, strong strokes, and crept up again. From this to Hammersmith Bridge the race was inexpressibly exciting. The boats were side by side, each crew looking only to the work they had in hand, and stretching to their oars with a power that made them bend like willows[3] and sent their craft forward with a visible leap at every stroke. Neither needed incentives to do their best; but they had them nevertheless, and the wild cries and hideous clamour

---

[1] Were in the crew of 1866.

[2] I cannot see why. 300 yards is a long distance to go before getting into form.

[3] If the oars *bent like willows* they were not fit to row with, and certainly could never make a boat *leap*.

of directions and encouragement from friends of each party came from all sides. But amid all this the stroke oars of the boats kept their own course, and increased or lessened as they thought best the pace by which they guided their crews. Before Hammersmith Bridge was reached, Cambridge had drawn nearly her length ahead. Under the bridge, which was black with spectators, the Cambridge boat led magnificently[1], amid a roar of applause, which was taken up by thousands on both banks of the river. After them, pell-mell, like a straggling pack of hounds, the steamers came rolling and tumbling on, swaying from side to side, as their passengers rushed about to cheer the competing crews, and volunteer, amidst a hopeless uproar, some well-meant words of advice, encouragement, or entreaty. Oxford again, however, increased her speed of stroke, though she was never within five or six a minute of that of Cambridge, and drew up again so fast alongside her opponents as to justify all the odds which then, amid the most tremendous cheers from boats and banks, were being offered in her favour. The struggle then was most exciting. It would be impossible, no matter what amateur critics may say, to witness anything better than the style of rowing in each boat[2]. Cambridge rowed quicker, but her style was beautiful. The oars rose and fell with the precision of machinery, and the low feathering, little more than clear of the surface of the water, was the very perfection of rowing[3]. The Oxford stroke, though less pretty to look at, was evidently that to win, and the heavy water over which both boats had to pass gave Oxford a decided advantage in her high feathering. At this time she began to take a decided lead, and, amid the almost frantic applause of her supporters, began to draw well ahead. Still, in spite of every

---

[1] As a Cambridge man I can appreciate the adverb, and hope this year to see the Cambridge boat *leading magnificently* about three-quarters of a mile above Barnes Bridge.

[2] As the rowing in the two boats was different, it is difficult to know what the writer means.

[3] It is an interesting question, what sort of *feathering* could be the *perfection of rowing*.

advantage both of tide, which was better in the course she took, and her style of rowing, which was admirably suited to the rough water, she could never draw her boat quite clear of Cambridge. The "spurts" which the latter put on cannot be too highly praised. At the moment when it seemed Oxford was to have her own way, the Light Blue again bent to their work and literally shot up beside their antagonists. These desperate efforts, however, began to tell on Cambridge, and when about half a mile before Barnes Bridge they were rowing somewhat "ragged," and steadily, but slowly, Oxford drew ahead. Here, however, a change took place that seemed almost unaccountable to those who witnessed it. The Oxford crew seemed to relax their efforts, just as Cambridge made another magnificent "spurt." None knew what the Oxford crew were about. They seemed to have slackened into idleness. Roars, shouts from the bank, entreaties from the boats around them, and a great hoarse cry from both sides of the river, "Row, Oxford, row[1]," seemed to have no effect upon them, while Cambridge drew on, and when near the railway bridge had got her boat ahead. Then only did the Oxford crew seem to realise their danger, and the struggle became one of the most intensely exciting ever seen. None believed that when so near home Oxford would be able to recover the advantage gained by the splendid burst which had put Cambridge a little ahead, and the efforts each crew made were almost painful in their earnestness to witness. They laid to their oars till the boats sprung stroke after stroke through the water. Every one of the spectators seemed more or less wild with excitement, and if entreaties and cries of encouragement could have effected anything, each must have come in first. It is difficult to describe the enthusiasm of their different supporters as Oxford at last, in spite of all the efforts of Cambridge, drew her boat level, and then began to get its bows ahead. They had, however, no easy task. As often as she showed a foot in front,

---

[1] It is doubtful whether such an exclamation as this (which surely has something of irony in it) would ever be uttered by any but a very limited number of persons.

Cambridge by a desperate effort dashed up again, and so they went almost stroke and stroke under Barnes Bridge amid such a roar of applause as has seldom before been heard on the Thames. Then it was evident, or, at least, said to be evident to experienced eyes, that the Cambridge crew were blown and exhausted by their repeated "spurts." The result showed that this must to a certain extent have been true, for the Oxford won, but never to the last second did the Cambridge crew relax in their struggle for victory. To the very winning-post they pushed the Oxonians almost to exhaustion to hold the very little they had gained, and never till the flag was actually passed did any of the friends of Dark Blue feel the race secure, for the bounds with which the Cambridge boat now and then rushed forward seemed to make it a doubt even when there was only 50 yards to row that Cambridge would not win. As it was, however, the Oxonians seemed too keenly alive to the strength and spirit of their antagonists ever to give them a chance again. With a sturdy, strongly-pulled stroke, every man pulling not only from his legs but apparently from every fibre and muscle in his body, they kept their boat just half a length ahead, and amid deafening shouts so passed the flag, winning one of the quickest and most desperately-contested races that have ever been rowed on the Thames. It is really hard to say which crew deserves most praise. Nothing could exceed the gallantry and determination with which each struggled to the end, and struggled, too, when the chances fluctuated almost every minute, and the hope of regaining the lead which each boat lost in turn seemed almost hopeless. Oxford has won for the seventh time, and Cambridge has been beaten, but after such a struggle as should make her more proud of her defeat than of many of her former victories. Actually it has been rowed in a shorter time. Relatively, when the state of the water, the force of the wind, and the almost entire absence of the tide are considered, it may be reckoned as one of the quickest. The pace from first to last, when these disadvantages are considered, was really tremendous. The boats started at 8h. 58min. 24sec., and finished at 9h. 21min.

3 sec., so that the whole course of nearly four miles and a half was rowed in 22 minutes, 39 seconds. Last year the chronograph registered 25 minutes 51 9-10 seconds, so that this year it was 3 minutes 12 9-10 seconds quicker. The ablest amateurs and the best professional watermen were alike surprised at the speed with which the race from first to last was rowed.

1868.

In December, 1867, the Trial Eights came off as usual at both Universities. At Oxford the two stroke oars were A. H. Hall (University), the winner, and S. D. Darbishire (Balliol), who lost the race chiefly through a mistake of his coxswain, who took the boat through the wrong arch of the bridge. Hall's boat was considered so much the slowest that it was decided to give him the Berkshire shore to make an even race.

The race was won by about two-thirds of a length : time 8 m. 42 s.

At Cambridge the race was rowed on one of the bitterest days imaginable. A freezing wind was blowing from N.W., which made any clothes that got splashed with water as hard as a board. The strokes were J. W. Pinckney, 1 Trin., and J. M. Collard, Lady Margaret. Mr Pinckney had the same No. 7 to back him as last year, viz. Mr Nadin, Pembroke, and was again victorious, winning easily by several lengths.

In the Lent term the challenge was sent as

usual from Cambridge, and practising went on as usual for the first few weeks of the term, which was a long one. Just as the crew were on the point of going into training a most melancholy event occurred; an event which caused the deepest sorrow and the greatest dismay among all Cambridge men. On Wednesday, Feb. 12, the Hon. J. H. Gordon, who rowed No. 4 in 1867, was found dying in his room, having been shot by his own rifle, which he appears to have been carrying loaded without sufficient care. The loss of this gentleman, whose qualities of heart and mind had endeared him to all, and whose prowess as an oarsman was looked up to with the highest admiration, caused a feeling of blank despair to pervade the whole body of undergraduates. It is not too much to say that this sad accident was more acutely felt by the whole University than anything of the kind that had happened for many years. It was not wonderful then that Mr Still and the other authorities of the Club, after mature deliberation, and after consulting those who were best able to give advice, should have at first come to the determination to ask leave to withdraw the challenge. Still less remarkable was it that, after a week or so had passed over, and after there had been received from Oxford an answer whose tone was very unsympathetic, the Club should rescind its former resolution and determine to row the race as usual.

Preparations were at once made for the race; and Mr Still endeavoured to get some one to train the crew. Messrs Griffiths and Bourke each came up for a week, but were unable to do more, and then Kelly the waterman was engaged for a short time; and finally, when the crew was found not to improve as it was expected to do, Mr T. S. Egan was persuaded to take it in hand for the last three weeks. All efforts however did not bring it to that state in which a University crew is expected to be when it arrives at Putney.

At Oxford the following crew went into training at about the usual time:

Bow, W. D. Benson, *Balliol;* 2 A. C. Yarborough, *Lincoln;* 3 R. S. Ross of Bladensburg, *Exon.;* 4 J. C. Tinné, *Univer.;* 5 J. J. Derrington, *Ch. Ch.;* 6 E. J. Carter, *Worc.;* 7 F. Willan (capt.), *Exon.;* str. R. G. Marsden, *Merton;* cox. C. R. Tottenham, *Ch. Ch.*

After some time it was found that this crew did not improve as it ought to do, and that there was little or no life about it. Mr Willan says, "I took the advice of some old men on the subject, and in the middle of training I made up my mind to make a most radical change in the boat—the result of which was that Darbishire of Balliol was placed at the stroke oar. This change at so late a period was considered by many as a very rash step, and one that would tell much against our chance of winning. It certainly was an almost desperate step to take, and one that ought never to be done without very strong reasons, and after much deliberation and consultation. However the change worked wonders, and we immediately went with more life and swing." The change resulted in the crew which rowed the race (see below).

"At Putney we luckily had the *invaluable* services of G. Morrison to coach us nearly every day, and sometimes also Woodgate, Brown, Risley and Henley; and under Morrison's care made great progress during the last week.

We did hard work at first, but had to ease a little, as some of the men were getting rather weak. However we came to the post eventually very fit, and as the following account from the *Times* will show, won the race in a canter."

The crews went down to the boatyards from their headquarters soon after 11 o'clock and embarked, the Oxford crew from the London Rowing Club boathouse at half-past 11, and the Cambridge men from the Leander boathouse some eight or ten minutes later. They paddled slowly to the starting place, and, turning their boats round, backed them down to the two gigs from which they were to be held. Their names and weights were as follows:

		OXFORD.		st.	lbs.
1	W. D. BENSON	*Balliol*		10	13
2	A. C. YARBOROUGH	*Lincoln*		11	8
3	R. S. ROSS of Bladensburg	*Exeter*		11	8
4	R. G. MARSDEN [1]	*Merton*		11	13
5	J. C. TINNÉ [1]	*University*		13	7
6	F. WILLAN [1] (captain)	*Exeter*		12	5
7	E. S. CARTER [1]	*Worcester*		11	8
str.	S. D. DARBISHIRE	*Balliol*		11	3
cox.	C. R. W. TOTTENHAM [1]	*Ch. Ch.*		8	7
	Average			11	11⅝

[1] Were in the crew of 1867.

Cambridge.

				st.	lbs.
1	W. H. Anderson[1]	....	*1st Trinity*...	11	2
2	J. P. Nicholls	....	*3rd Trinity*	11	3
3	J. G. Wood	....	*Emmanuel*...	12	6
4	W. H. Lowe	....	*Christ's*	12	4
5	H. T. Nadin	....	*Pembroke* ...	12	11
6	W. F. MacMichael	....	*Downing* ...	12	$1\frac{1}{2}$
7	J. Still[1] (captain)	....	*Caius*	12	1
str.	W. J. Pinckney	....	*1st Trinity*...	10	10
cox.	T. D. Warner	....	*Trin. Hall.*	8	4
	Average	....		11	$11\frac{3}{4}$

Cambridge, for the first time these many years, won the toss for choice of station, and of course took the Fulham side. They certainly on the present occasion derived no advantage from it, because the boats from which the start was to be made were moored so close in to the Middlesex bank of the river—far too close indeed—that they had much less tide than their opponents. The Fulham station boat ought properly to have been placed where the Surrey station boat was stationed, and the latter should have occupied the position of the Conservancy steamer, which could easily have brought up in mid stream. Mr J. W. Chitty, of Exeter College, Oxford, was as usual umpire, and was conveyed by Citizen T, a fast boat, from which he was enabled to view the race throughout. Mr Edward Searle officiated as starter, and John Phelps of Fulham acted as judge at the flagboat at Mortlake.

Just as Fulham Church clock was striking 12, the starter gave the word to go, and the University Boat Race of 1868 commenced. The oars of the two crews caught the water as nearly as possible at the same instant, but as there was most "lift" in the Oxford eight, the latter may be said to have been the first off. As soon, however, as both boats were well under way the Cambridge crew, pulling a slightly quicker stroke

---

[1] Were in the crew of 1867.

than Oxford, at once showed in front, leading, as well as could be judged, by a quarter of a length off Simmons's yard, and by rather less than half a length at the London Rowing Club boathouse. The Oxford crew in their turn now began to hold their own, and almost as soon to make up their leeway, so that on passing the Leander Club Rooms they had reduced the lead of Cambridge to a third of a length. The two boats continued racing nearly abreast of one another up the Reach towards Craven Cottage, the Oxonians steadily though slowly gaining ground, and on passing the Cottage they showed ahead of Cambridge. A spurt from the latter once more appeared to leave the issue doubtful, but as the effort died away the Oxford crew again led, no more to be repassed. Both eights were taking a long shoot across the river for the Surrey side, the Cambridge coxswain steering a good course in the full strength of the flood tide, but Mr Tottenham suddenly fetched his boat in towards the towpath, probably mistaking the position of the Soap Works Point, which was indistinguishable in the prevailing haze. He soon discovered his error and kept away, having lost ground by the manœuvre, but still not enough to jeopardize his crew's chance of success. At the Crab Tree Oxford led by perhaps half a length, the Cambridge crew becoming unsteady as they were headed.

At the Soap Works Wharf the Oxford crew were a length in front, and they passed under the Surrey arch of Hammersmith Bridge two lengths before their adversaries, who were taken outside the steamboat pier and through the centre span. Time 7 min. 40 sec. Above the bridge a large fleet of rowboats had collected on the Surrey side of the river, and in making way for the Oxford eight several of them placed themselves in the track of the Cambridge boat, which was compelled to make a slight detour to avoid them. Round the bend of the river, opposite the Doves, Oxford continued to hold a lead of about two lengths, which on entering the straight reach past the Oil Mills was a trifle increased, the Cambridge coxswain sheering out to avoid the backwash of the leading boat. Half way up to Chiswick Eyot Mr Pinckney made a brilliant effort to retrieve the fortunes of the day, in which he was pretty well backed up by his crew, and reduced the lead of Oxford to two lengths or thereabouts. The spurt was answered by the Oxonians, and then the Cambridge crew, who had been rowing more or less wildly from the time they passed the Crab Tree, fell "all to pieces," their shape and time, especially on the stroke side, being wretched. There is little more to tell, for the Oxford crew maintained and increased their lead, passing under Barnes Bridge about three lengths in front in 16 min. 50 sec., and reaching the flagboat at the foot of the Kew meadows in 20 min. 56 sec. from the time of starting, easy winners by upwards of four lengths, having rowed over the upper half of the course 36 strokes a minute to 40 on the part of Cambridge.

The rowing in both boats was indifferent—indeed, it is doubtful whether the University match, to which every one is accustomed to look for good oarsmanship, has ever previously been contested by less finished crews. Of course the Oxford crew rowed the better of the two, but it is one thing to row a winning race and another to row a losing one, so that allowance must be made on that score. At the same time few persons who had witnessed the daily practice of the rival eights at Putney were prepared to see the Cambridge crew, who in their training had rowed a long slow stroke, fall so utterly to pieces as they did during the race. They not only got wild, but "short" also when the pinch came, and it is needless to point out that on a long trying course like that between Putney and Mortlake, to get short and "scratchy" is to meet with certain defeat.

"In conclusion, I must again testify to the splendid steering of Tottenham, who for the fifth and I am sorry to say for the last time has contributed mainly to our victory over Cambridge.

"FRANK WILLAN,
"*President.*"

1869.

The trial eights at the end of 1868 were rowed as usual. At Oxford the two strokes were Darbishire (*Balliol*), and Yarborough (*Lincoln*). The former won a most exciting and plucky race by about three-eighths of a length. At Cambridge a new feature was introduced, which, as it has given rise to a great deal of strong feeling and talk, I think I had better say a few words about.

The long chain of disasters which Cambridge had suffered from 1861 to 1868 had resulted in a state of utter demoralisation on the part of the University Boat Club, and Mr Anderson, who succeeded Mr Still as president, came to the conclusion that the state of the Club was such as rendered some extraordinary action necessary. Therefore, having taken the advice of some old men, he invited Mr G. Morrison, of Balliol College, Oxford, to come to Cambridge to coach the trial eights of 1868 and the University crew of 1869. When this action became generally known, Mr Anderson received many letters containing very strong remonstrances from old Cambridge men, who remembered the days when the C.U.B.C. was victorious and triumphant, and who were pained to think that she should have recourse to Oxford for instruction in the art of rowing. They considered it a disgrace to the Club. After the race of 1869, when we were again beaten, other Cambridge men, not quite so old nor yet so discreet, expressed their opinions in the public papers, and not only abused Mr Anderson, and his immediate predecessors, but did not scruple to fall foul of Mr Morrison himself.

I feel sure, however, that Cambridge men generally, whatever may have been their opinions or feelings with regard to the policy of obtaining assistance from the sister University, had but one sentiment of regard and gratitude towards Mr Morrison for the pains and trouble he had taken with the crew, and were sorry that other Cambridge men should have given expression to any other feeling.

With regard to the *policy* of Mr Anderson's action, I may express my own opinion that, though it had not the immediate result of making us victorious last year, it has had and is now having a very beneficial effect on the rowing of the University, and has inspired new life into the Club at large. The ideas of men generally about rowing have improved wonderfully,—if at least the "coaching" on the bank is any criterion,—and the style of rowing in the college boats has changed very much for the better in the last twelve months.

It will be remembered that in 1852 the O.U.B.C. in like circumstances asked and obtained the aid of a Cambridge coach, Mr T. S. Egan. In each case the ruling consideration on both sides was the common interests of rowing, which seemed for the time being to require the adoption of a course which, as is obvious, neither University would consent to adopt except under pressure of necessity. It may be safely left to the judgment and spirit of the Club to decide whence that necessity has arisen.

At Cambridge there were altogether five refusals to row this year, and the state of affairs was such that Mr Morrison advised that no challenge should be sent; the Club however determined not to give in, and the challenge was sent in due course.

The following is from the Secretary's book:—

"Morrison did not come up till the beginning of February, but we of course began practising with Anderson for coach at once, Blake Humphrey rowing for him. Regular training began on Ash Wednesday, and the log of the crew is given below.

"We began training on Wednesday, Feb. 10, with the following crew:—

"1 P. H. Mellor, *1st Trin.* 2 W. H. Anderson, *1st Trin.* 3 J. W. Dale, *Lady Margaret.* 4 F. J. Young, *Christ's.* 5 W. F. Macmichael, *Downing.* 6 J. H. Ridley, *Jesus.* 7 J. A. Rushton, *Emmanuel.* 8 J. H. D. Goldie, *Lady Margaret.* Cox. H. E. Gordon, *1st Trin.*

"The average weight was 11 st. 12 lbs.

"Our general practice was to have coaching in pair-oar gigs in the morning. Then to walk down to the Bridge in the afternoon, and either row twice up and down the course, or go to Bottisham; have the boat rowed up from there to Clay Hythe, and thence paddle to Baitsbite, whence we walked home.

"During training Anderson and Ridley changed places, and so did Rushton and Mellor."

The race was fixed for Wednesday, March 17. The Cambridge crew went up to town on Wednesday, March 3rd. The following is the log of the last 10 days' training on Putney water :—

Saturday, March 6th. Heavy wind against tide. Could not row higher than Chiswick. Thence rowed hard to the Aqueduct. Got the boat jammed across two of the piers of Putney Bridge. Fortunately no harm done to the boat, but No. 7 caught cold.

Monday, March 8th. Rowed hard from Simmond's Yard to Barnes Bridge against the ebb. A Leander eight picked us up in Putney Reach, but could not hold us at all: time 21 m.

Tuesday, March 9th. Rowed hard from Simmond's Boat Yard to the "Ship:" time 21 m.

Wednesday, March 10th. Rowed sharply to Hammersmith, and paddled back.

Thursday, March 11th. Mellor's cold got worse. J. Still, who happened to be up at Putney, rowed for him: only rowed to Hammersmith and back.

Friday, March 12th. Mellor's cold a little better. Rowed to Chiswick and back.

Saturday, March 13th. Mellor much worse, and obliged to go home. Still was telegraphed for and arrived at about 5 o'clock. Paddled out in a heavy fall of snow.

Monday, March 15th. Rowed hard from the Bathing Place Creek to L.R.C. Boat House. Rowing good.

Tuesday, March 16th. Rowed sharply from the Aqueduct to Hammersmith Bridge on the flood.

The following account of the race is from the *Field*.

About half-past three o'clock the crews proceeded from their hotels to their boats. The weather was not the most agreeable for a boat-race, as there was a raw wind from the southward of east, dull, leaden-coloured clouds overhanging the river; but, although rain had fallen during the early part of the afternoon, it cleared up before the embarkation of the crews commenced. At a quarter to four the Dark Blue crew pushed off and paddled down towards the Aqueduct, followed at an interval of five minutes by the Cambridge crew, who were vociferously cheered as they left the shore. The tide, which was about three-quarters flood, was running hard, and this, coupled with the force of the south-east wind, led to the prediction amongst frequenters of the river side that the match would be completed in unusually quick time. The two small boats, from the sterns of which the competing eights were held at the start, were moored about a hundred and fifty yards above Putney Aqueduct. The Fulham station was occupied by the Oxford boat, the Cambridge eight being on the Surrey side of them; but the direction of the wind and the state of the tide were such that one place was as good as the other, especially as the Surrey side boat was moored a trifle ahead of its fellow, so as to equalise matters. And here it may be stated that the Cambridge crew were instructed to take the outer, or Surrey station, if they won the toss, in order that they might have the advantage of the long turn to the left in the bank of the river between the Crabtree and the top of Chiswick Eyot, where the tug of war was expected to take place—and with justice, as the sequel proved. The two crews were soon in readiness to start after taking up their positions, and a couple of minutes before four o'clock Mr Edward Searle, of Lambeth, gave the signal, and the race commenced, the crews and their latest weights being as follows:

OXFORD.

			st.	lbs.
1	S. H. Woodhouse	University	10	13½
2	R. Tahourdin	St John's	11	11
3	T. S. Baker	Queen's	12	8
4	F. Willan[1]	Exeter	12	2½
5	J. C. Tinné[1] (Captain)	University	13	10½
6	A. C. Yarborough[1]	Lincoln	11	11
7	W. D. Benson[1]	Balliol	11	7
str.	S. D. Darbishire[1]	Balliol	11	8½
cox.	D. A. Neilson	St John's	7	10¼
	Average of crew		12	0¼

CAMBRIDGE.

			st.	lbs.
1	J. A. Rushton	Emmanuel	11	5
2	J. H. Ridley	Jesus	11	10½
3	J. W. Dale	St John's	11	12
4	F. J. Young	Christ's	12	4
5	W. F. MacMichael[1]	Downing	12	4
6	W. H. Anderson[1] (Captain)	1st Trinity	11	4
7	J. Still[1]	Caius	12	1
str.	J. H. D. Goldie	St John's	12	1
cox.	H. E. Gordon	1st Trinity	7	8
	Average of crew		12	0

The Cambridge crew got hold of the water first, but the Oxford boat, as soon as it was well under way,

---

[1] Rowed in 1868.

drew up to them, and so even was the speed of the two boats, that they passed Simmons's yard as nearly level as possible. In the next few strokes the nose of the Oxford boat forced itself in front, and off the London Club boathouse led by ten or twelve feet—the Cambridge eight at the same time, in its turn, crept up rapidly, and half-way up the willows, opposite the first bridge on the tow-path, led by three or four feet. The Oxford crew, meanwhile, were not to be denied, and rowing very steadily, whilst their opponents got a little wild and short, once more drew up alongside them, and led by a trifling distance off the site of the old half-mile post, with every appearance of increasing their advantage. The Cambridge boat was here kept wide, but in the strength of the flood, whilst the Oxford eight hugged the shore too close at the Point; the former thus again went ahead, and had drawn their boat's nose as much as a third of a length in front. The Oxford crew, after passing Craven Cottage, again overtook the Cambridge, and, racing them hard in Crab Tree Reach, led at the end of the first mile. In the centre of the Reach the Cambridge crew held their own until breasting the Crab Tree itself, where the Oxford coxswain suddenly sheered his boat's nose out towards the Middlesex side of the river. Notwithstanding this, the Cambridge crew seemed unable to take advantage of the opportunity, so that Oxford led at the Soapworks Wharf by three-quarters of a length. In the next hundred yards, the Cantabs commenced to overhaul the leading eight, going up to it hand over hand, and half-way to the bridge they showed a trifle in front; both boats being steered slightly across the tide, which here sets strongly towards the Surrey arch, in order to clear the steamboat pier at Hammersmith. On the two boats sped for the centre arch of the Suspension Bridge, amidst the greatest excitement from the multitudes assembled on the bridge and in its immediate neighbourhood, where the cheering was deafening—the Cambridge boat inch by inch increasing its advantage, until, as it shot under the archway, it led by, as nearly as may be, one-third of a length. Directly after passing the bridge, the Oxford crew presented a very threatening appearance, although their pulling was not regular. Above the bridge the Oxford steersman lost no little ground by sheering off to the Middlesex shore. The consequence was that the Cambridge crew still held the lead off the Doves, and round the bend of the bank opposite the Mall. As soon, however, as the Oxford boat was again put into her proper course, she commenced once more to overhaul the Cambridge crew, the latter being kept too close to the bank out of the full set of the tide. In entering Corney Reach, the steering in both boats was rather erratic; but the Oxford crew, whose strength was beginning to tell against their opponents, got up alongside the Cambridge eight, and at the Waterworks led by a third of a length, the rowing in both boats at the lower end of Chiswick Eyot being open to considerable improvement. In passing Chiswick Eyot, the Oxford crew slowly but surely drew their boat away, inch by inch, and it became only too evident that the match was no longer in doubt. Off Chiswick Church, where the Cambridge boat was taken too close into the Surrey shore, out of the strength of the tide, the Oxford crew led by half a length, and, in spite of a plucky spurt on the part of Cambridge, added surely to their lead in rounding the turn in the bank, drawing themselves clear, for the first time during the contest, off the White Cottage in the Chiswick fields. At the bathing-place they had increased their lead by another half length, the Cambridge boat keeping out very wide. From the bathing-place to Barnes Bridge the Oxford crew increased their advantage, finding themselves rowing a winning race. Along the osier beds opposite the road between Mill Lodge and Lord Lonsdale's grounds the Cambridge crew made several plucky efforts to retrieve their ill-fortunes — especially when they heard a well-known voice close astern of them—but to no purpose, as the Oxford crew passed under Barnes Bridge leading by two lengths or thereabouts, and, slightly adding to this distance over the remainder of the course, reached the Ship first, clever winners by three lengths, or a trifle over. Time, 20 min. $4\frac{4}{5}$ sec. This time is the fastest on record; but, that it may not mislead in comparing the pace of the winning crew of 1869 with that of some of its predecessors, we may observe that the favourable wind and strong tide contributed materially to shorten the duration of the race, irrespective of which the crews did not row the whole course through, and for the reason that the winning flag was planted immediately opposite the Ship at Mortlake, although the start took place a hundred and fifty yards above Putney Aqueduct. On previous occasions the flagboat has sometimes been placed at a corresponding distance above the Ship, but in the present instance it was not so. Both crews rowed in boats built by the Salters of Oxford, and the betting at starting may be quoted at 5 to 2 and 3 to 1 on the winners (taken and offered).

In remarking on the race the *Field* says:

Without in the slightest degree wishing to detract from the well-known abilities of Mr Still, we cannot help thinking that, if the crew had not lost their trained man at the eleventh hour, they would have made a better fight of it to the end. As he was without any training or practice whatever, it could not be expected that he would be able to row the whole punishing distance of $4\frac{1}{4}$ miles as effectually as if he had been thoroughly fit. The gallant manner in which he responded to the call of duty, and the plucky way in which he rowed from first to last, are above all praise.

Mr Morrison during the whole of the practice on the Thames coached from the Ariel steam yacht, which was kindly lent to the C.U.B.C. by Mr Blythe, of Downing College.

It was disputed whether the time was 20′ 20″ or 20′ 5″, but all were agreed that it was the fastest on record.

The following observations are from the O.U.B.C. Book.

"The above is a fairly accurate account of the

race. At the last moment I believe the betting reached 4 to 1 on Oxford. In the account of the dinner there is one report which I must contradict; in returning thanks to the company for drinking the health of the Oxford crew, I am reported to have said that the race might have had a very different result if Mr Mellor (No. 7) had not been obliged to relinquish his seat in consequence of illness. Nothing was farther from my thoughts, for I believe that the absence of Mr Mellor from the boat and the addition of Mr Still, untrained, to it, made far less difference than people think. Lord Justice Selwyn had been requested to take the chair at the dinner, but as he was prevented from coming, it was agreed that the winning captain should preside. Before closing the account I must add a word of gratitude to the Thames Conservancy for the assistance they gave us in keeping a clear course, and for the arrangements in general, which were admirable. More especially are our thanks due to Mr Lord, the working manager, for his assiduous attention.

"It was thought advisable to keep guard over the boats the night previous to the race; consequently three policemen kept watch over both the Oxford and Cambridge boathouses throughout the night.

"There was a report previous to the race, that an attempt would be made by blacklegs to damage the chance of Oxford by smashing the boat when going down to the start; but if proper care be taken surely all such attempts can be frustrated; at all events I hope the time is far distant when the University Boat Race is moved away from the Metropolitan course."

The Oxford and Harvard Boat Race.

In the winter of 1867—8 there was some correspondence between the O.U.B.C. and the rowing men of Harvard College, Massachusetts, U.S. The latter were desirous of making up a match for the ensuing long vacation. They proposed to row an eight-oared race on a straight course three miles long without coxswains.

The Oxford men expressed their willingness to make a match on terms similar to those on which the Oxford and Cambridge annual race is rowed, but declined to row without a coxswain. Chiefly on this account the race fell through for the year, but in closing the correspondence the Harvard men challenged Oxford to row

"A three mile straight away race at Lynn, Norfolk, on the Ouse, some time between the 15th of August and 1st of Sept. 1869.

"Each boat to contain eight rowers and a coxswain.

"The exact time and date to be mutually agreed upon by the captains of the respective crews."

The officers of the O.U.B.C. pointed out that they could not pledge their successors, but suggested that the challenge should be renewed early in 1869.

Mr Tinné, President 1869, says:

"Towards the end of the Michaelmas term, 1868, I heard that very probably a challenge would come over from America to row a race with Harvard University. I therefore got promises from all the men who rowed in Trial Eights and from several 'Varsity oars to row if called upon."

Soon after the commencement of the summer term challenges were received both at Oxford and Cambridge to row a four-oared race with coxswains from Putney to Mortlake in the latter half of August. The Americans suggested that all three should row together.

After much discussion the O.U.B.C. accepted the challenge by a bare majority of the Captains' meeting. The Cambridge President made every effort to get a crew, but failing to do so, was obliged to decline the challenge.

The following is from the Oxford Book.

"After the conclusion of the eights, I entertained an idea for some time of putting on a crew at Henley, by way of practice for the American race, and for a few days a crew composed of Darbishire, Tinné, Yarborough, and Benson practised between Oxford and Ifley; circumstances prevented the above from going to Henley, so it was arranged that nothing for the present should be done, but I asked the following to be at Eton, where we spent the first part of the training, by July 9th: Darbishire, Yarborough, Willan, Woodhouse, Crofts and Burgess. I also asked Benson, but he was unavoidably prevented coming, and so I had to give up all idea of obtaining his services. On July 7th we met at Eton, and for the first few days I had an eight out, made up of the fellows mentioned, with some Eton boys to fill up. On July 12th Darbishire, Tinné, Yarborough, Willan and Woodhouse went into training, Woodhouse being 5th man. The course we rowed was from Romney locks to the wooden bridge in Windsor lock Cut. Our day was divided thus: Out of bed at 7, walk and 100 yards run, cold bath, breakfast at 8, gig practice at 10, paddle in four at 12, lunch at 2, hard row at 6, dinner at 8, bed at 10.30 or not later than 11. Under the experienced eye of Mr Warre the crew soon shook together, and sometimes the rowing was thoroughly satisfactory. On July 28th, we tried the racing boat for the first time; she was very long, 44 feet, with no flat in the bottom: she was built purposely for going with the stream, and Salter particularly requested us not to row her hard against the stream. On July 31st we left Eton for Pangbourne, where we remained for about 10 days; the course we rowed was from Chertsey lock to Whitechurch lock, about 4 miles. G. Morrison coached us from the time we left Eton up to the time of the race. On August 11th we went to Putney and lodged at No. 93, High Street, a very comfortable house, the only drawback being that it was so far from the river. I had great difficulty in settling a day for the race; I had paid a visit to the Harvard captain when they first arrived at

Putney, when he was unwilling to come to any arrangement, because, as he said, he had not brought his crew over to England 3000 miles to row a 'rough and tumble race.' I told him that I was quite as anxious as he was for a calm day, but that I could not guarantee it, that it was quite necessary to settle on one day in order to allow the Thames Conservancy to carry out their arrangements for keeping the course clear; after some time we at last arranged to row on Friday, August 27th, on the evening tide.

"The weights of the Oxford crew at the beginning and end of training were as given below:

July 12th.				*August* 27th.	
st.	lbs.			st.	lbs.
12	2	......	WILLAN	11	11
11	12	......	YARBOROUGH	12	0¾
14	2	......	TINNÉ	13	7
11	10	......	DARBISHIRE	11	5

"I made a special point of leaving it entirely in the hands of the Harvard captain, Mr Loring, to choose a judge, a starter, the number of umpires, and in fact every arrangement that I thought he might like to have. He proposed to me that we should agree 'if an oar be broken in either crew during the first 12 strokes of the race, the race shall be called back, and the start made afresh.' This was quite an innovation to our English notions of rowing, but I thought it best to act up to the principle to which I had adhered throughout, viz. giving in to their wishes on every point, and so made no objection."

The race was rowed on Friday, August 17. The following account of it is taken from *Bell's Life* of the next day :—

A more gallant and determined contest—one honourable alike to victors and vanquished, and worthy in every respect of the first meeting between the amateur oarsmen of the Old and New Worlds—it has never been our lot to chronicle, and we imagine that few of those who had the good fortune to witness the struggle from start to finish will readily forget the scene presented yesterday evening on the Thames between Putney and Mortlake.

As a spectacle alone it was a marvel ; indeed, we have no hesitation in saying that the like has never been witnessed on the Thames—for though the surroundings bore a general family resemblance to the scene which the great annual eight-oared match between the two English Universities has made familiar to all lovers of aquatic sports, everything in connection with the memorable match of yesterday was on such a colossal scale as to render it impossible to draw any comparison between the two. To describe the externals of this eventful contest is, however, foreign to our present purpose, inasmuch as the task is altogether incompatible with the limited time at our disposal and the exigencies of the "composing-room ;" so, under the circumstances, we shall offer no apology to our readers for plunging incontinently *in medias res*, and proceeding without further preface to our record of the race itself.

A bright August morning, with a burning sun and scarcely a breath of wind, ushered in the eventful day, but towards afternoon a light air sprang up from the north-east, which, though scarcely sufficient to crisp the surface of the tideway, nevertheless had the effect of rendering the temperature somewhat more endurable. The start had been fixed provisionally, and subject to the state of the tide, for 5 p.m., and within a few minutes of the appointed hour the Oxford men got afloat at the yard of the Leander boathouse, and paddled leisurely down towards the starting-place, amid a burst of cheering from the spectators. The Harvard crew followed suit about six minutes later, and were equally well received; indeed, it seemed to us that the enthusiasm of the British public preponderated somewhat in their favour, more particularly when it became known that they had won the toss for choice of stations. Both crews lost no time in taking up their allotted positions at the stern of a couple of skiffs which were moored in a line with the pier, about five-and-twenty yards apart, but somewhat further towards the centre of the stream than usual, the Harvard crew of course selecting the Middlesex side, where they had a considerably better tide than their opponents.

The following are the names and weights of the two crews:—

OXFORD.

			st.	lbs.
1	F. WILLAN	(*Exeter*)	11	11
2	A. C. YARBOROUGH	(*Lincoln*)	12	0¾
3	J. C. TINNE	(*University*)	13	7
4	S. D. DARBISHIRE	(*Balliol*)	11	5
cox.	J. HALL	(*Corpus*)	7	4
	Average of crew		12	2¾

HARVARD.

		st.	lbs.
1	J. S. FAY	11	7
2	F. O. LYMAN	11	2
3	W. H. SIMMONDS	12	4
4	A. P. LORING	10	13
cox.	A. BURNHAM	7	6
	Average of crew	11	6½

For some reason or other the Harvard men have declined to supply an official return of their latest weights, but we had the above on excellent authority, and believe they will be found to be pretty nearly correct. The betting had fluctuated considerably during the few days immediately preceding the race, the odds ranging between 7 to 4 and 5 to 2 on Oxford, but yesterday morning the latter price was currently offered, and 2 to 1 and 9 to 4 were readily obtainable up to the moment of the start. In accordance with the excellent arrangements of the Thames Conservancy, which were admirably carried out under the immediate supervision of Mr Lord, of whose energy and firmness we cannot speak in too high terms of praise, two steamboats only were permitted to accompany the match, one carrying the officials, and the other devoted exclusively to the press, the latter having on board about fifty representatives of the leading English and American journals. Mr Tom Hughes, M.P., officiated as referee, and Mr Chitty and F. S. Gulston as umpires for Oxford and Harvard respectively, the above somewhat obsolete arrangement having been made, we understand, in compliance with the expressed wish of the American gentlemen. Mr Blakie (the hon. sec. of the Harvard Boat Club) acted as starter from the deck of the umpires' steamboat (Citizen T), and as soon as the crews had taken up their positions for the start dismissed them on level terms at 5.14.10 precisely. Both caught the water at the same moment, but the Harvard men were the quicker of the two in settling down to their work, and dashing away with lightning-like rapidity showed almost immediately with a perceptible lead. Foot by foot they improved their advantage up to Simmonds's, where the Harvard boat was fully half a length in front, their stroke being nearly on a level with No. 1 of the Oxford crew, who, however, were rowing a considerably slower stroke than their opponents, not exceeding 39 a minute, while the others ranged up to 44. As might be expected, this great disparity speedily told a tale, the Harvard men going away from the Dark Blues hand over hand with such amazing rapidity that they were within a foot of being clear as early as Bishop's Creek. At this stage of the race both boats were right in the centre of the stream, the Harvard coxswain gradually bearing a trifle out towards Oxford, whose coxswain gave way a little, apparently under the apprehension of a foul. The same relative positions were maintained up to the

Point, where the Harvard crew quickening up to 45 strokes to the minute drew themselves clear, and for a moment there was a palpable gap between the two boats, but a bit of faulty steering on the part of their coxswain lost them this advantage, and the next instant the nose of the Oxford boat slightly overlapped the leader's stern. They rowed in this position up to the Crab Tree, which was reached in 5 m. 15 s. from the start, but here another fine burst on the part of the Americans again brought them clear, and by the time they were well across the water the stern of the leading boat was fully half a length in advance of the stem of Oxford. At this critical moment the Harvard coxswain was guilty of a fatal act of indecision. For a moment he turned the nose of his boat over towards the Surrey shore, as though with the object of taking the Oxford's water, which to all appearance might have been effected without much danger, but either he misjudged his distance, or his nerve failed him at the critical point, as the next instant he put the rudder on hard in the contrary direction, and came out wide, the Oxford coxswain very wisely holding on his course, and refusing to give way the fraction of a foot. This momentary hesitation materially altered the complexion of the race, as before the Harvard coxswain could get his boat straight the "clear half length" was lost for ever, and just above the Soap Works the Oxford crew, with slightly-quickened strokes, once more came up with the leaders, and overlapped them a foot or two. At this moment the difference between the styles of the two crews was particularly noticeable; the long, machine-like Oxford drag, and faultless form and swing, exhibiting a marked contrast to the flurried rush forward and short, scratchy arm-work of their opponents, whose tremendous efforts to force the pace during the early part of the struggle were now beginning to tell the inevitable tale. Inch by inch the Oxford crew crept up, but it was only by inches, for the Americans disputed every foot of water with most dogged determination, and though falling palpably "ragged," more particularly on the stroke side, every moment, never slackened their killing stroke for an instant. Hammersmith Bridge was reached in 8 m. 45 s. from the start, Harvard leading, as nearly as we could judge, by about four-fifths of their own length; but here their coxswain again took them out somewhat wide, and by the time both boats were well through the bridge there was scarcely more than half a length between them. Off the Doves, however, the Americans, by a desperate spurt, momentarily improved their position, but the effort speedily died away, and they gradually "came back" to Oxford, whose long, telling stroke seemed fairly to break the hearts of their opponents. Still they struggled on with most unflinching pluck, and held their lead gallantly to the bottom of Chiswick Eyot; but here it was palpable that the day was against them, as Oxford, without the slightest perceptible quickening of their stroke, came up hand over hand, and for the first time in the whole of this eventful race drew themselves level. All was now over. Halfway up the Eyot Oxford were well ahead, and, going right away as though the others were standing still, drew themselves clear, without the slightest apparent effort, at the top of the island taking the Americans' water about 50 yards higher up. From this point the race calls for no detailed description, as the Harvard men were now palpably "all to pieces," while the others were to all appearances going better than when they started, and increasing the gap between the two boats with every stroke. At the bathing-place Oxford led by two clear lengths, going well in front of the Americans, and giving them the full benefit of their backwash, the Harvard coxswain, for some inscrutable reason, keeping right in the wake of their leaders, and following them wherever they went. Passing under Barnes Railway Bridge (time 18 m. 20 s.) the Oxford boat led by fully three lengths, rowing easily within themselves, the Harvard men being by this time hopelessly beaten, and their coxswain in vain essaying to restore their failing energies by the novel expedient—novel at least on this side of the Atlantic—of splashing them liberally with cold water. Between the Bridge and the winning-post Oxford added another length to their lead, and (after a narrow escape of being fouled by an idiot in a gig, who coolly rowed right across them) came in first by three clear lengths, having covered the whole distance in 22 m. 17 s.

A more magnificent race for the first two miles it has never been our lot to witness, and we scarcely know to which side we ought to award the higher praise—to the winners for their splendid exhibition of form, style, and patient endurance, or to the losers for the indomitable pluck and unwavering resolution they displayed throughout the whole of this trying struggle. That the best crew won, and won fairly on its merits, we think there can be no two opinions, and it is equally certain that the victory was a triumph of good form and good style over superior physical strength less scientifically applied. From the first, as our readers are well aware, we never anticipated any different result, but at the same time we must candidly confess that the really good fight the Harvard men made of it took us completely by surprise. It was truly a magnificent race, and though beaten the losers have assuredly lost no laurels in the contest; on the contrary, they will have the satisfaction of feeling that their opponents found them "foemen worthy of their steel," and that they themselves have measured oars not ingloriously against one of the finest amateur crews that has been seen on the Thames for many a long year.

The distance by which the race was won was stated as above in all the newspapers, but Sir Aubrey Paul, the judge, stated that there was a gap of three-quarters of a length only between the boats at the finish.

This discrepancy, which arose from a mistake of the reporters, was clearly explained at the time, but it is not worth while entering now into the reasons of its occurrence.

APPENDIX I.

TECHNICAL AND SCIENTIFIC TERMS.

Page 4. *A maiden over.* An over at cricket in which no runs are made off the bat.

ibid. tub. A boat built for steadiness rather than swiftness, and consequently broad and heavy. Men learning to row are at first taken out in pair-oared 'tubs,' and taught how to sit, and swing their bodies, and feather their oars.

Page 5. *ship,* is the word generally used to express merely the boat in which the crew are put, as the word *boat* is constantly used to include the crew.

Page 10. *stretcher.* A board inclined at a small angle to the vertical, against which the rower plants his feet.

Page 11. *extensor muscles.* Muscles whose action *extends* or stretches out a limb to its fullest extent; they generally lie over the convexities of the joints. *Flexors* are those whose contraction *flexes* or draws in a limb which is extended. 'Flexors' are consequently *antagonistic* to 'extensors.'

Page 13. *feather.* An expression taken from the action of the feathers on a bird's wing. When the oar is in the water the blade is at right angles to the surface of the water. To 'feather' the oar is to bring the blade by a turn of the wrist to the horizontal position. The meaning of the word is often extended so as to include all that part of the motion of rowing in which the oar is out of the water.

Page 15. *psoas* and *iliacus.* Two muscles of the loins attached at their lower ends to the thighs. If the trunk be fixed, they raise the thighs as in the act of running; if the thighs be immovable, as in rowing, they bring the trunk forwards on the hip-joints as a pivot.

ibid. serratus magnus. A large muscle on the side of the chest whose action is to draw the lower part of the scapula forwards.

Page 15. *scapula.* The shoulder-blade.
  ibid. pectoralis minor. A muscle assisting the 'serratus magnus.' It draws the scapula forwards and downwards.
  ibid. triceps. An extensor muscle on the back of the arm, by means of which the fore-arm is brought into a perfectly extended position.
  ibid. anconeus. A small muscle which assists the triceps in extending the fore-arm.
Page 16. *Erector spinae.* The muscle or set of muscles whose action straightens the backbone, and makes it a firm column.
  ibid. pelvis (πέλυξ, a basin). The bony basin which supports the entrails, and to which the thigh-bones are jointed.
Page 17. *trapezius.* A large muscle the office of which is to draw the scapula towards the back-bone. It is antagonistic to the serratus magnus.
  ibid. latissimus dorsi. A large muscle bringing the arm backwards and downwards, and through it having a corresponding action on the scapula.
  ibid. rhomboidei, have much the same action as the trapezius.
  ibid. pectoralis major. A muscle at the side of the front of the chest, which draws the arm inwards, and perhaps to some extent assists the trapezius and rhomboidei.
  ibid. biceps. A muscle lying on the front of the arm, and flexing the fore-arm, and thus antagonistic to the triceps.
  ibid. brachialis anticus. A supplementary to the biceps.
  ibid. pronation. The reverse of *supination,* which is the action of turning the palm of the hand upwards.
  ibid. retractors. Those which draw backwards; in this case the trapezius and rhomboidei.
  ibid. quadriceps. A muscle on the front of the thigh, which extends the leg and whose action is therefore similar to that of the triceps in the arm.
  ibid. fulcrum. Properly the point about which a lever turns, here used inaccurately for any fixed point which exerts resistance.

APPENDIX II.

MR STANIFORTH, the stroke of the Oxford boat, who kept a diary of what took place in 1829, has kindly furnished me with the following particulars :—

He finds no mention of Mr Snow's first letter, but got a second letter from him on March 14th. On March 16th they went down in the eight-oar for the first time; and on the 17th "with the crew picked for the match." On the 21st they went to Sandford; and on the 28th to Newnham. The next day they deliberated whether to send Stephen Davis, the boatman, to Cambridge; from which day till May 7th there is no further notice.

From the last-named day practising went on with considerable regularity till the race. Several men were tried beside those who eventually rowed. For some time Garnier was at stroke. A few days before the race Mr Staniforth and Stephen Davis went to reconnoitre the water at Henley. They came to the conclusion that the best course to take was to go between the island and the Berkshire shore. This is not the most direct course, and was wholly unknown at Henley before that time; but there is hardly any stream on that side, so that a boat rowing up the river saves more in time than it loses in distance by taking that course. This in some measure explains how the foul occurred which happened soon after the first start, as I think what follows will show. I have made inquiries of several gentlemen who rowed in the two crews as to the facts which actually occurred. The accounts are somewhat contradictory, but I believe that the statement in the text is substantially correct, with the exception of the sentence to which this note is appended. The umpire for Oxford was Mr Cyril Page; I cannot make out who was umpire for Cambridge. Mr Page gave his decision as in the text, but when Mr Staniforth asked the Cambridge umpire what he said, he declined to answer, as he was not appealed to by the Cambridge captain. I merely mention this for the sake of accuracy. It seems probable that the Cambridge men, who were on the inside, intended steering, according to the usual custom, outside the island, the Oxford men, who were on the outside, had made up their minds (or, rather, Mr Staniforth had) that the true course was inside the island. This necessitated crossing, and as neither boat was clear of the other, the foul occurred when they had got fairly round the corner, just when the two opposite ways of steering were bound to clash. After the boats were started the second time the Oxford were a good while longer in getting sufficient lead to cross over.

INDEX.

The Page refers to that in which the Biographical Notice is given.

Cambridge.	PAGE
Abercrombie, J., 1839 ...	63
Agnew, S. A., 1854	214
Alderson, F. C., 1856 ...	224
Anderson, W. H., 1867, 8, 9	
Archer, F. H., 1862, 3, 4, 5	
Arnold, F. M., 1844, 5 ...	128
Bagshawe, W. L. G., 1849	155
Baldry, A. T., 1849	167
Bayford, A. F., 1829......	40
Beebee, M. H. L., 1865	
Benn, A., 1857	235
Blake, H., 1853, 4, 5 ...	215
Blake, J. S., 1860, 61 ...	278
Booth, G., 1849............	155
Borthwick, G., 1864, 65..	
Bourke, J. U., 1866, 67..	
Brandt, H., 1851, 2	195
Branwell, A., 1853	
Brett, W. B., 1837, 8, 9	64
Brooks, H., 1844	
Buchanan, J. G., 1862 ...	
Budd, G., 1837	
Chambers, J. G., 1862, 63........................	
Chaytor, H. J., 1859, 60, 61........................	267
Cherry, B. N., 1860	278
Clissold, S. T., 1846......	139

Oxford.	PAGE
Aitken, J., 1849, 51	167
Arbuthnot, E. J., 1829 ...	39
Arkell, J., 1857, 8, 9......	235
Austen, H., 1858	252
Awdry, W. 1863, 4	
Baillie, W., 1836	52
Baker, T. S., 1869.........	
Bates, J. E., 1829	39
Baxter, H. F., 1859, 60...	266
Bennett, G., 1856	225
Benson, W. D., 1868, 9...	
Bethell, R., 1841	91
Bewicke, C., 1839.........	65
Blundell, T. H., 1854 ...	214
Bourne, G. D., 1842......	101
Bowman, W. P., 1867 ...	
Breedon, E. A., 1842......	101
Brewster, W. B., 1842 ...	101
Brown, M., 1864, 5, 6 ...	
Buckle, W., 1845	129
Buller, R. J., 1852.........	194
Burton, E. C., 1846, 7, 8, 9, 51	139
Burton, R. E. L., 1862...	
Carr, C. R., 1862, 3	
Carter, J., 1829............	39
Carter, G., 1836............	52
Carter, E. S., 1867, 8 ...	
Champneys, W., 1861 ...	
Chitty, J. W., 1849, 51, 2, 3	156

INDEX.

Cambridge.	PAGE
Cloves, W. P., 1844, 5, 6	128
Cobbold, R. H., 1841, 42	90
Collard, J., 1867	
Collings, H. H., 1861, 62	
Courage, E., 1853, 4	214
Coventry, M., 1860, 61	278
Cowie, H., 1851	
Croker, J. M., 1841	91
Croker, W., 1841	90
Crosse, C. H., 1851, 2	195
Cunningham, F. E., 1867	
Dale, J. W., 1869	
Darroch, D., 1858, 59	251
Davis, J. C., 1854	214
Denman, Hon. G., 1841, 42	90
Denman, Hon. L. W., 1841, 42	90
De Rutzen, A., 1849	155
Egan, T. S., 1836, 9, 40, 4	51
Entwisle, T., 1829	41
Fairbairn, A. H., 1858, 9, 60	252
Fairrie, H. E., 1855, 6	225
Fitzgerald, R. U. P., 1861, 62	
Fletcher, R., 1837	
Foord, H. B., 1852	195
Forbes, A., 1866, 67	
Formby, R., 1851	
Forster, G. B., 1853	
Fortescue, J., 1866	
Freshfield, E., 1853	
Galton, R. C., 1854	214
Garfit, A., 1847	
Gaskell, T. K., 1861	
Gisborne, T., 1847	
Goldie, J. H. D., 1869	
Gordon, Hon. J. H., 1867	

Oxford.	PAGE
Clarke, R. F., 1859	266
Cocks, J. J. T. S., 1840, 41	75
Codrington, T. S., 1855	
Compton, B., 1839	64
Conant, J. W., 1846	140
Cotton, R. W., 1849, 52	167
Coventry, G. C., 1865	
Cox, J. C., 1842	101
Crowder, F., 1866, 7	
Cruste, T. H., 1855	
Darbishire, S. D., 1868, 9	
Davis, D. T., 1836	52
Denne, R. H., 1852, 3, 5	195
Dry, W. J., 1844	
Elers, F. W., 1856, 57	225
Everett, C. H., 1855	
Fish, J. H., 1867	
Fooks (? Foulkes), 1839	65
Freeman, W., 1866	
Fremantle, W. R., 1829	40
Garnier, T. F., 1829	39
Garnett, W. J., 1839	64
Garnett, W. B., 1840	76
Gurdon, P., 1856, 57	225
Greenall, R., 1851, 2	194
Griffiths, E. G. C., 1847	
Haggard, M., 1845, 7, 8	129
Harris, T., 1836	52
Halsey, T. F., 1860	278
Henley, E. F., 1865, 6	
Heygate, W. U., 1846	139
Hoare, W. M., 1861, 2, 3	
Hobhouse, R., 1839	65
Hodgson, H. W., 1841	91
Hooke, A., 1854, 5	214
Hooper, E., 1854	
Hopkins, H. G., 1861	

INDEX. 377

Cambridge.	PAGE
Gordon, H. E., 1869......	
Gorst, P. F., 1862.........	
Gough, W. R., 1838......	
Granville, A. K. B., 1836, 7	51
Green, F., 1836, 37	50
Griffiths, W. R., 1865, 6, 7	
Graham, E. C., 1855......	
Hall, J., 1858, 59, 60, 61	252
Harkness, W., 1845	128
Harkness, R., 1845, 6, 7	128
Hartley, P., 1836	50
Havart, W. J., 1858......	251
Hawkins, W. W., 1864...	
Hawkshaw, J. C., 1863, 4	
Hawley, E., 1852, 3	195
Heath, B. R., 1829	42
Heathcote, S., 1860	278
Hill, C. G., 1845, 46 ...	129
Hodgson, W. C., 1849...	155
Holden, J. C., 1849, 51	155
Holdsworth, A. B. E., 1829........................	40
Holley, W. H., 1857 ...	235
Holme, A. P., 1857	235
Holroyd, G. F., 1846 ...	139
Ingles, D., 1860............	278
Jackson, F., 1847	
Johnson, F. W., 1851, 2, 4, 5	195
Jones, H. C., 1840, 41 ...	75
Jones, H. R. M., 1855, 6	225
Jones, W. J. H., 1849 ...	155
Jones, W. M., 1836	51
Keane, J. H., 1836, 37 ...	51
Kinglake, R. A., 1863, 4, 5, 6	
La Mothe, C., 1863	
Lawes, C. B., 1865	

Oxford.	PAGE
Hopwood, F., 1862, 3 ...	
Hornby, J. J., 1849, 51...	167
Houghton, W., 1849, 51, 2	167
Hughes, G. E., 1842......	101
Isham, J. V., 1836	52
Jacobson, W. B. R., 1862, 3, 4	
Kelly, F. H., 1863, 4......	
King, W., 1847	
King, W., 1853	
King, W. O. M., 1852, 3, 4	195
Lane, C. G., 1858, 9......	252
Lane, E., 1858	251
Lawless, Hon. V., 1859...	266
Lea, Wm., 1841............	91
Lee, S., 1839	64
Lewis, G. B., 1844	
Lewis, H., 1845............	129
Lonsdale, A. P., 1856, 7	225
Maberly, S. E., 1839, 40	64
Macdougall, F. T., 1842	100
MacQueen, J. N., 1860 ...	278
Mansfield, A., 1848, 9 ...	156
Marsden, R. G., 1867, 68	
Marshall, T. H., 1853, 4, 5	214
Martin, R., 1857	235
Medlicott, H. E., 1861 ...	
Mellish, 1854	214
Menzies, F. N., 1842......	101
Menzies, R., 1842	101
Merriman, E. B., 1861 ...	
Meynell, G., 1840, 41 ...	75
Milman, W. H., 1845, 6, 8	129
Moon, E. G., 1847	
Moore, G. B., 1829	40
Moore, P. H., 1853	
Morgan, H., 1844	

INDEX.

Cambridge.	PAGE
Lloyd, R. L., 1856, 7, 8, 9	224
Lloyd, T. B., 1846	139
Lockhart, W. S., 1845	128
Longmore, W. S., 1851, 2	195
Lowe, W. H., 1868	
Lubbock, H. H., 1858	251
McCormick, J. 1856	225
MacMichael, W. F., 1868, 69	
Mac Naghten, E., 1852, 3	195
Mann, G., 1845	128
Massey, W., 1840	74
Maule, W., 1847	
Merivale, C., 1829	40
Miller, H. J., 1849	168
Morgan, R. H., 1863	
Morland, J. T., 1858, 9, 60	267
Munster, H., 1845	129
Murdock, G. F., 1846, 7	139
Nadin, H. T., 1868	
Nairne, S., 1854	214
Nichols, J. P., 1868	
Nicholson, C. A., 1847	
Nicholson, W. N., 1837, 44	
Norris, W. A., 1852	195
Page, A. S., 1851	
Paley, G. A., 1858, 9	267
Paris, A., 1838, 9	63
Pearson, P. P., 1855, 7	236
Pellew, H. E., 1849	167
Pennant, see Pearson	
Penrose, C. T., 1837, 8, 9	64
Penrose, F. C., 1840, 1, 2	74
Pigott, E. V., 1864, 5	
Pinckney, J. W., 1868	
Pollock, A. B., 1842	102
Proby, H., 1849	155
Raven, T., 1844	
Richards, G. H., 1861, 2	

Oxford.	PAGE
Morrison, G., 1859, 60, 61	267
Morrison, A., 1862, 3, 5	
Mountain, J. G., 1840, 41	75
Moysey, F. L., 1836	52
Neilson, D. A., 1869	
Nind, P. H., 1852, 3, 4, 5	194
Nixon, W., 1851	
Norsworthy, G., 1860	
Oldham, J., 1847	
Parsons, J., 1864	
Penfold, E. H., 1846	140
Pennefather, J., 1836	52
Petch, 1853	
Pinckney, W., 1854, 5	214
Pocklington, D., 1864	
Pocock, I. J. J., 1840	75
Polehampton, H. S., 1846	139
Poole, A. R., 1861, 2	
Powys, P. L., 1839	65
Prescott, O. K., 1852, 3	194
Raikes, R. T., 1865, 6	
Rich, W. G., 1848, 9, 51	156
Richards, E. V., 1841	91
Richards, F. J., 1845	130
Risdale, S. O. B., 1861	
Risley, R. W., 1857, 8, 9, 60	235
Robarts, A. J., 1859, 60	267
Roberts, C., 1864	
Robertson, W., 1861	
Rocke, A. B., 1856	225
Rogers, W., 1840	75
Ross of Bladensburgh, 1868	
Royds, E., 1840, 1	75
Royds, F. C., 1845, 6, 7, 8	129
Salmon, R. I., 1856	225
Schneider, H., 1865	
Senhouse, H. P., 1865, 6	
Seymour, A. E., 1864	

Cambridge.	PAGE	Oxford.	PAGE
Richardson, J., 1844, 5...	128	Shadwell, A. T. W., 1842	101
Ridley, J. M., 1840, 1, 2	74	Shepherd, R., 1863	
Ridley, J. H., 1869		Short, W. F., 1853, 4, 5	214
Royds, J., 1842	102	Soanes, C. J., 1846, 7, 8,	
Royds, N., 1858, 9	267	9	140
Rushton, J. A., 1869 ...		Spankie, J., 1844	
		Spottiswoode, W., 1844	
		Staniforth, T., 1829	40
Salter, J. P., 1856	224	Stapylton, H. E. C., 1843,	
Sanderson, E., 1862		4	
Schreiber, H. W., 1855		Stapylton, W. C., 1845, 6	129
Selwyn, G. A., 1829......	41	Stephens, F. T., 1836 ...	52
Selwyn, J. R., 1864, 6 ...		Steward, C. H., 1849......	156
Sergeantson, J. J., 1857	236	Stocken, W. F., 1856 ...	225
Shadwell, A. H., 1838, 9,		Strong, C. I., 1860	279
40............................	63	Sykes, J. J., 1848, 9, 51	156
Smyly, W. C., 1862, 3 ...			
Smith, C. T., 1854	215		
Smith, A. L., 1857, 8, 9	236	Tahourdin, R., 1869	
Smyth, W. W., 1838, 9	63	Thomas, G., 1859	267
Snow, H., 1856, 7.........	225	Thompson, W. S., 1836	52
Snow, W., 1829............	42	Thorley, J. T., 1856, 7, 8	225
Solly, W. H., 1836	50	Tinné, J. C., 1867, 8, 9...	
Stanley, E., 1836, 9	50	Toogood, J. J., 1829	39
Stanning, J., 1863		Tottenham, C. R. W.,	
Steavenson, D. F., 1864,		1864, 5, 6, 7, 8	
5, 6		Townsend, R., 1856	225
Stephenson, S. V., 1853,		Treherne, see Thomas.	
4		Tremayne, H. H., 1849...	156
Still, J., 1866, 7, 8, 9 ...		Tuke, F. E., 1845	130
		Walls, R. G., 1839, 40 ...	64
Tarleton, W. H., 1861 ...		Walpole, H. S., 1858 ...	251
Taylor, S. B., 1840	74	Wauchope, D., 1849......	155
Thompson, W. T., 1829	41	Warre, E., 1857, 8	235
Tower, F. E., 1842	102	Willan, F., 1866, 7, 8, 9	
Tuckey, H. E., 1851, 2	195	Wilson, F. M., 1845......	129
Tomkinson, H., 1853 ...		Winter, G. R., 1847, 8 ...	
		Wodehouse, J., 1849......	167
		Wood, T., 1865	
Upcher, A. W., 1836 ...	51	Wood, W. H., 1857, 8...	235
Uppleby, G. C., 1840 ...	74	Wood, W. W., 1866, 7...	
		Woodgate, W. B., 1862, 3	
		Woodhouse, S. H., 1869	
Venables, T., 1844.........		Woolaston, C. B., 1841	91

Cambridge.	PAGE
Vialls, C. M., 1840, 1 ...	75
Vincent, S., 1847	
Waddington, W. H., 1849	155
Warren, C., 1829	40
Warner, T. D., 1868......	
Watney, H., 1865, 6, 7	
Watson, W., 1842	102
Watson, H., 1864	
Wharton, R., 1857, 8 ...	
Wilder, E., 1846	139
Williams, H., 1855, 6, 8, 9	251
Wilson, J., 1863............	
Wingfield, W., 1855, 6...	225
Wolstenholme, E. P., 1846, 7	139
Wood, J. G., 1868.........	
Wray, J. C., 1849	168
Wright, J., 1854	215
Yatman, W. H., 1838, 9	63
Young, F. J., 1869	

Oxford.	PAGE
Wordsworth, C., 1829 ...	39
Wynne, O. S., 1862	
Yarborough, A. C., 1868, 9	
Young, J. F., 1860	279

www.ingramcontent.com/pod-product-compliance
Lightning Source LLC
Chambersburg PA
CBHW032148010526
44111CB00035B/1244